THEODORE THE STUDITE

Writings on Iconoclasm

Ancient Christian Writers

THE WORKS OF THE FATHERS IN TRANSLATION

No. 69

THEODORE THE STUDITE: WRITINGS ON ICONOCLASM

TRANSLATED AND INTRODUCED

BY

THOMAS CATTOI

THE NEWMAN PRESS
New York/Mahwah, NJ

Caseside by Sharyn Banks
Book Design by Lynn Else

Library of Congress Cataloging-in-Publication Data

Theodore, Studites, Saint, 759-826.
[Works. Selections. English. 2014]
Writings on iconoclasm / Theodore the Studite ; translated and introduced by Thomas Cattoi.
pages cm. — (Ancient Christian writers ; 69)
Includes bibliographical references and indices.
ISBN 978-0-8091-0611-0 (hardcover : alk. paper) — ISBN 978-1-58768-424-1 (e-book)
1. Iconoclasm. 2. Icons—Cult—History of doctrines—Middle Ages, 600-1500. 3. Icons—Cult—Byzantine Empire. 4. Byzantine Empire—Church history. I. Title.
BR238.T4413 2014
246`.53—dc23

2014018123

ISBN 978-0-8091-0611-0 (cloth)
ISBN 978-1-58768-424-1 (e-book)

Published by The Newman Press
an imprint of Paulist Press
997 Macarthur Boulevard
Mahwah, New Jersey 07430

www.paulistpress.com

PRINTED AND BOUND IN THE UNITED STATES OF AMERICA

CONTENTS

INTRODUCTION

> "The icon masters of old were never concerned with earthly matters...but always raised their spirit and their thoughts toward the light which is divine and immaterial."
>
> Joseph of Volokolamsk,
> Message to an Iconographer[1]

In Defense of Orthodoxy: Theodore the Studite and the Second Iconoclastic Crisis

Theodore the Studite (759–826) is one of the most important personalities in the period of Eastern Christian theology that followed the Second Council of Nicaea (787). The purpose of this volume is to offer to an English-speaking public all the writings of Theodore that were devoted to the question of the veneration of sacred images. Iconoclasm was Theodore's chief preoccupation during the second part of his life; it led to the composition of his chief polemical works—the three *Antirrhetici* and the *Seven Chapters against the Iconoclasts*—as well as his refutations, in verse, of different poetic compositions by members of the iconoclastic party.

Theodore the Studite lived and worked at the very end of the Patristic era and brought together in his vision different elements from the trinitarian theology of the Cappadocian fathers and the great Neo-Chalcedonian synthesis of Maximos the Confessor as well as from the great monastic tradition. While the scholarly literature on the iconoclastic crisis is immense, and interest in the theological, aesthetic, and spiritual significance of Eastern Christian iconography shows no sign of abating, comparatively little has been published on the second wave of iconoclasm that struck the Byzantine Empire after the Second Council of Nicaea had apparently enshrined the legitimacy of icon veneration at the heart of orthodox Christian practice. This volume attempts to fill a lacuna and to increase scholarly interest for a period of Eastern Christian theology that came after the great trinitarian and christological efflorescence of the first centuries, but also preceded the great mystical syntheses of authors such as Symeon the New Theologian and Gregory Palamas. Theodore was the most important thinker in the decades that followed the Second Council of Nicaea, and while his writings proved to be very influential in steering the iconoclastic debate toward its final resolution, they have received far less attention than the works of John Damascene (676–749), his great predecessor in the struggle against iconoclasm.[2]

Theodore the Studite grew up in an aristocratic milieu in the capital of the empire, and many members of his family covered important positions in the administration of Emperor Constantine V (741–75).[3] His privileged social location at the center of Byzantine political and religious life places him in the long Eastern tradition of influential, urban clerics that stretches back all the way to the Cappadocian fathers and John Chrysostom. Theodore's involvement in a series of high-profile politico-religious disputes—including the infamous moechian controversy concerning the serial marriages of Emperor Constantine VI (780–97)—ensures that we have a detailed knowledge of the different stages of his career.[4] A *Vita* that survives in four different versions, and that can be dated to forty years following Theodore's death, describes his earlier life in considerable detail. Many details of this biographical composition, however, cannot be considered reliable, as the authors follow the established conventions of Byzantine hagiography, which by the ninth century was already a well-developed genre of literature.[5] A second source of information about Theodore's life is an anonymous sermon preached around the year 850 on the anniversary of the transfer of Theodore's relics to the monastery of Studios in Constantinople from the place of his initial burial on the island of Prinkipo.[6] This sermon, which is preserved in the *Analecta Bollandiana*, corrects or integrates the information in the *Vita*.

According to these different sources, Theodore was educated by a private tutor, who imparted to him lessons on composition, rhetoric, and philosophy, and ostensibly prepared him for a career in the imperial administration. Theodore's very influential figure during his formative years was his maternal uncle Plato, who after an initial stint as a civil servant had been tonsured as a monk and had become the abbot of the Symbola Monastery in Bythynia.[7] Around the year 780, Theodore chose to follow his uncle's example and moved to Bythynia with his mother and his sisters, where they all embraced the monastic life. Theodore would eventually inherit his uncle's position at the head of his monastic community and would go on to become one of the most influential church figures of his time, devoting a great part of his life and energies to the question of monastic reform. His addresses to his monastic community, which were later collected under the titles of *Magna* and *Parva Catechesis*, played a pivotal role in the institutionalization of coenobitism as the normative form of monastic life. His catechetical works offer us an extraordinary wealth of information on the theological debates of the time, and they also allow us to catch a glimpse of the ongoing struggles between ecclesiastical and political authority in Byzantium at a time when Eastern and Western monasticism had already started to develop their very distinct character.[8]

Theodore first came to prominence around the year 795, after Emperor Constantine VI had decided to divorce his wife, Maria, and marry one of his mother's ladies-in-waiting. Along with many other church leaders, Theodore thought Constantine's remarriage was illegitimate, as the emperor had not produced any proof of his wife's alleged adultery. Theodore accused the church hierarchy of compromising on the truth of the gospel out of fear of the emperor's reprisal.[9] His opposition to the acceptance of the imperial marriage on the part of the patriarchal authorities resulted in his first period of exile, which ended only after the Dowager Empress Irene had her son blinded and assassinated during a palace coup.[10] In 809, when a decision of the Constantinopolitan synod effectively ratified the legitimacy of remarriage after divorce as an expression of *oikonomia*, Theodore condemned again what he perceived to be the laxity of the church hierarchy, calling their decision "a dogma against the Gospel, against the Forerunner, and against the Canons."[11]

Even this second crisis, which was known as the second moechian controversy, would eventually be overshadowed by the events of the political and religious crisis that started a few years later and would continue for over three decades. In the spring of 813, after laying waste to large swaths of the empire's European territory, the ruler of the neighboring Bulgarian kingdom entered into peace negotiations with Emperor Michael I Rhangabe. Michael chose to reject the requests of the Bulgars, fearing that a policy of appeasement might actually give them the time to regroup and strike again with renewed strength. The result of this impasse, however, was a resumption of the hostilities in which the imperial army suffered a series of humiliating defeats and could not stop the advance of the Bulgarian army well into Byzantine territory. The emperor returned to the capital in July, having lost the support not only of the more high-ranking officers in the army, but also of the palace administration and of the church hierarchy. Immediately afterward, an Armenian-born *strategos* from the Anatolian region (or *theme*) staged a palace coup and ascended to the throne with the name of Leo V, forcing Emperor Michael and his immediate family to receive the tonsure and to embrace the monastic life. Later historians would go as far as to allege that the new sovereign had actually engineered the victory of the Bulgars so as to dethrone Michael I, who had already come to be seen as a weak ruler by many of his collaborators.[12]

One of the first signals that the new monarch intended to embrace a new political course was his immediate decision to affirm in a symbolic but highly significant manner the independence of state authorities from ecclesiastical oversight. As he ascended the throne, Leo performed the customary ceremonies, but at the moment of his coronation, he refused to swear the traditional public oath to defend the church from heresy and schism. This event, however, was only a small prelude to the more momentous decisions that the emperor would take the following year. In July 814, Leo contacted John the Grammarian, abbot of the Monastery of Sts. Sergios and Bacchos in Constantinople, and asked him to form a commission that would investigate whether the recent military defeats in the Balkans might not be connected with the practice of icon veneration.[13] The fact itself that the emperor could establish such a committee indicates how, a quarter of a century after the Second Council of Nicaea, there were still considerable portions of the church that would not fully accept the legitimacy of image worship. The historical sources of the time do not disclose whether the emperor had always held on to this position, or whether he sensed that it would be politically expedient to take this stance so as to strengthen his position under the threat of foreign invasion and in a tense political climate. What we know is that the report of the commission substantially sided with the iconoclastic position. The emperor did not take any immediate action, thereby allowing the iconoclastic party to become more vocal and to start demanding the removal of images from public places of worship. Around Christmas of the year 814, however, Leo ordered the removal of an icon of Christ from the façade of the imperial palace, allegedly to save it from being defaced by the mob.[14] The situation grew increasingly tense: other churches started to take down many portable icons that had been the object of particular devotion, and the Patriarch Nikephoros, who had voiced his opposition to this trend, was forced to resign and leave the capital.

At this point Theodore chose to intervene, organizing a procession around the Studios monastery with icons of Christ, the Mother of God, and the saints who were protectors of his community. The procession appears to have taken place in March 815, and Theodore's hope was to rally the church of Constantinople against what he saw as a sly attempt to subvert the conciliar decisions of 787. In fact, the newly appointed patriarch seized the opportunity to convene a synod that declared the Second Council of Nicaea null and void, and reaffirmed the validity of the iconoclastic Council of Hieria as the Seventh Ecumenical Council.[15] The result of this decision was the beginning of a period of persecution for all those who persisted in upholding the legitimacy of religious images. Theodore was arrested and had to undergo repeated flogging, but he refused to recant and was exiled from the capital. When Emperor Michael II ascended the throne in 821 and the first wave of persecution relented, Theodore was released from imprisonment, but at the time of his death in 826, he had still not been allowed to return to his monastery in Constantinople.[16] It was only at the Synod of Constantinople, which was held in 842, sixteen years after Theodore's passing, that the legitimacy of icon veneration was reestablished for all time, and the theological vision of the abbot of the Studios was finally vindicated.

In his study of Theodore's life and thought, Ukrainian scholar Roman Cholij acknowledges the wide-ranging impact of Theodore's writings on iconoclasm, and while he asserts that his works on this theme "do not evidence any original creative thinking," he is at least willing to concede that Theodore was "a highly intelligent practical theologian."[17] Many of the arguments present in the *Antirrhetici*, Theodore's chief work on the topic of the images, had already been deployed by John Damascene in his orations against iconoclasm, despite the rather surprising fact that in none of his extant writings does Theodore ever seem to quote directly from them. Like John, Theodore takes it for granted that his readers will be familiar with the trinitarian theology of the Cappadocians as well as with the Chalcedonian Christology of the fifth century and its later Neo-Cyrillian interpretations. Theodore is also familiar with the christocentric theology of the spiritual life that had emerged in the centuries after Chalcedon and had found a comprehensive expression in the writings of Maximos the Confessor. In a style that echoes John Damascene's *De Fide Orthodoxa*, the text of the *Antirrhetici* and his other work rely on the canonical authority of earlier authors, whose views are often presented without particular attention being paid to the historical context that occasioned their formulation and without consideration for their chronological location.[18] While John Damascene's way of arranging material in a streamlined, logical fashion already prefigured the style of the later *Summae*, Theodore's more "lateral" way of theologizing recalls the more traditional Cappadocian models, such as the orations of Gregory of Nazianzos or the treatises of Basil of Caesarea.[19] Basil is actually quoted very frequently in the *Antirrhetici* and in Theodore's remaining iconophile works, even if some citations are difficult to identify with any certainty. The other prose works by Theodore follow the same stylistic pattern of the *Antirrhetici*, albeit on a smaller scale. His works in verse, on the contrary, are more explicit exercises in apologetic, responding to the poetic production of iconoclastic authors of the time; their style is less measured, more charged, and they often move into the realm of the invective.

The phenomenon of Byzantine iconoclasm in its theological as well as its historical and cultural aspects has been the object of a vast body of literature, while the growing number of academic and popular publications on the subject of the icons attests to the enduring appeal of Eastern Christian iconography. Rather than attempting a chronological reconstruction of the phenomenon of iconoclasm, this introduction offers a conceptual genealogy of Theodore's theological understanding of the veneration of images; it explores the intrinsic link between Christology and the theology of the icon, but it also seeks to outline and elucidate some of the iconoclastic positions that Theodore himself set out to refute. To this purpose, I focus on the theological vision of three authors: Evagrios Pontikos (345–99), Leontios of Byzantium (485–543), and Maximos the Confessor

(580–662). Evagrios's highly idiosyncratic Christology and his rejection of mental images as hindering the achievement of union with the Divine introduce us to the enduring current of Neo-Platonism that continued to flourish in certain monastic milieus long after the condemnation of Origenism in 553,[20] and which, perhaps unsurprisingly, resurfaced in eighth- and ninth-century iconoclasm. Leontios's reflections on the nature of Christ's subjectivity—which actually integrated Evagrian elements into the orthodox christological paradigm—paved the way for the "asymmetric" reading of Chalcedon that Theodore deploys in the *Antirrhetici* to defend the concreteness of Christ's humanity as well as the possibility of portraying it in an image. Finally, Maximos's theology of the spiritual life and his presentation of the life of Christ as the paradigm of individual asceticism provided the basis for the christological vision that undergirds Theodore's understanding of spiritual life and that emphasizes the ultimacy and the irreducible quality of every individual subject.

Considered in the light of these protracted debates on the hypostatic union and its salvific impact on humanity, the iconoclast crisis can be seen as the final episode in a long-drawn battle between an "Origenist" or "Neo-Origenist" approach to the incarnation and spiritual practice that calls for a spiritualizing flight from the material, and a Chalcedonian narrative that affirms instead the salvific import of the created order and gestures toward its eschatological endurance. We will not find any explicit reference to Origenism in the pages of Theodore's iconophile works, but it is in his passionate defense of the images that the century-long fight around the meaning and the import of the incarnation finally comes to an end. Theodore's theological vision is a passionate defense of the Chalcedonian worldview, one in which Christ's assumption of humanity brings about an irreversible change in the structure of the universe and in which icons allow us a glimpse into the final deification of the cosmos.

The Spirituality of "Origenism" and the Danger of Images

In his outline of the development of Greek Christology, John Meyendorff notes that, during the second and third centuries, the question of images was a cause of great embarrassment to both

Christian and educated "pagan" apologists.[21] On the one hand, Christian authors who preached the mystery of the death and resurrection of the incarnate Word were utterly adamant in their opposition to the veneration of images. On the other hand, Neo-Platonic writers, whose philosophical worldview asserted the intrinsic inferiority of matter, found themselves obliged to defend the legitimacy of the images of the Olympian gods. The strategy used by non-Christian apologists was to resort to the Platonic dialectic of prototype and image: the prototypes belonged to the immaterial realm and existed on an ontologically higher plane than the idols of stone and metal, but material images were necessary as long as human beings remained in the fallen world of the flesh, since they had no other access to the divine prototypes.[22]

In an extant fragment of *Contra Christianos,* Porphyry acknowledges that, for some simple people, the gods truly dwelt in the idols of stone and gold. While this distortion is merely the result of their poor education, Porphyry claims that uneducated pagans are actually less incoherent than Christians. The latter may reject images, but they believe that the Godhead entered the womb of a virgin—something far more unsuitable—and chose to "become a fetus, be born and be swaddled in cloths drenched in blood, membranes, bile, and even more vile substances."[23] In his *Sermo Verus,* the Latin author Celsus follows a similar line of argument when he says that the human flesh of Jesus was made of mud, which is of lower dignity than metals or precious stones; therefore, the Christian belief in the incarnation was even more unworthy of the Divine than the pagan practice of idol veneration. "Do the Christians have the right to criticize idols," Celsus asks rhetorically, "when they themselves venerate a God who became flesh?"[24]

Christian writers such as Clement of Alexandria[25] and his followers were well acquainted with these arguments, and of course they understood that educated pagans did not identify images with their divine prototype. Origen actually uses the classical distinction between prototype and image in the text of *De Principiis,* in which he compares the relationship between the Father and the Son (who is the image of the Father) and the relationship between the Son and humanity, which is said to be the image of the image.[26] The very fact that this kind of reasoning could be used in Christian theology—after all, it appeared to provide the philosophical backbone of the most Platonic of New Testament texts, the Letter to the Hebrews—

indicates that the popularity of Neo-Platonic reasoning was not limited to pagan apologetics.

One early author who addresses the question of images in some detail, albeit from a different perspective than we might initially expect, is Evagrios, who explores the role of mental images in the context of spiritual and monastic practice.[27] As noted by Elisabeth Clark in her monograph on fourth-century Origenism, Evagrios played an important role in the rediscovery and popularization of Origen's ideas within the monastic culture of the Egyptian desert.[28] Evagrios had spent the earlier part of his life in Constantinople, but a series of events had led him to abandon the capital and to seek refuge in Jerusalem until he chose to move to Egypt and embrace the monastic life. His theological vision contained a few distant echoes of the thought of the Cappadocians, but it was primarily a synthesis of Neo-Platonic philosophy and Origenist spirituality, transplanted into the barren landscape of Egyptian monasticism. Evagrios's theology of the spiritual life proved to be enormously influential, and it was a theology that anyone with an interest in iconoclasm should consider with the utmost seriousness, since, according to Evagrios, mental images were a major hindrance to Christian spiritual practice.

Evagrios's theological and spiritual vision is grounded in a constant dialectic between unity and multiplicity, university and particularity, the absolute and the contingent. In the writings included in the first volume of the *Philokalia,* he envisages the spiritual battle as an ongoing struggle against inner distraction and fragmentation in which the individual moves gradually away from the created order and ascends toward an undifferentiated intuition of the Divine. According to the *Texts on Discrimination in Respect of Passions and Thoughts,*[29] the first step in the spiritual battle is to learn how to "recognize the difference between angelic thoughts, human thoughts, and thoughts that come from demons." While "angelic thoughts" are concerned with "the true nature of things" and with searching out their "inner essences" so as to learn how to use the created order for the greater glory of God, "demonic thoughts" look forward to "the wealth and glory" that the individual can gain through a selfish use of the same material goods.[30] The chief way in which our thoughts influence our behavior is by way of mental images. Evagrios tells us that "all thoughts inspired by the demons produce within us conceptions of sensory objects," so that the intellect "bears the forms of these objects within itself." Evagrios will concede that not all mental images originate from the activity of the demons; indeed, he states that it is the very nature of the intellect to "bring forth the images of past events." Whenever thoughts produce anger or desire "in a way that is contrary to nature," however, this is the work of the demons.[31]

Evagrios's theology of the image was influenced by the Aristotelian notion that all knowledge begins in the senses. Where he differed from Aristotle, of course, was in his view that all cognitive processes culminating in mental images are also a supernatural battlefield on which good and evil spirits try to sustain or impede our progress toward God. The individual who heeds the suggestions of the demons is thus filled with impassioned images that tie him to this world and prevent his spiritual ascent. As illustrated by medieval paintings of the temptations of St. Anthony, the monastic is the object of the special attention of the demons, who are eager to disturb his prayer and ensure that his intellect "commits adultery" with the created order.[32] "Impassioned thoughts" (*pathētikoi logismoi*) caused by demons leave an imprint in the intellect that produces anger (*thymos*) and desire (*epithymia*). If the individual heeds these disordered passions, the related mental images become ever more vivid, making it more and more difficult to resist the temptations associated with them. This is a vicious circle that can only be broken by a sustained practice of the virtues of detachment: *epithymia* is destroyed "through fasting, vigils, and sleeping on the ground," and *thymos* is tamed "through long-suffering, forbearance, forgiveness, and acts of compassion." The individual has to achieve radical detachment from material possessions and self-esteem, and even come to despise his or her body, since "it is through the body that the demons often attempt to attack us."[33]

Evagrios likens the ascetic engaged in this process of struggling against images to the sailors who are in danger at sea and who throw overboard everything they can, because of the violence of the winds and the threatening waves. If we follow these injunctions, God, "the Physician (*therapeutēs*) of souls," will create "the new Adam" in every one of us—an Adam characterized by dispassion (*apatheia*), where there will no longer be any distinction, "neither Greek nor Jew, circumcision nor uncircumcision, barbarian, Scythian, bond nor free."[34] Indeed, where images and impassioned thoughts are swept away by detachment, "Christ is all and in all."[35]

What is interesting in Evagrios's analysis is the close correlation between emotional and behavioral tendencies, on the one hand, and the presence of images in the intellect, on the other. According to the treatise *On the Spiritual Law* by Mark the Ascetic, a monastic author of the fourth century who was clearly influenced by Evagrios, a habitual pattern of sinful activity results in the "involuntary presence of former sins in the memory," which he terms "prepossession" (*prolēpsis*).[36] "Prepossession" conditions our behavior so that, even if we have freed ourselves from voluntary sins of the mind, we still need to fight against the passions that flow from the visual memory of earlier sinful actions. According to Mark the Ascetic, if we experience a temptation, but the temptation does not give rise to a new intellectual image and it fails to bring back images from the past, the "experienced" ascetic is able to repulse the temptation quite easily. Such imageless stimuli, or "provocations" (*prosbolai*), are not accompanied by any guilt, as they attack individuals from outside, in complete independence from their will. If one begins to "entertain" the provocation, however, turning it over in one's mind and considering with some pleasure the possibility of heeding the temptation, the provocation will eventually give rise to a mental image. Once the image has arisen, the individual is no longer free of responsibility; in the words of the Gospel, "anyone who looks at a woman lustfully has already committed adultery with her in his heart."[37]

For Evagrios, the condition of inner *apatheia*, which is the goal of the practice of the virtues, must thus be accompanied by the shedding of intellectual images. As he points out in his teachings *On Prayer*, "One who has attained dispassion has not necessarily achieved pure prayer (*kathara proseuchē*)," because his mind may still be occupied with thoughts, "which, though dispassionate, distract him and keep him away from God."[38] Neutral—human—thoughts are also to be shed, as they tie us to the world of plurality, which we need to leave entirely behind. Of course, this approach will have an important impact on the way Evagrios understands the role of the imagination in the spiritual life. "When you are praying," warns Evagrios, "do not shape within yourself any image of the Deity, and do not let yourself be stamped with the impress of any form." What is immaterial can only be approached in an immaterial manner; anything else will merely be a trick of the demons. The natural tendency of the intellect to dally with thoughts ensures that we are easily distracted: the intellect will be unable to pursue "immaterial and formless knowledge," and shall "mistake smoke for light."[39] The most startling expression of Evagrios's "inner iconoclasm" is found in the *153 Texts on Prayer*, which warns us: "while you are praying purely and calmly (*apathetikōs*)," the demons will "bring before you some strange and alien form, making you imagine in your conceit that the Deity is there." This is because the demons want you to believe that "the object suddenly disclosed to you is the Deity," when in fact "the Deity does not possess quantity or form."[40]

Evagrios's radical rejection of images may also have been influenced by the particular religious landscape of fourth-century Egypt, where traditional Egyptian polytheism was still practiced by a substantial proportion of the population of the rural areas and the deserts in which Evagrios and his followers had settled.[41] The fear that monks who had only recently embraced Christianity could revert to their ancestral practices may have intensified Evagrios's distrust of the imagination. However, if we turn to another work by Evagrios, the *Kephalaia Gnostika*, we will see how his reflection on the role of images goes far deeper than a mere response to social and historical circumstances.

The two extant versions of the *Kephalaia Gnostika* are Syriac translations of a lost Greek original, and while it may be corrupt or incomplete, the text they preserve offers a fascinating entrée into Evagrios's reflections on cosmology and Christology, a theme virtually absent from the writings included in the *Philokalia*. Evagrios envisaged the first creation as a world of eternal and incorrupt intellects (Syr. *hawna*, most likely a translation of the Greek *nous*), who enjoyed a full and unqualified knowledge of the Godhead. The latter is eternal and immutable, whereas the former are distinct from God's being; because of their ignorance or carelessness (Syr. *mahmianuta*, Greek *ameleia*), they are no longer in union with God, but turned their attention to the material world that God had created after their fall.[42] In this vision, the created order is both a punishment and a medicine; the *noes* become entangled by the passions because of their attachment to the world of matter, but they can also contemplate God's activity in creation. In a twist that sets the *Kephalaia Gnostika* apart from the writings of the *Philokalia*, the way their return to unity is accomplished is through the mediatory work of the Logos.[43]

According to Evagrios, ontological plurality is the outward manifestation of an underlying ethical deficiency that is destined to be superseded at the end of time when the unity of the *noes* with the Godhead will be restored. The role of Christ in this *exitus-reditus* dynamic is instrumental to the restoration of this intellectual unity. For Evagrios, the *nous* of Jesus is the only one that remained in communion with God even after its descent into the flesh, preserving a simultaneous link with both dimensions.[44] As such, this *nous* is deemed worthy to enter into a union with eternal Logos, so that the person of Christ emerges out of the encounter between these two distinct ontological realities. For the author of the *Kephalaia Gnostika,* the goal of the incarnation is not the redemption of humanity within the framework of the natural order, but the dissolution of this world of multiplicity and the retrieval of the *noes*' communion with the Divine.[45] Ordinarily, *noes* that dwell in the world of the flesh are unable to discern the providential character of the natural world because of their attachments to material reality, but Christ's descent into the flesh reveals God's plan for the world, helping the *noes* leave behind the realm of disordered plurality and become coheirs of the *nous* of Jesus.

This worldview is dramatically very different from the classical model of creation of atonement that we find, for instance, in Athanasios's writings on the incarnation. According to Evagrios, the body or, indeed, the humanity of Christ is a mere tool that is abandoned once its task has been fulfilled.[46] Conversely, attachment to the body is a clear sign that one is unable to transcend the world of plurality or to return to communion with the Divine. If the *153 Texts on Prayer* and the treatise *On Discrimination* are read against the background of the *Kephalaia Gnostika,* Evagrios's rejection of mental images acquires a different significance: relying on your imagination while praying will tie you to the world of multiplicity and plurality, which Christ himself is encouraging you to leave behind.

For Evagrios, Jesus' *nous* was a sort of ontological glue that brought together the eternal Word with the flesh of humanity, while Christ's subjectivity came into being as the encounter of two distinct ontological realities, one of which was eventually destined to be left behind and was thus unworthy of being the subject of meditation or devotion.[47] Eventually, however, the councils of Nicaea and Chalcedon would hone the foundations of what would become the orthodox christological consensus, while "paganism" in its various forms and guises gradually ceased to pose a threat to the Christian churches. The emphatic definition of the consubstantiality between Father and

Son at Nicaea and the later assertion of Christ's full humanity at Chalcedon could not coexist with the subordinationist Christology of Evagrios, nor could they be reconciled with the Origenist call to flee the world of contingency and multiplicity.[48] When the Iconoclast Council of Hieria met in 754 to condemn the veneration of images, the language of its pronouncements was reminiscent of Evagrios's understanding of the incarnation.[49] At the same time, Evagrios's notion of Christ's composite subjectivity would also have a long and unexpectedly orthodox progeny, some of which would be used in defense of the veneration of images.

By the late fifth century, however, the incarnational turn of Chalcedon had led to an irreversible shift in the theology of the hypostatic union, resulting in a greater emphasis on the historical, concrete character of the incarnation. In the old dispensation it was possible to say with Evagrios that "the Deity has no shape or form," but in the words of the Chalcedonian definition, Christians now confess

> *one and the same Son, our Lord Jesus Christ, the same perfect in Godhead and also perfect in manhood;*
>
> *truly God and truly man, of a reasonable [rational] soul and body;*
>
> *consubstantial [co-essential] with the Father according to the Godhead, and consubstantial with us according to the Manhood;*
>
> *in all things like unto us, without sin;*
>
> *begotten before all ages of the Father according to the Godhead, and in these latter days, for us and for our salvation, born of the Virgin Mary, the Mother of God, according to the Manhood.*[50]

Christ's Composite Subjectivity and the Ontological Status of His Humanity

The Chalcedonian definition, of course, did not represent the conclusion in the development of christological doctrine; indeed, the debate on the meaning and implications of Chalcedonian Christology continued to dominate the theological landscape for centuries to come. In an article on the philosophical nature of the conciliar *horos*, Sarah Coakley points out that the council fathers did not seek to offer an exhaustive account of the hypostatic union, but merely selected some conceptual and terminological tools to mark a legitimate theological "space" in which reflection on the mystery could continue.[51] In this perspective, the claim that the person of Christ rests in two distinct natures (or *physeis*) should not be seen as a univocal description of an ontological reality, or as a linguistic strategy to articulate a specific religious experience; and it is equally mistaken to regard it as a metaphor or as an invitation to leave behind all preoccupation with conceptual or terminological coherence. For the council fathers, the incarnation was a historical event, and the conciliar definition was analogically grounded in this event, which was something that transcended and challenged our cognitive categories but that could not cease to be the subject of our speculative reflection.

Indeed, nestled within the analogical margin of the conciliar *horos* are many unexplored issues that the council fathers unwittingly or deliberately chose to bypass. One such issue is the question of the principle of subjectivity and agency within the person of Christ—a problem that we saw Evagrios had tried to address in the *Kephalaia Gnostika.* While the Chalcedonian definition appeared to suggest that the hypostatic union possessed one single center of subjectivity, the council passed no judgment as to this subject's actual identity. Was Christ's subject fully identical with the eternal Logos, or did it emerge only in the wake of the hypostatic union? Did Christ's principle of subjectivity undergo change in the course of his earthly life or after the event of the resurrection? And finally, if the subject of the incarnation was a divine subject, what was the salvific import of Christ's humanity? These questions appear very abstract and remote from the later debate on the veneration of the images, but the way Christ's subjectivity as well as Christ's humanity were conceptualized in the wake of Chalcedon would play a crucial role in determining the outcome of the debate on the legitimacy of icons.

In the earlier part of the fifth century, Cyril of Alexandria (376–444) had insisted on theopaschite formulations that postulated the suffering of the Second Person of the Trinity via his assumption of our common humanity. In his treatise *De Unitate Christi,* the Alexandrian bishop had introduced the important mechanism of the *communicatio idiomatum,* in virtue of which the hypostasis of the eternal Son could experience the physical torment and death that were proper to his humanity while preserving the unchangeable and impassible character of his divinity.[52] In the post-Chalcedonian period, quite a few authors attempted to reconcile Cyril's assertion of *mia physis* with the Chalcedonian assertion of Christ's two distinct natures, trying to offer a new, comprehensive account of the question of Christ's subjectivity and agency. One of the most intriguing treatments of this issue—even if not, perhaps, the most accessible—can be found in the writings of Leontios of Byzantium (485–543).[53] His *Contra Nestorianos et Eutychianos* postulates a sort of infra-christological dialectic or *perichōrēsis* that echoes Cyril's discussion of the *communicatio idiomatum* but modifies it in a number of important respects.

Leontios's work proceeds in the usual dialogical fashion that Theodore himself would adopt in the *Antirrhetici*, with a "heretic" asking questions that allow the author to expatiate on a variety of different topics. One of Leontios's "heretics" is a Nestorian, who wonders why it should be so improper to postulate two principles of subjectivity in the person of Christ, as long as it is truly the case that neither the eternal Logos nor the flesh of Christ's body underwent any alteration in the moment of the incarnation.[54] The question is couched in semi-Cyrillian terms, reflecting the preoccupation with the preservation of Christ's natures that was typical of the Christology of the time. A simple answer would point to the fact that the lack of alteration in the persons of Christ makes a second principle of subjectivity redundant: the panoply of divine attributes flowing from the hypostasis of the eternal Son do not displace their human counterparts, and as a result Christ's human nature is in no need of a supplementary crutch to support itself in the face of the divinity of the Word. Leontios, however, points out that the relationship between humanity and divinity in the person of Christ could be conceptualized in different manners, drawing inspiration from the relationship between Father and Son.[55]

Choosing this different perspective, Leontios paves the way to a different kind of insight. He notes that certain nouns denote the essence of the subject to which they refer (*eidos*), while other nouns intimate the existence of a relationship (*schesis*).[56] While certain beings are identical in essence, others are distinguished one from the other by number; yet another set are "joined to each other by definition." In this way, Leontios distinguishes two types of relation: one that is characterized by sameness and another that is characterized by difference. The notion of double consubstantiality is thus rephrased in dialectical terms, since within the same Logos, one can discern two manners of relations: "in one, the Logos is in a relationship of sameness with the Father, whereas in the other, the Son is distinguished from the Father." Leontios will apply the term *ousia* to the former, and the term *hypostasis* to the latter.[57]

The distinction between union by nature (*enōsis kat'ousian*) and union according to the principle of subjectivity (*enōsis kath'hypostasin*) puts Leontios in the position to say that Christ "as a whole" (*holos*) is a hypostasis with respect to the Father, in virtue of his divinity joined with his humanity, while he is also a hypostasis with respect to all members of the human race, in virtue of his divinity joined with his humanity.[58] What Leontios has accomplished is the de facto creation of a relational anti-Nestorianism: relational, as the subject of Christ emerges out of a relationship; anti-Nestorian, as there is still only one hypostasis. Postulating an individual human hypostasis in Christ would question the ontological ability of the divine Logos to sustain Christ's humanity, but what really sets Christ's flesh apart from ours is not the preexistent divine reality: rather, it is the *schesis* of relationship that the flesh of Christ has with our own flesh. In this perspective, the principle of unity that sustains and informs the life and mission of the incarnate Christ comes into being, *kata synthesin.* The resulting, composite principle of subjectivity, which is brought together by the blending of distinct ontological realities, is ostensibly in line with the Chalcedonian definition, but it also echoes the Evagrian contention that the *nous* of Jesus mediates between the eternal Logos and the flesh of Christ, so the principle of Christ's action also comes into being by composition.[59]

What happens then to the natures that rest in this newly created reality? Interestingly enough, this composite subject is said to carry the *idiōmata* of both natures.[60] Leontios introduces the notion of *enousion* when he deals with the existence of a subject "within an essence" and develops the parallel notion of *enhypostaton* when he deals with the existence of a nature within a hypostasis. At the same time, Leontios asserts that there is "no nature without a hypostasis" (*ouk estin physis anypostatos*); a nature cannot be contemplated in itself, and while a nature cannot be "accidental (*symbebēkos*)," it always exists within another being.[61] A hypostasis, for its part, indicates an individual who is identified on the basis of certain characteristics. Leontios introduces the term *enhypostaton* to indicate the way in which a particular nature comes to rest within a particular hypostasis. As Christ's humanity cannot be "contemplated" in an abstract sense, Leontios will say that it is enhypostatic, or in other words, that it is manifested through an individual principle of subjectivity. To complete the picture, it is then possible to say that the humanity of Christ is also anhypostatic, as it lacks its own principle of subjectivity. The hypostasis of the eternal Word, for its part, emerges out of the two natures (*ek duo physesin*), and it is known to us by way of the mediation of their properties.[62]

The question of Christ's subjectivity and its relationship with the two different natures would be taken up again in the seventh century in the writings of Maximos the Confessor (580–662).[63] Maximos's vision was steeped in the wisdom of Chalcedon, but his theological vision was not a mere repetition of Chalcedonian *obiter dicta*, as he also drew elements from unexpected sources: one element was the "Origenist" thinkers whom he had set out to refute, and another was the writings of Leontios. Maximos's preoccupation with the synergy of two distinct, and yet perichoretically interacting wills ensured that his understanding of Christ's hypostasis pays particular attention to the relationship of unity and the duality. As such, Maximos could actually borrow a phrase from Leontios and write that the hypostasis of Christ is not merely subsisting in two natures (*en duabus naturis*) but actually emerges out of two natures (*ex duabus naturis*).[64] At the same time, Maximos emphasized that the subject of Christ's actions preserved an utter continuity—and indeed, identity—with the hypostasis of the eternal Son. While the divine nature of the Second Person of the Trinity is preserved from all shadow of change, the hypostatic union ensures that the divine agency of the Logos can be active in the cosmos in a way that is utterly unprecedented.[65]

In his study of Maximos's theology, Lars Thunberg underscores how for Maximos the hypostatic union involves a reciprocal relationship of complementarity between the two natures of the Logos: God's love for humanity (*philanthrōpia*) makes sure that the eternal Son assumes our common nature, while humanity assumes the divine properties or *idiōmata*. The expression "beautiful reciprocity" (*kalē antistrophē*) intimates this marvelous reversal, whereby the incarnation accomplishes the descent of divinity into the human condition, while the process of *theōsis* brings about the deification of humanity.[66] Maximos mentions that, in the person of Christ, the union of the two natures results in a "new" theandric energy; drawing on a text by the Pseudo-Denys, Maximos notes in the *Opuscula Theologica et Politica* that this energy is not a previously nonexistent reality brought about by the incarnation, but represents the commingling of two ontologically distinct realities.[67]

How does this take place? If the energy of the divine nature has been humanized (*androtheisa*), we no longer see a naked God (*gymnos Theos*), and at the same time we cannot say that in Christ we contemplate a "mere human being" (*psilos anthrōpos*). The Cyrillian reading of the Chalcedonian definition that Maximos embraces here conflates the *hypostasis* of the Word with Cyril's *mia physis*.[68] While Leontios's notion of a subject emerging *kata synthesin* intimated the appearance of a "mixed" ontological subject that was discontinuous with God's pre-incarnational reality, Maximos's composite hypostasis purifies the notion of "composite hypostasis" from its more problematic association and associates composition, or synthesis, with the mode of cognitive access to the incarnate Logos. In other words, according to Maximos, human beings are not able to perceive the divine nature of the Logos directly, but they do so thanks to the mediation of Christ's humanity, which acts as *trait-d'-union* between the Second Person of the Trinity and fallen humanity.

This "asymmetric" reading of Christ's subjectivity, purified of its Origenist taint through Maximos's Chalcedonian understanding of relationality, would gradually become part of the christological tradition. The absence of a human hypostasis is not the "unfortunate" price of the incarnation; it is actually a soteriological necessity, as it guarantees that the hypostasis of the eternal Logos indwells our common human nature and is able to infuse it with the divine energy. At the same time, the relational character of anhypostasy entails that the eternal Logos *acts* in the world through the medium of both natures; and indeed, that the eternal Logos *is known* to us only by way of the medium of both natures. Eventually, it was to this "salvific asymmetry" of the incarnate Christ that Theodore the Studite would turn as he sought to defend the particularity and the representability of Christ's humanity. Before he could do so, however, he had to ensure that anhypostasis would not be hijacked, and systematically misused, by the iconoclastic camp.

Anhypostasis and the Icon: A Fraught Relationship

Anhypostasis, indeed, soon proved to be a double-edged sword, as a number of opponents of the images argued that the absence of a human hypostasis in Christ indicated clearly that his humanity was not like our humanity, and as such, it could not be represented in an image. The supporters of this idea, who were very active in the eighth and ninth centuries, although they did not leave behind any theological treatises of great weight, would go down in history with the rather peculiar name of *agraptodocetae*: those who believe that Christ cannot be circumscribed and therefore cannot be represented in an icon.

If we read the writings from many of the participants in the second iconoclastic controversy toward the end of the eighth century, we will see that the different parties routinely accused each other of resurrecting the heresies of the past and of falling back into Nestorianism, Monophysitism, and all possible shades of Docetism. In addition, despite the fact that over two hundred years had elapsed since the condemnation of Origenism, the latter was far from dead. From the correspondence of Germanos of Constantinople, who was patriarch under Emperor Leo III, we learn that the emperor had surrounded himself with numerous Asian bishops who had Origenist or semi-Origenist leanings and were therefore suspicious of the use of imagery in all forms.[69] Their influence at court continued under the reign of Emperor Constantine V Copronymous, who earned his less-than-flattering sobriquet thanks to his strenuous opposition to the veneration of icons. According to Patriarch Nikephoros, who would become one of his harshest critics, the emperor questioned how the humanity of Christ could be represented in any way. Constantine claimed that if the images represent the humanity of Christ and not his divinity, they introduced a division in his person;[70] if the image truly represented Christ in the fullness of both natures, the two natures were mingled—and the supporters of the images fell into the Monophysite heresy of Severus[71]—or the divinity was said to be fully circumscribed in the humanity, which of course was a logically untenable proposition. Paradoxically, the iconoclastic emperor was appealing to Chalcedon to defend his position; he claimed that the icon brought to the person of Christ that very "confusion" and "separation" that had been ruled out by the council fathers, so that, to defend orthodoxy, one had to reject the images.[72]

Many of the opponents of the images, however, were actually looking back to an earlier, pre-Chalcedonian understanding of the hypostatic union—one where the humanity of Christ was not preserved in the totality of its characteristics but rather became fully spiritualized and virtually fused into the divinity. If we look at the christological definition of the Council of Hieria, we will find not only a return to an earlier understanding of Christ's composite subjectivity, but even a throwback to an Evagrian reading of infra-christological relationships:

> *As the divinity of the Son has assumed into its own hypostasis the nature of the flesh, the soul of Christ becomes the intermediary between the divinity and the thickness of the flesh; and the soul is also the soul of the divine Logos. The soul and the body have now been deified, and the divinity is now inseparable from either; wherever is the soul of Christ, there is the divinity; and wherever is the body of Christ, there is the divinity.*[73]

As in the *Kephalaia Gnostika*, the soul of Christ mediates between the eternal Logos and the lowly world of the flesh.[74] While Chalcedon affirmed the preservation of both natures in the totality of their characteristics, the Council of Hieria, which claimed to defend orthodox Christology from the alleged Nestorianism of the iconophiles, unwittingly dissolved the humanity of Christ in the embrace of the divinity of the Logos.[75]

It is easy to see why the notion of anhypostasis, which, after all, developed out of Leontios's qualified retrieval of the earlier Origenist vision, would be appropriated by the supporters of this position. The absence of a human center of subjectivity in Christ offered a seemingly reasonable justification to the claim that, in the hypostatic union, the humanity of Christ was radically disembodied—indeed, it is almost deontologized. For the opponents of the images, if Christ were not an individual human being and his body, no less than his soul, had become intimately associated with the person of the Word, the conclusion was inescapable: his body and his soul had become indistinguishable from his divinity, and as such, they could no longer be represented in an image.

Nikephoros's *Antirrhetici*, like many apologetic works, takes great pleasure in highlighting the absurd beliefs of the *agraptodocetae*.[76] Agraptodocetism differed from Docetism because it does not claim that Christ's humanity was a phantasm; however, it also went further from Aphthartodocetism, which affirmed Christ's humanity but denied that it could suffer, since according to the *agraptodocetae*,

Christ "lacked individual characteristics" (*acharaktēriston*), because he was "a man in general" (*anthrōpos katholou*). Nikephoros tells us that according to the *agraptodocetae*, even the womb of the Virgin Mary "had come to escape description" as soon as it had become the dwelling place of the eternal Word.[77]

When Theodore the Studite, alongside all the defenders of the images, finds himself addressing the claims of the iconoclasts, he cannot fail to consider the challenge posed by Agraptodocetism. An understandable temptation would be to let go of the notion of anhypostasy, which had opened the way to all these conceptual distortions. Theodore, however, chooses not to do so, but actually reaffirms Leontios's claim that the humanity of Christ lacks its own hypostasis. To counter the notion of christological agency revived at Hieria, with all its attendant agraptodocetic problems, it was necessary to reaffirm the teaching of anhypostasis, but to do so in light of Maximos's "sanitized" version of Christ's composite subjectivity. In this way, it was possible to assert the general character of Christ's humanity, which undergirded its universal salvific reach, while simultaneously asserting that Christ's human nature was enhypostatized in a particular subject and was therefore representable. At the same time, this strategy underscores the pedagogical value of Christ's two natures: while we cannot have direct access to the hypostasis of the eternal Son, we do so via the mediation of the two natures. The iconic representations of Christ's humanity continue the mystery of the incarnation in time, opening a window into the mystery of the hypostatic union where our humanity partakes in the glory of the divine energies.

Evagrios had taught his followers to escape mental representations of the Godhead, as the latter was above the world of contingency and plurality.[78] The *agraptodocetae* appear to echo his concerns, as they claim that Christ lacks individual characteristics—which would be below the dignity of the Logos—and should only be contemplated "noetically."[79] Theodore adamantly rejects this claim. On the one hand, he agrees with his opponents when they reject the suggestion that Christ was a "mere man" (*psilos anthrōpos*), or that the eternal Logos had "assumed an individual man" (*ton tina tōn anthrōpōn*). The Second Person of the Trinity is the one and only subject of the hypostatic union. At the same time, Theodore insists that the humanity of Christ is enhypostatized in the person of the eternal Logos, and as such it possesses a whole set of characteristics like any other human individual.[80] The salvific mission of Christ took place at a particular time in history, and in a particular geographic location; Christ ate, and drank, and slept, and did everything that pertains to our common humanity.

The way Theodore addresses the agraptodocetic objections to the representability of Christ's humanity is to reaffirm the notion of anhypostasis in line with the Chalcedonian understanding of Christ's agency, and subsequently to apportion the properties of Christ between the two natures by way of the teaching of *communicatio idiomatum*. Within this christological vision, the subject of Christ's actions is the eternal and unchanging Word of God, which now exists and is known to us "out of two natures."[81] At the same time, through the mechanism of the exchange of properties, Christ's hypostasis preserves all the characteristics of Christ's divinity, such as uncircumscribability and unrepresentability, but it also acquires the properties of Christ's humanity, such as circumscribability and, indeed, representability.[82] In this way, Theodore can respond to the objections raised by Emperor Constantine against the sacred images: in the icons there is no blending or fusion of the natures in a Monophysite manner, as both sets of properties are preserved intact, and there is certainly no Nestorianizing division between the natures, as the properties of both natures are ascribed to the hypostasis that is represented. Theodore even retrieves the old Nestorian term *synapheia* ("association") to talk of the ontological relationship between the natures, but he uses it in an irreproachably orthodox sense, to assert the perichoretic exchange of properties of two distinct realities within the same, undivided subject.[83]

The paradoxical endpoint of this tortuous intellectual process sees a Christology such as that of Leontios—characterized by a problematic Origenist ancestry—turn into a building block for a theology of the hypostatic union, which is almost "Antiochean," to use a well-worn cliché, in its defense of Christ's concrete humanity. Maximos's more "Chalcedonian" interpretation of anhypostasis, and his understanding of Christ's composite subjectivity, allow Theodore to use the *communicatio idiomatum* as an overarching conceptual template to describe the way in which the two natures of Christ relate to each other, thereby securing the legitimacy of Christ's pictorial representation. The implication of this theological vision is that pictorial images of Christ are truly capable of capturing the reality of his individual humanity, and they can be considered legitimate portrayals of the incarnate Logos.

Imitatio Christi and Deification in the Wake of Chalcedon

One of the reasons why the question of the veneration of images was so controversial was their centrality in the context of individual religious practice no less than in the liturgical life of the church. As icons were the focus of private and public devotion, their role in the spiritual progress of the individual had to be carefully considered. In the wake of the christological controversy of the fourth and fifth centuries, as well as of the condemnation of Origenist spirituality in the sixth, the debate on the nature of spiritual practice hinged on the question of the purpose and destiny of the particular humanity of the individual Christian. After the debates of the fifth and the sixth centuries on the ontological status of Christ's humanity had led to a more careful articulation of the relationship between the two natures within the mystery of the hypostatic union, it was also important to determine in what way the dialectic of humanity and divinity would unfold in the life of the individual believer as he or she underwent the gradual process of deification.

While for Evagrios the ultimate *telos* of practice was a return to the undifferentiated noetic insight, later "orthodox" Christology would affirm the enduring quality of individual subjectivity, while also noting that individual practitioners could never attain the spiritual level, or the ontological condition, of the incarnate Logos.[84] If salvation is communicated to everyone through the sacrament of baptism, the process of deification (*theōsis*) discloses a different mode of "using" one's own individual nature and is achieved in proportion to the individual's receptiveness to divine grace.[85] This soteriological vision presents Christ's glorified humanity as the ontological paradigm for the deification of the individual, who is called to follow Christ in the simultaneous pursuit of contemplation and the virtues. The notion that the saints partake in the divine attributes lavished on the humanity of Christ through the mystery of the hypostatic union is the reason why saints are worthy of veneration. When, in the *Antirrhetici*, Theodore the Studite offers a rationale for the veneration of the icon of the saints, he is relying on a theology of deification and of the spiritual life that is rooted in the Chalcedonian paradigm and that, again, finds its highest expression in the works of Maximos the Confessor.

Maximos retrieves the notion of *apatheia* developed by Evagrios and notes that the process of deification cannot take place in us unless our natural abilities have been purified from sin and we have become detached from the passions.[86] Earlier studies of this theme published in the 1940s and 1950s were colored by a Scholastic understanding of the dynamics of grace and nature, as well as by a tendency to view salvation as an extrinsic gift bestowed on humanity in virtues of the sacrifice of Christ.[87] In the *Liber Asceticus*, however, Maximos observes that the saints are those who truly believed in Christ and thus, "through the practice of the commandments, have made Christ himself come to live in them."[88] This understanding of deification is fundamentally christocentric; the eternal Logos is the ontological ground as well as the paradigm of the virtues, so that in those who follow the commandments, Christ becomes incarnate anew. Given that the eternal Word encompasses the *logoi* of the virtues, the saints appear to be "repeated incarnations" (so to speak) of the one eternal Word that became fully manifest in Christ.[89]

Maximos's *Ambigua*—a collection of commentaries on problematic passages from scripture or the church fathers—highlight the connection between deification and obedience, and underscore how our own individual deification is patterned according to the example of Christ's own *kenōsis.*[90] Following the commandment to love one another brings us closer to Christ's own transfigured humanity; letting go of our own ascetic desires and inclinations by way of ascetic practice is a sort of self-emptying that mirrors the kenotic abasement of the eternal Son. This profound symmetry between our ascent and Christ's own descent is paradigmatic of the synergy between divine and human initiative that shapes the spiritual progress of the individual. In a letter to John the Cubicularius, Maximos goes as far as to say that God's incarnation in the virtues of the individual Christian takes a different quality in line with the ethical and existential choices that the individual makes.[91] In this way, it is possible to say that in the persons of the saints, the unique and unchangeable Godhead becomes manifest in an infinite number of different and ever-changing ways. In a startling passage of the *Capita Theologiae et Oeconomiae,* Maximos goes as far as to say that to the extent that "I remain imperfect and refractory, neither obeying God nor obeying the commandments" (through *praxis*), "nor becoming perfect by way of spiritual contemplation" (through *theōria*), "Christ himself also appears imperfect and refractory," as "I diminish and cripple Him by not growing in spirit."[92]

Within the boundaries of the Evagrian paradigm, the goal of spiritual practice was the elimination of all difference (*diairesis*), whereas in the theology of Maximos the incarnation is actually what secures the preservation of diversity and plurality.[93] The entire world of contingency is redeemed in the incarnation; in the same way as the two natures of Christ continue to exist within the mystery of the hypostatic union, all different members of the human race will be deified but they will preserve their distinct ontological character even after the passing of this world. At first, the notion that ascetic practice and holiness accomplish a sort of "renewed incarnation" might appear to echo the early "Christology by degrees" that was championed by authors such as Paul of Samosata but eventually condemned as incompatible with the Nicene assertion of divine consubstantiality between Father and Son.[94] Nothing, however, could be more distant from Maximos's intentions than a blurring of the ontological distinction between Christ and the individual practitioner. His understanding of *theōsis* asserts the ultimacy of each human hypostasis, and the deification of the individual person is an instance of "mystical symmetry," which miraculously renews, but simultaneously reverses, the event of the hypostatic union. The individual assumes the properties of the divinity, all the while preserving the unbridgeable ontological distinction between the human nature and the divine nature.

The images of the saints that the church offers to the veneration of the faithful are thus a gesture toward the celestial Jerusalem, where the saints are transfigured by the divine energies and dwell with the Lamb for ever and ever. According to Evagrios, our destiny is to return to the embrace of the primordial unity; if this is the case, the images of the saints could not represent the eschatological destiny of the human race, which is called to leave behind the realm of shape and form. According to Maximos, however, our destiny is to share in the glory of Christ, who was crucified and is now risen, and who graciously allows us to partake in the glory of his glorified humanity.[95] As each of us is a different individual, Christ will be manifest in each one of us in a different way; heaven will be a kaleidoscope of infinite kinds of holiness, and the images of the saints on this earth will be a support and a consolation as we struggle to reach what is our true, eternal homeland. If the saints are deified, their images also partake in the divine energies, and the honor that is due to their prototypes should be due to their pictorial representations here on this earth.

Toward the end of the first *Antirrheticus*, when Theodore reminds us that it is right to depict and to honor the images of the saints, he must address the iconoclasts' objection that the memory of saints should rather be honored by following their example and transmitting their teaching.[96] Theodore does not disagree with this point, but he adds that the saints earned this honor by way of martyrdom, or by way of a holy life. In other words, it is their very life that becomes a channel of the divine grace; their very being has been ontologically transformed. If we were merely to commemorate them in words, without honoring their image, we would fail to pay due respect to the extraordinary transformative power of the divine grace that transfigured them and ensured that they would participate in the divine glory.

THE *ANTIRRHETICI*: A CHRISTOLOGICAL TREATISE

Theodore's *Antirrhetici* are not a systematic exposition of a theology of the image; this work, as well as the other occasional writings on icon veneration authored by Theodore in the course of his life, blends together Christology and spiritual theology in a synthesis characterized by an overarching apologetic thrust.[97] His terminology is the classical terminology of the Chalcedonian controversies: *physis* ("nature") and *prōsopon* ("person") are actually used in preference to *ousia* ("essence") and *hypostasis* (which also indicates the person, as well as the center of subjectivity). A variety of terms are applied to the images in a way that defies consistency: *eikōn* ("image"), *typos* ("type"), *morphē* ("form"), *schēma* ("pattern"), *charaktēr* ("feature"). As noted by Catherine Roth in the introduction to her 1981 translation of the *Antirrhetici*, the term *eikōn* can indicate sacred images, profane paintings, or the relationship of similarity in an abstract sense.[98] At the same time, the term *omoiōma* ("likeness") is sometimes used to indicate the relationship between icon and prototype, and sometimes it is virtually synonymous with the image itself.[99] A crucial terminological choice, however, is the distinction between *latreia* ("adoration," or "worship," in the strict sense of the term), which is due to God alone, and *proskynēsis* ("veneration," or "worship," in a broader sense), which is due to the Virgin Mary and the saints but can also be given to relics and other holy objects—such, indeed, as icons.[100] Theodore buttresses his claims with numerous references to scriptural passages in the Septuagint version and to works by earlier fathers, although, as already noted, some of the citations cannot be identified with certainty.

After the customary disclaimer in which Theodore protests his unworthiness to approach such a lofty topic, the first *Antirrheticus* opens with an affirmation that faith (*pistis*), adoration (*latreia*), and veneration (*proskynēsis*) are all equally due to the three persons of the Trinity, even if the three persons are perceived distinctly because of their hypostatic properties.[101] The text then continues as a conversation between a heretic, who voices the iconoclastic objections to image veneration, and a representative of the orthodox position, who tries to highlight the self-contradictory nature of the iconoclast position or its inconsistency with the tradition of the fathers.

The first *Antirrheticus* touches on a variety of arguments, many of which will be taken up by Theodore over and over again throughout the whole corpus of his writings. The first observation of "the heretic" is that the veneration of images is "a wile that has been transferred by some demonic wile from the Greek tradition into the universal church," thereby taking us back to the times of the veneration of idols. It is certainly no accident that the heretic should repeat the claims of the Council of Hieria almost verbatim, as that council, which had presented the veneration of images as coming from the wiles of the devil, had become the doctrinal benchmark of the iconoclast movement.[102] Theodore agrees with "the heretic" that the divine is "utterly incomprehensible (*aperilēpton*) and uncircumscribable (*aperigrapton*)," and actually strengthens this claim by pointing out how it is manifest to all that the divine nature lacks in "boundaries, limits and forms."[103] Christians are right in condemning the foolishness of the Greeks, who were deceived by demonic cunning, and who, instead of giving the due honor to God, the Creator of all, bowed down to the products of God's creation; to apply circumscription (*perigraphē*) to the divine in the order of theology, as opposed to the new dispensation inaugurated by the incarnation, would be an invention of Greek sophistry (*epinoia*). The error in the iconoclasts' position, however, is that they do not distinguish between *theologia* and *oikonomia*.[104] Because of his great condescension, one of the persons of the Trinity has chosen to assume humanity and to become like one of us, and as a result, "a mingling came into being of what is uncircumscribed with what is circumscribed, of what has boundaries with what is boundless." What is naturally without circumscription because of his divinity has now accepted the natural circumscription of our body: echoing Maximos's dythelite theology,[105] Theodore notes that both humanity and divinity in the hypostatic union become manifest in virtue of their distinct actions (*pragmasin*), without either suppressing the other.

Theodore does not claim that the irruption of the divine realm into our shared human nature at the moment of the incarnation eliminated the Old Testament injunctions against images.[106] The event of the hypostatic union, however, enjoins us to reconsider the context of these prohibitions, which reflected an era when God had not yet chosen to become incarnate and was thus not yet visible in the flesh. The repeated juxtaposition of opposites—the limited and the unlimited, that which is characterized by form and that which is formless, the circumscribed with the uncircumscribable—invites the reader to appreciate the incarnation's disruption of human philosophical categories, much as the adverbs of the Chalcedonian definition—*adiairetōs, asynchytōs, atreptōs,* and *achōristōs*—underscore the inability of human discourse to capture the mystery of the incarnation.[107] In this perspective, the error of the heretics is their unwillingness to accept that the philosophical terms used to hint at the reality of the divine nature must reflect the way in which the latter chooses to relate with the created order.

Another objection that Theodore places in the mouth of "the heretic" shows us again how some iconoclasts resorted to the Chalcedonian definition in an attempt to legitimize their position.[108] "The heretic" notes that if the deity has been united to the flesh by means of the hypostatic union, the uncircumscribable divinity would also have to share in the circumscription of the flesh; to deny this, he alleges, would introduce a kind of *diairesis* in Christ, which is something the fathers at Chalcedon had denied. This is the first time in the *Antirrhetici*, but not the last, that Theodore's defense of icon veneration turns to the issue of the *communicatio idiomatum*.[109] The argument of the iconoclast is that if the divinity can be portrayed in an image of Christ, what is uncircumscribable can be circumscribed, and what is circumscribable is no longer subject to circumscription. This would be a clear logical contradiction, showing that images oppose reason, no less than revelation. Theodore, however, points out that in the hypostatic union, neither nature "ceases to be what it is," nor is it "transformed into the other," since this would cause the confusion (*synchysis*) that Chalcedon condemns. Christ is "one and the same" in hypostasis (*tē hypostasei*) and is characterized by a "lack of confusion" (*to asynchyton*) in his two natures, "within the limits of their proper boundaries."[110]

Theodore's contention is that the properties of either nature are ascribed to the one hypostasis that sustains them, without in any way being mingled or confused; the divinity of Christ does not die, nor is his humanity immortal; rather, the hypostasis of Christ experiences death in virtues of his human nature, and the same hypostasis is immortal in virtue of his divine nature.[111] Paradoxically, if the locus of the *communicatio idiomatum* were in the natures of Christ, the iconoclasts' objection would be quite correct, and Christ's humanity could not be portrayed in an image. The locus of the *communicatio idiomatum*, however, is the hypostasis, and as a result what we see in the icons is Christ's hypostasis dwelling in a glorified humanity.[112] Theodore's theology of circumscribability and uncircumscribability is merely a development of the Cyrillian strategy of partitive exegesis, which had paved the way for the Chalcedonian definition of a duality of natures, and is now deployed to defend the concreteness of Christ's incarnate humanity.[113]

This issue is taken up again as soon as "the heretic" claims that it is "absurd" to call Christ a "mere man" (*psilanthrōpos*), because "mere men" are characterized by circumscription, and Christ most certainly is not circumscribed.[114] Theodore not only agrees that Christ is not a "mere man" but adds that it would be utter impiety to claim that Christ assumed "one of the members of the human race" (*tōn tina anthrōpōn*), as Christ assumed humanity as a whole, or "the whole nature" (*tēn holēn physin*). The iconoclasts are accusing the orthodox of semi-Nestorianism. From their point of view, if Christ can be portrayed in an image, Christ must have had an individual human nature, but, the iconoclasts continue, we know from Cyril of Alexandria and from Leontios of Byzantium that Christ did not have an individual human nature; hence, they conclude, Christ cannot be portrayed in an image, and those who believe that he can are guilty of heresy. For Theodore, this is a *non sequitur.* Christ, it is true, did not have an individual human nature; yet, at the same time, Christ's nature was seen "in an individual manner" (*en atomō*), since we read in the Gospels that Christ was seen and was touched by his disciples, and that he went through all the usual activities that are typical of members of humanity.[115]

According to this argument, it is absurd to associate the assertion of Christ's circumscription with a revival of Nestorianism. Christ is circumscribed even if he is not a *psilanthrōpos*; he is not "one of many" but "God made man."[116] Rather predictably, Theodore turns this argument around, and he accuses his opponents of heresy. If they do not accept his position, they are saying that Christ came only "in phantasy," and they are falling back into some sort of Docetism.[117] Theodore is adamant that Christ became incarnate only once, at a particular moment in time and in a particular geographical location, and while Christ had assumed the totality of the human nature through his divine hypostasis, his humanity was invested with specific characteristics that made it distinguishable from other members of the human race.

Some iconoclasts took a different line and claimed that it was degrading to represent Christ using images that were "taken from the material world" (*hylikais hypotypōsesin*); in their opinion, the eternal Word should be considered "only by way of a noetic contemplation" (*en tēi kata noun theōriai*).[118] To this purpose, the iconoclasts even cited the word of the Prophet Habakkuk: "What is the purpose of a sculpture when someone has sculpted it?"[119] It is interesting that the language of "the heretic" should be almost Evagrian, and while there is no explicit reference to Evagrios or to any other Origenist author, the fact that this point should be made in these terms—indeed, in a way that seemingly questions the legitimacy of mental as well as physical imagery—is indicative of the lingering Origenist undercurrent in a lot of iconoclast apologetics. Theodore responds by citing Luke 14:11 and observes that while it is shameful for those who are lowly to exalt themselves, it is equally glorious for those who are above to undergo humiliation. As a result, what we may find repugnant—such as Christ's descent into "blood, bile, and other vile substances" that so appalled Porphyry[120]—actually underscores God's utter glory and condescension toward us. If "noetic contemplation" had been sufficient for our salvation, it would have been enough for Christ to come to us in that manner. As a result, "we would have been deprived of the appearance of his deeds" and of his suffering, which is so much like ours. Instead, Christ came into the flesh and chose to undergo everything that is typical of humanity; and while the eternal Word did not assume an individual human being, he still chose to become incarnate in the flesh and endure everything that is typical of our circumscribed nature.[121] Theodore's appropriation of the notion of anhypostasis allows him to claim that Christ's humanity had exploded the dialectic of generality and particularity; its generality was made manifest through its particularity, but its particularity in no way impinged on its generality.[122] Indeed, as Theodore reminds us, "as flesh he suffered in the flesh, he drank, and in the same way he ate."[123]

To use more contemporary language, Theodore's overarching concern is the dissolution of the concrete scriptural narrative into a disembodied intellectual intuition, where the incarnation is ultimately redundant. If the story of Christ's life in the flesh is crucial for our salvation, and if this story unfolded in the world of matter, it is certainly not unsuitable to represent it to us by drawing upon the example of nature. The iconoclasts' use of scripture is deeply misguided, as they focus on Old Testament injunctions against idolatry and apply them to images of Christ when the incarnation has brought about an irreversible transformation in the relationship between the divine and the created orders.[124] Theodore contrasts those who are under the law and those who are under grace, and notes that "the things of old" (*ta palai*), such as Sabbath and circumcision—and hence the prohibition against images—cannot be imposed on those who are no longer subject to the law.[125] A radical embrace of visual apophaticism fails to appreciate Christ's very concrete soteriological strategy.

Throughout the *Antirrhetici*, Theodore is always very careful to distinguish what can be said of the Son and what can be said of the Father; it is the incarnate Godhead "in human shape" that can be depicted using "material pigments," not the hypostasis of God the Father, who dwells beyond the realm of matter and form.[126] Theodore mentions the acts of the Quinisext Council, which, in the late seventh century, had addressed this very question and had condemned the practice of representing God the Father as an old man, as well as the custom of painting Christ as a lamb.[127] While these practices were not entirely unscriptural—the former relied on the description of the Ancient of Days in the Book of Daniel, whereas the notion of Christ as lamb is clearly present in John 1 and in Revelation—the council thought that the warrant of custom was insufficient to justify iconic representations that were not grounded in Christ's assumption of our common humanity. By recalling this decision, even if just in passing, Theodore reminds his readers that his position is in continuity with the broader tradition of the church. At the same time, he is also telling us that the heretics are confusing what can be said of the Father with what can be said of the Son; as the Father never became incarnate, the Old Testament injunctions against images continue to apply to him.

The *Antirrhetici* also discuss the relationship between the Eucharist and the sacred images, which was a highly controversial matter during the first as well as the second iconoclastic crisis.[128] Emperor Constantine V had claimed that Christ could be "represented" only in the liturgical action of the Eucharist, following the command of Christ "to do this in memory of me"; other forms of "representations" were instead illegitimate, because Christ had not commanded them. Theodore's answer is twofold: on the one hand, he notes that it is impossible to apply the term *image* to the eucharistic species, which are not the types (*typoi*), but rather the sacraments (*mystēria*) of truth. On the other hand, as the Eucharist is the synthesis of the economy of salvation, Theodore claims, rather imaginatively, that we are not only enjoined to celebrate this particular mystery—indeed, this can only be done by those who received holy orders—but also to commemorate all mysteries of Christ's life through liturgical actions or other celebrations; commemoration can also take the form of writing down the actions of Christ's life, either by way of ink on a parchment or by way of pigments on some other material. In the words of Basil of Caesarea, "The art of painting silently shows by imitation those things which the words of the story narrates."[129] Christ's injunction to "make memory" of all the events of his life—and therefore not just of the Eucharist—inspired the evangelists to compose the four Gospels. Theodore then asks why nobody ever questioned the decision of the sacred authors to put the actions of Christ in writing, and yet the iconoclasts now question the decision to depict the same actions in an image. Clearly, the composition of the Gospels and the "writing" of the icons are different but equally valid ways to commemorate Christ. Theodore goes even further and claims that it is perfectly legitimate to depict scenes from scripture that no human eye has ever seen—such as the Last Judgment, where "those standing on the right or on the left have a sadder or more joyful countenance"—as well as angels, about whose aspect the Word of God gives us few and scant information. Theodore justifies this practice, noting that there is no substantial difference between what is apprehended by the mind and what is apprehended by the senses such as hearing and sight; hence, we can complement with the imagination what we learn from the scriptures by the way of the intellect.[130]

A final important point in the first *Antirrheticus* is the question of whether, or in what way, the divinity of Christ is ontologically present in the image.[131] "The heretic" wonders whether the divinity of Christ indwells the icon according to the nature (*physikōs*), so that icon and divinity would become the object of joint veneration, as is already the case with the divinity of Christ and his flesh (*sarx*). Theodore responds that the way in which the divinity of Christ is present in the image is very different from the way in which the two natures of Christ are joined in the hypostatic union. In the former case, the connection (*synapheia*) of the two natures ensures that the divine hypostasis is subject to the circumscription of the flesh; as such, the two natures are honored jointly (*synaptikōs*), even as each nature preserves its own ontological integrity. In the case of the image, however, the flesh of Christ is not ontologically present. As a result, the divinity of Christ indwells the sacred image in the same way as it is present in all beings: "on the basis of the analogy (*kata analogian*) of the natures that receive it." The divinity is not present in the image in virtue of a natural union (*physikē enōsei*) but in virtue of a relational participation (*schetikē metalēpsei*).[132] As the natures that receive the divinity differ, so will veneration (*proskynēsis*) be of many different types (*polyschidēs*); while proper worship (*latreutikē*) belongs to God alone, veneration will differ according to the intention (*dia tēs dianoēseōs*).

The organization of the second *Antirrheticus* differs from the first, as every paragraph of this second treatise begins with a statement of the "orthodox" interlocutor. This is immediately challenged by "the heretic," giving rise to a rejoinder by "the orthodox" at the beginning of the following paragraph. While there is a substantial amount of repetition, the second *Antirrheticus* helps us understand the role and the function of tradition in the mind of Theodore, who constantly stresses that his theological position is in continuity with the legacy of the earlier church fathers. A recurrent point in the second *Antirrheticus* is the claim that Christ, having become like us in all things, is also "the prototype of his own image," even if "this is not written in these very terms" (*tē lexei*).[133] "The heretic," of course, observes that nowhere in scripture is it said that Christ is the prototype of his own image; in a similar way, this claim was not included in the Nicene Creed (which is here called "the profession of faith," *homologia tēs pisteōs*). Theodore responds that many teachings that are not included in scripture are of the same weight as teachings that are: the obvious example is the teaching of *homoousia*, but Theodore also mentions the divinity of the Holy Spirit and the teaching that Mary is the Mother of God—both of which, he adds, were formally defined when the church needed to oppose certain heretical teachings.[134]

Continuing on the same point, "the heretic" tries to defend his claim from a different angle, observing that Christ is not a mere man and therefore cannot be a prototype.[135] Theodore responds that Christ's universal humanity does not deny his circumscribability, and as such he can be the prototype of an image in the same way as every human being can be a prototype. For "the orthodox," the adoration of Christ and of his imprint (*ektypōma*) are one and the same; everything that can be said "synonymously" of the prototype will then be said "homonymously" of the image.[136] Theodore also applies this to the images of the cross: if images receive the same veneration as their prototype, the crosses we use for private devotion, or in liturgical contexts, should be given the same veneration as the true cross of Christ.[137] In support of this point Theodore cites a number of passages from the Pseudo-Denys, Basil of Caesarea, and Athanasios of Alexandria.[138]

The third *Antirrheticus* does not follow the dialogical structure of the previous ones, and Theodore himself notes at the very beginning that he composed this work sometime after the first two sections. Theodore develops his argument by way of a series of syllogisms, thereby summarizing the chief points of discussion from the first and second *Antirrhetici*. Part A reviews the arguments for Christ's pictorial representability using the customary strategies derived from the Christology of Chalcedon but also resorting to more speculative arguments from philosophy and linguistics. The chief point is, once more, the claim that in virtue of the *communicatio idiomatum*, Christ can be circumscribed and as such he can be portrayed in an image without any injury to the unity of the natures or to the distinction of their properties. The earlier debate on the difference between image and prototype provide the chief focus of Part B, in which Theodore reflects on the nature and purpose of artificial images. While emphasizing the difference in essence between the image and the prototype, Theodore also stresses that image and prototype share the same likeness (*homoiōsis*); the likeness of Christ is ontologically present in the icon, and the likeness of the icon is ontologically present in Christ. Part C builds on the preceding section and concludes that as there is an ontological relationship between image and prototype—albeit the relationship is not one of consubstantiality or of equality in dignity—the veneration of images is justified, as the honor that is paid to the icon ultimately ascends to the prototype. Part D insists that the veneration that is due to the icon and the veneration that is due to Christ are actually one and the same, and this in no way constitutes idolatry, as those who venerate an image are venerating a reality that is already ontologically present in the prototype.

Once more, this final *Antirrheticus* focuses on the dialectic of circumscribability and uncircumscribability that flows from a careful deployment of the *communicatio idiomatum.*[139] Theodore uses this notion to challenge the iconoclastic claim that the incarnate Christ cannot be depicted in an image—a claim reflecting the iconoclasts' poor understanding of the ontological relationship between humanity and divinity. On the one hand, the third *Antirrheticus* deploys a very high christological rhetoric, underscoring the anhypostatic character of his humanity as well as the role of the eternal Logos as the subject of Christ's every action. On the other hand, as already noted, Theodore's driving intention is to defend a very "concrete" understanding of the hypostatic union, which not only affirms the presence of the Son's full-fledged divinity in the person of the incarnate Christ, but also emphasizes the presence of a very concrete, and thus "describable" and "representable," humanity.[140]

Theodore's theology is therefore a theology of the image to the extent that it is also a theology of the incarnation; and it is a theology of the incarnation not only because it explores the inner dynamics of the hypostatic union, but also because it underscores the soteriological import of this event for the members of the Christian community, who are able to access the ongoing redemptive value of the life of Christ through the iconic representation of the events of his life. As noted in the previous section, Theodore's theology of the icon is also a profoundly spiritual theology, presenting the veneration of images as a devotional and liturgical entry point into the eschatological reality where our humanity will be embraced and transfigured by the divine.

Theodore's Other Apologetic Writings and the Invention of the Iconophile Tradition

Theodore's remaining works on iconoclasm are less widely known than the *Antirrhetici*, largely because of their unavailability in modern translations. What we find in Migne's *Patrologia Graeca* is probably only a selection of his theological production on the topic, much of which probably took the form of occasional writings that have not been preserved.[141] After the ninth century, once the memories of the iconoclastic crises faded away, Theodore was remembered mainly for his work of monastic reform; his writings on the question of the images tended to receive far less attention, and John Damascene's *Treatise on the Holy Images* became the standard reference work for the orthodox teaching on the icons.[142] While the *Antirrhetici* contains the most extensive treatment of his theology of the image, the other works afford us a glimpse into the world of Byzantine apologetics, where epigrams, letters, and theological pamphlets were the chief vehicles for theological discourse and polemic. The *Seven Chapters against the Iconoclasts*, the *Questions Posed by Theodore to the Iconoclasts*, as well as the collage of verse and prose that carries the title *Refutations and Subversions* (*Elegchos kai Anatropē*), show us Theodore at the very center of the controversy on the icons. They also show how Theodore envisages his theological position: much as Maximos the Confessor in the seventh century had presented himself as working in perfect agreement with the Chalcedonian tradition, Theodore understands his work as firmly in continuity with the teaching of the seven ecumenical councils that have come before him. While John Damascene had passed away in the year 749, long before the Second Council of Nicaea proclaimed the legitimacy of sacred images, Theodore is writing after the highest deliberative organ of the universal church had already pronounced itself in favor of icon veneration; because the iconoclasts rejected the decisions of this assembly, Theodore felt that it was his duty to emphasize the perfect congruence between the practice of venerating images, on the one hand,

and the faith of the church as it had been proclaimed by the earlier councils, on the other.

The *Seven Chapters* is a sort of systematic summary of the *Antirrhetici*;[143] each section addresses the question of icon veneration from a different perspective, in response to a particular objection on the part of the iconoclasts that is mentioned in the heading. An important theme, as in the first *Antirrheticus*, is the contrast between the old and the new economy; enemies of the images fail to appreciate the progressive nature of God's revelation to humanity, as well as the fact that there is a fundamental difference between the purviews of *theologia* and *oikonomia*. The second chapter contains another attack against the *agraptodocetae*, who complain that the Gospels are silent about Christ's physical appearance but forget that there are many details of Christ's life that are not described explicitly, and yet no one questions that they actually took place. Theodore also launches on a rather fanciful exegetical analysis of the passage in Matthew 22 where Christ tells Peter to pay the tribute "for me and for you," which Theodore interprets as meaning "for my image and for yours"—arguably the least convincing aspect of Theodore's argument in favor of Christ's pictorial representation. While many of the arguments in the *Seven Chapters* are not particularly original, the fourth and the fifth chapters give us a glimpse of the impact of iconoclasm on liturgical life: the enemies of the images thought that blessings of children or exorcisms could only be carried out with a cross and not with an icon. Theodore observes, of course, that as the priest is himself a type of Christ, the cross and the icon are in an ontological relationship.

The *Questions Posed by Theodore to the Iconoclasts* is a brief text in fifteen paragraphs, in which Theodore sets out to expose the inconsistency and the untenable consequences of the teaching of his opponents by way of a *reductio ad absurdum*.[144] As in the third *Antirrheticus*, Theodore frequently resorts to the teaching of the *communicatio idiomatum*, exploring the way in which the dialectic of circumscribability and uncircumscribability makes the pictorial representation of the incarnate Christ ontologically possible, while also furnishing a rationale for legitimizing its veneration.[145] Paragraphs seven and nine, in particular, attack the claims of those iconoclasts for whom Christ is characterized solely by uncircumscribability and therefore cannot be represented in any way. Theodore associates this position with "the heresy of Mane the Persian" and accuses them of denying the reality of the incarnation. As mentioned above in the discussion of the *Antirrhetici*, the ascription of the properties of the natures to the hypostasis of the eternal Word ensures the dual consubstantiality of the incarnate Christ, while also preserving the integrity of both natures.

The *Letter to Plato* gives Theodore the opportunity to reflect one more time on the relationship between the veneration of the image and the veneration of the prototype.[146] Theodore cites *De Ecclesiastica Hierarchia*, in which the Pseudo-Denys reflects in high Neo-Platonic terms on the relationship between image and archetype.[147] He then goes on to expatiate on the difference between a natural and an artificial image: while the former does not have a natural distinction from its prototype, but merely one of identity, the latter shares a hypostasis with its prototype but is distinct from it in terms of substance. Of course, the paradigmatic example of a natural image is the eternal Son, who is the image of the Father, whereas icons of Christ and the saints are examples of artificial images. The problem with some iconoclasts is that they follow Origen in thinking that the only true image is a natural image, when in fact artificial images, while ontologically different, are also legitimate.

The *Refutations and Subversions*, for their part, are quite different from all other works included in this volume.[148] In the first part of this work, Theodore refutes the argument brought forth by a number of iconoclastic authors in a series of poems that are reproduced at the beginning of the work. The identity of the authors cannot be determined with certainty, although "John" may be John the Grammarian (780–847), who is also the target of harsh criticism in the *Celebratory Canon*. It is also not impossible that the author of these compositions may be Theodore himself, seeking to set up a target for his own apologetic eloquence. At the same time, the iconoclastic poems do not address the question of sacred-image veneration directly, but contrast the fabrication and the veneration of the icons with the practice of venerating the cross. Most of the poems by the iconoclasts, as well as some of the poems expressing the "orthodox" point of view, follow an elaborate pattern, where the first, middle, and last letter of each line, as well as the middle word of each stanza, compose a sentence that is used by the author as the title.

The first poem—attributed to "John"—is of particular interest, as the author claims that in refusing to honor the images, but in giving honor to the cross alone, the iconoclasts—represented by the emperors "who carry crowns"—are actually following the example of the authors of the Gospels, who praised Christ "in golden letters" but did not pay any attention to "lowly matters"—presumably details such as Christ's physical appearance.[149] This is the position of the *agraptodocetae* lambasted by Nikephoros in his *Antirrhetici.* Theodore responds that the authors of the Gospels did not think it beneath their dignity to describe Christ reclining in the manger, eating, or sleeping; in fact, so as to describe these events, belonging to the economy of our salvation, they actually had to raise "the eyes of their minds" to what they were contemplating. Theodore neither addresses the claim of the iconoclast from a theoretical point of view, as in the *Antirrhetici,* nor does he try to highlight their inconsistency, but he comments in a style that is close to a theological stream of consciousness, citing from the scripture and the fathers as he sees fit, and frequently directly attacking his adversaries. This different style of argumentation—veering away from the speculative toward the genre of the invective—gives Theodore more leeway to expatiate on the viciousness of the iconoclasts' views, which are presented as conceptually mistaken, but also as ethically and spiritually flawed. The enemies of the images are endangering their own salvation, and Theodore feels he has a duty to expose their views for what they really are.

Another interesting poem in the *Refutations and Subversions* is the one by "Sergios," who recounts how Moses raised a type of the cross and with this type defeated the enemy, while in the present the true cross of Christ will save from perdition those who are "spiritually wounded" by the sacred images.[150] While a reader may initially associate Moses raising the type of the cross with the episode of the bronze serpent,[151] it becomes clear from Theodore's comment that Sergios is referring to the episode of Moses praying with his arms outstretched in the shape of the cross and thereby defeating the Amalekites.[152] Theodore responds that it is foolish to honor the cross, but not the image of the one who triumphed on the cross; the iconoclast, whose teaching is as dangerous as a violent flood, detaches the image of Christ from the weapon he used to defeat evil, so that Christ, echoing Matthew 12:26, "is now divided against himself." The belief that one may venerate the cross but withhold honor from the image of the Savior is thus exposed as inconsistent, since it was the incarnate Christ who procured our salvation through his suffering. To call the sacred images "arrows thrown with an evil intention" is not only illogical but utter blasphemy.

While the *Refutations and Subversions* preserve some of Theodore's poetic compositions on the question of the images, the more interesting part of the work arguably begins at paragraph 17, where Theodore reproduces an iconoclastic profession of faith and goes on to refute it point by point, only to conclude with his own "orthodox" profession. The iconoclastic "declaration" (*hypographē*) professes to accept the six ecumenical councils; it does, however, reject "the meeting held under Tarasios"—a transparent reference to the Second Council of Nicaea that was held in 787—and accepts as binding the decisions of the iconoclastic Council of Hieria, which had met in the year 754 at the church of Hieria and at St. Mary in Blachernae.[158]

This text is clearly a product of the second wave of iconoclasm that shook the empire in the early ninth century. While at the time of the first iconoclastic crisis no ecumenical council had officially affirmed the legitimacy of images, even if the Quinisext Council had addressed some questions of iconography, by the time of Theodore, opponents of the images had to confront the fact that the church's highest deliberative body had pronounced itself in favor of icon veneration. As a result, iconoclasts found themselves in need of an alternative ecclesial genealogy for their position—a narrative that would establish the orthodoxy of their views and brand their opponents with the mark of heresy. The enemies of the images stressed, of course, that they accepted everything that the first six councils had taught but regarded the Second Council of Nicaea as canonically irregular, and they chose to view as binding the two iconoclastic assemblies held during the reign of Constantine V.

In the rest of the *Refutations*, Theodore exposes the untenable nature of this narrative and replaces it with an orthodox alternative that alone, in his opinion, is in line with the tradition of the earlier fathers. Theodore notes that it is typical of heretics to claim that they accept the teachings of the holy fathers who came before them, but this display of deference toward the tradition will not fool those who truly live according to the orthodox faith. Both scripture and the fathers, however, teach the legitimacy of icon veneration. Theodore proves this once more with a series of citations from the Letter to the Hebrews, the writings of the Pseudo-Denys and the Cappadocian fathers, and other more obscure texts that he attributes to Athanasios and Gregory of Nyssa but are now generally regarded as spurious.[154] The assembly at Hieria—which, as we know, had actually retrieved an older, semi-Evagrian understanding of Christ's subjectivity—cannot possibly represent the true orthodox faith, as its decrees fell outside the consensus of what constitutes orthodoxy.

According to Theodore, there is only one faith that has been taught from the beginning to the present, and this faith is the faith of the Council of Nicaea, which was merely expanded by the later councils as the need arose from time to time to counter the threat of heresy.[155] Nicaea did not immediately teach the truth of Mary's divine maternity, which was proclaimed at Ephesus; and even Chalcedon, which asserted that Christ was fully consubstantial with the Father in terms of his divinity and fully consubstantial with us in terms of his humanity, did not pronounce itself on the question of Christ's wills, which would only be defined by the Sixth Ecumenical Council in the seventh century. Whatever was not taught earlier, however, was already implicit in the teaching of the earlier councils. As such, according to Theodore, the First Ecumenical Council, in asserting that Christ had become incarnate and had embraced the fullness of humanity, had already asserted the legitimacy of icon veneration. The faith of the First Council of Nicaea is the same faith as that of the Second Council that was also held in Nicaea over four hundred and fifty years later; the faith of Hieria, however, is a different faith—one that places itself outside the boundaries of orthodoxy, as it does not fully accept the real import of the incarnation.

Theodore's chronological position at the end of what could be called without exaggeration the great adventure of early Christian thought ensures that he can take a long view of the history of doctrinal development. The fact that he can look back with confidence at a conciliar definition of the legitimacy of icon veneration places him in a different position from his great predecessor John of Damascus, whose writings on the icon were composed at a time when no official pronouncement on the question had yet been made. What we find in Theodore's writings against iconoclasm is a great work of synthesis, carried out by someone who knows how to weave together different insights from the great spectrum of the Chalcedonian tradition, and who never wavers in his conviction of the fundamental coherence of his vision. In the dialectic of circumscribability and uncircumscribability, as well as in the theology of anhypostasy whose ancestry went all the way back through Maximos and Leontios to the mysterious pages of the *Kephalaia Gnostica*, Theodore found a way to assert the general character of Christ's humanity while simultaneously affirming the salvific particularity of the incarnation and the propaedeutic value of the sacred images. If, more than four hundred years earlier, Evagrios had warned his fellow monks ensconced in the depths of the Egyptian desert that "the Deity had no quantity or form" and that all representations of the divine had to be rejected as demonic,[156] Theodore can reassure us that God did not disdain to enter into the world of matter and that sacred images afford us a glimpse of this encounter between humanity and divinity. Like few other theologians, Theodore could make his own the words of the First Letter of John, "That which was from the beginning, which we have heard, which we have seen with our eyes, which we have looked at and our hands have touched—this we proclaim concerning the Word of life."[157]

The Triumph of Orthodoxy

In the year 842, sixteen years after Theodore's death, the veneration of icons was definitively restored by a synod held in Constantinople under the leadership of the Dowager Empress Theodora (815–67) and Patriarch Methodios (788–846). On February 19 of that year, at the end of the first session, all members of the synod took part in a triumphal procession from St. Mary in Blachernae, which had been the scene of the iconoclastic Council of Hieria in 754, to the Basilica of Hagia Sophia, carrying the icons of Christ, the Theotokos, and numerous saints. This procession took place on the First Sunday of Great Lent, which until that time had been devoted to the commemoration of Old Testament figures such as Moses, Aaron, and Saul. The synod held in Constantinople decreed, however, that from that year onward, this day should be marked by a perpetual feast commemorating this event. This inaugurated the liturgical tradition of the Triumph of Orthodoxy, which the Christian East celebrates to this day.[158]

Theodore could not witness these events, as he had passed away sixteen years previously. The Byzantine tradition, however, would forever associate his name with this liturgical celebration and would attribute to his pen one of the most important liturgical texts used by the church on this day. As the faithful process around the church carrying the icons, a canon is sung that begins:

> *Let us sing, O faithful, a song as an action of grace to the God and benefactor of all, because He raised a horn of salvation, and a great power, to protect the true faith.*
>
> *Truly the divine grace has been shown to the world, and glory and honor are manifest; and for this reason the Church rejoices, having put on the stole, of which she had earlier been stripped.*
>
> *The holy fathers, having woven again the garment of Christ, which had earlier been torn apart by John, the seducer and the maker of poisons, gave it back to the church.*[159]

It is highly unlikely that Theodore should be the author of this text, which stretches over eight odes and could only have been written after the battle for the legitimacy of the icons had been definitely won. A more likely author is Patriarch Methodios, who had prevailed over the iconoclastic faction and had restored peace to a church torn apart by decades of strife; or perhaps this celebratory hymn is the product of some unknown iconophile monk, who had endured long persecution for his convictions and was now expressing his joy in seeing his position vindicated. Yet, in the same way as Maximos the Confessor had been the target of harsh persecution for his dythelite conviction but had been rehabilitated posthumously at the Third Council of Constantinople,[160] Theodore's struggle in defense of the images was now finally acknowledged to be no less and no more than an expression of the unadulterated faith of the church. During the procession for the Triumph of Orthodoxy, the faithful sing:

> *Having taken back the incarnate form of the Lord, the Church exults and rejoices with her children; it has received from him the ensigns of victory, the symbols of orthodoxy.*

It was only fitting then that on this day the liturgy should mention the name of Theodore as one of the holy fathers who had preserved the treasure of the orthodox faith.

WRITINGS ON ICONOCLASM

FIRST REFUTATION OF THE ICONOCLASTS

Since a new-fangled heresy is up in arms against us, barking against the truth, and instilling agitation in unstable minds by way of vain talk,[1] it is only proper that whosoever has the ability to speak should do so, rather than remain silent.[2] A speaker might conceivably decide to perform the two following tasks: he could strengthen his own discernment somewhat, exploring and bringing together the supporting arguments of the matter at hand; and he could then share his discoveries with others, if there be any who would lend their ears. Thus, while I am utterly inadequate to both endeavors, relying on the prayers and the exhortations of my elders, I will attempt to express my opinion (*hypolēpsis*), for what the latter is worth.[3] The theologian claims that "it is better to offer one's modest contribution than to let go of the whole matter";[4] this is all the more true as the issue at hand was not explained exhaustively in my *Invective (Stēliteutikos)*.[5] Thus, this debate will be continued by opposing our teaching to that of our adversary, hoping that through the juxtaposition, as through some kind of investigative procedure, the corrupt and deceitful mark of impiety may be cast off from the pious and undefiled character of truth. Yet, "The Lord will grant speech to those who bring the good news to a great power," if, unworthy as I am, I may quote scripture as I begin my treatise.[6]

I. *Orthodox*: You should know, my hearers, that among us Christians there is one faith (*pistis*), and one adoration (*latreia*), and one veneration (*proskynēsis*): the one that is addressed to the Father, and to the Son, and to the Holy Spirit;[7] because concerning the nature (*physis*)[8] of the deity, what is venerated is one, and in the same way, according to tradition (*synepeia*),[9] those that are intellectually perceived according to their hypostatic character (*idiotēta*) are three.[10]

II. *Heretic*: "It is not one at all, as our piety has proved to have a multiplicity of objects (*polyproskynēton*) in virtue of the erection of images, a tradition that has been transferred by some demonic wile from the Greek tradition into the whole church, bringing about the veneration of idols."[11] The divine is utterly incomprehensible and uncircumscribable, as every theologian agrees.

Orthodox: To the claim that the divine is incomprehensible (*aperilēpton*) and uncircumscribable (*aperigrapton*),[12] one may add that the divine is also lacking in boundaries, limits, and forms, and one may also use any other term signifying the privation of what is not proper to God; this is evident to everybody. It is only appropriate to say with scripture, "What fellowship does light have with darkness, or what agreement does Christ have with Belial?"[13] Or indeed, what agreement do sacred images have with idols of demons? Before the effects, it would then be appropriate to honor and venerate their causes, such as Astarte, and Chamos, the curse of the Sydonians.[14] And similarly, we should also honor Apollo, Zeus, Chronos, and the other various gods of the Greeks, and as the latter, because of demonic cunning (*kakotechnia*), had transferred their ignorant veneration from God the creator to the products of his creation, scripture says that "they gave honor to the creation instead of the creator,"[15] and that they plunged into the same abyss of polytheism.[16]

For us, however, there is only one God, whom we venerate as Trinity. As far as the teaching of theology is concerned,[17] beware, lest you devise some kind of circumscription or comprehension—this was an invention of Greek thought (*epinoia*)[18]—when one cannot even have a grasp of God's very existence, or what it consists of, as the Godhead alone can have an understanding of itself. But because of his great goodness (*agathotēta*), one of the Trinity has come into human nature, becoming like us; and in this way, there came to be a mingling of what cannot be mingled, and a joining of what cannot be joined; in other words, [a union] of what is uncircumscribed with what is circumscribed, of what has boundaries with what is boundless, of what is limitless with what has limits, of what escapes form with what is comfortably subject to form. Truly, this is a paradox; for this reason Christ is depicted in images, and what is invisible is seen; he who in his proper divinity exists without circumscription accepts the natural circumscription of our body. Both aspects reveal what they are by means of their actions, and neither falsifies what it is, as is alleged by your claim.[19]

III. *Heretic*: But when the iconophiles circumscribe God bodily, they deny that God remains uncircumscribed. If the deity had been united to the flesh by means of a hypostatic union, it is necessary that the uncircumscribable divinity should share in the circumscription (*perigraphē*) of the flesh. It is not possible to divide one from the other, otherwise one would introduce some detestable manner of division (*diairesis*).[20]

Orthodox: According to your erudite claim (*philologēma*),[21] neither was it the case that what became circumscribed could remain uncircumscribed even as it was wrapped in swaddling garments, nor could the same remain invisible in the act of being seen, even as it was beheld, nor could it remain intangible in being touched even as it was touched, nor could it remain impassible as it suffered even as it was crucified, nor could it remain immortal as it was put to death even as it was crucified. In the same way, you should consider that the divine nature remained uncircumscribed even as it was circumscribed. Indeed, these are properties (*idiōmata*) in the same way as the others are: the ones belonging to the uncircumscribable nature are those wherein Christ is acknowledged to be God, whereas the ones of the circumscribed nature are the ones in which Christ is acknowledged to be divine.[22] Neither modifies the other, or ceases to be what it was; nor is it the case that either is transformed into the other, as in this case the confusion (*synchysis*) would arise from that which we have fled; but he is one and the same in his hypostasis, and he is characterized by a lack of confusion (*to asynchyton*) in his natures, within the limit of their proper boundaries.[23] Thus you must accept the notion of circumscribability; otherwise, you must let go of terms such as *visible*, *tangible*, or *comprehensible*, as well as all other similar terms; if you did that, it would be clear that you would have rejected the very notion that the Word became flesh, which is utter impiety.

IV. *Heretic*: To call Christ a mere human being (*psilos anthrōpos*) is neither here nor there. The fact of being circumscribed is a characteristic of a mere human being; but given that Christ is not circumscribed, he is clearly not a mere human being.[24]

Orthodox: You appear to indulge in a word game when you bring forth your beloved term *uncircumscribable* (*philaperigrapton*), or when you counter our argument with a non-argument, or try to prove what is not subject to proof, or deploy your logical reasoning against what cannot be demonstrated.[25] Hence, you should by all means get out of here. Christ has not been generated as a mere man; no one who belongs to the number of the pious would ever say that he assumed one out of the members of the human race (*tōn tina anthrōpōn analabein*);[26] rather, he assumed human nature as a whole, or the whole nature (*kath'holou, tēn holēn physin*); and yet this nature was seen in an individual manner (*en atomō*)—for otherwise how could he be seen?—and according to this nature he is then seen and described, touched and circumscribed, he eats and drinks, he grows and matures, works and takes a rest, sleeps and walks, experiences hunger and thirst, weeps and perspires, and does whatever else one who is a human being may experience at all. Therefore Christ is circumscribed, even if he is not a mere human being (he is not one of the many, but God become a human being); else those whom you follow, and who say that Christ only came in appearance and as it were in a phantasy, would be attacked by the swift dragons of heresy.[27] And yet, if he is truly God made man, he is also uncircumscribed, so the impious dog who laughably suggests that Christ had his origin from Mary may be chased off.[28] This is indeed the new mystery of the economy: an encounter (*synodos*) has taken place between the divine and the human nature in the one hypostasis of the eternal Word, which preserves in an intact manner the properties of each in the undivided (*adiairetō*) union.

V. *Heretic*: In the scriptures, however, the erection of simulacra is utterly forbidden, for it says, "Thou shalt make no idol for thyself, nor any likeness or whatever is in the heaven above or on the earth below or in the waters under the earth; thou shalt not venerate them; nor shalt thou worship them, for I am the Lord thy God."[29]

Orthodox: But when was this spoken, and to whom? Before grace was given, and to those who were under the law[30] and were being inducted into the monarchy of one person;[31] when God had not yet appeared in the flesh, and the ancients were protected from the idols of the Gentiles; indeed these things were laid down as law for those who through their forefather Abraham had formed a chosen people, having fled the abyss of polytheism. Indeed one is God and Lord of all, "whom no one has seen or can see," as scripture says; of him there is no description, or likeness, or circumscription, or determination, nor any of the things that come within comprehension by way of human reasoning (*dianoia*).[32] About this scripture could say most clearly, "To whom did you compare the Lord? And to which similitude did you liken him?"[33] I forego to point out that what was utterly proscribed in the case of God was not proscribed in all other cases. Indeed, he who had issued this prohibition to Moses during his vision (*tō hierophantē Mōsei*) would then command him, "Thou—He indeed said—shalt make two chiseled Cherubim in gold, on the two extremities; the cherubim shall extend their wings above, overshadowing with their wings the seat of mercy, their face turned one toward the other...and there I will make myself known to you, and I shall speak to you."[34] And in Leviticus: "Make yourself a serpent, and set it on a sign post; and if a serpent were to bite a man, whoever was bitten, looking at it, would be saved. And so Moses made a bronze serpent, and set it on a sign post; and it came to pass, that if a serpent bit a man, and he would look at the bronze serpent, he would live."[35] Mark well what we find in scripture: even if the angels are not in the flesh like us, and even if the serpent differs in appearance in virtue of its monstrous shape, the latter was represented in a mysterious manner (*ainigmatōdōs*) as a type of Christ.[36] So, if God in ancient times condescended to disguise himself in such manner so as to heal those that were bitten, how could it not be seemly or pleasing to him to raise up the icon of the bodily form (*idea*) in virtue of which he has become a human being? And if the monstrous type merely by the act of being seen could cure, how could the sacred image of Christ, by being looked at, not hallow those who look at it?

VI. *Heretic*: God then falls into contradiction and opposition with himself.

Orthodox: What folly! The negative command (*apophasis*) concerns the likening of the Godhead to those objects of creation such as, for instance, the sun, the moon, the stars, or whatever else is used to model idols; the positive command (*kataphasis*) aims at leading Israel symbolically, as far as possible, toward the contemplation and worship of the one God by means of sculpted and shaped supports. Is the very pattern of the whole tent not a clear foreshadowing of worship in the Spirit, adumbrated by means of symbolic visions to the great Moses by the God of all?[37]

VII. *Heretic*: It is an offense and a degradation to represent Christ in types drawn from the material world (*hylikais hypotypōsesin*). Let him rather remain in a noetic contemplation (*en tēi kata noun theōriai*), so that he should be formed (*morphoutai*) in us as the Holy Spirit inspires in us some sort of divine formation through sanctification and righteousness. Scripture says, in fact, "What is the purpose of a sculpture when someone has sculpted it? He has made something of metal, and a liar, because the maker trusts its own creation."[38] And further, "Because it is a tree cut from a forest, the work of a craftsman, the result of fusion, of gold and silver."[39]

Orthodox: You obviously love not to move away from repetition, or perhaps even blindness, maliciously moving from one thing to the next. What you call indecent and repugnant is indeed worthy of God and elevated because of the sublimity of the Divine Mystery. Is it not the case indeed that it is glorious for those who are above to undergo humiliation, in the same way as it is shameful for those that are lowly to exalt themselves?[40] In this way, the circumscription of our own body, embraced out of a most magnanimous condescension toward us, is to the glory of Christ, who remains on the pinnacle of his proper divinity, adorned by his immaterial indescribability. He who had established everything became matter, or indeed, flesh. And he did not disdain what he had chosen to become or what he had chosen to be named after, namely, matter, and the fact that matter can be circumscribed. Concerning the claim that intellectual contemplation is sufficient, or that Christ would be formed in us again by the Holy Spirit—this belongs to the discussion of the topic of baptism.[41] And, in any case, we are not talking of the impression onto us of the very stamp of the hypostasis of God the Father but of the representation for us of the image in human shape using material pigments. If indeed the noetic contemplation were to suffice, it would have been enough for him to come to us in this manner, and thereby we would have been deprived of the appearance of his deeds, if he had not come in a bodily manner, and of his sufferings, which were undeniably like ours. But we have said enough of this. As flesh he suffered in the flesh, he drank, and in the same way he ate; he did all the things that each human does, except for sin.[42] And so what in your opinion is unseemly is truly honor to the highly praised and exceedingly glorious Word. Cease then to cast scriptural passages against us in an ignorant manner, taking those that are spoken against the Greeks in regard to the idolatrous shapes and misapplying them to the image of Christ! Who then who has a sane mind (*noun echōn*) would not distinguish the difference (*diaphora*) between an idol and an icon?[43] The fact that one is darkness and the other is light? That the one is deceitful and the other lacking in deceit? That one is the mark of polytheism and the other the clearest mark of the divine economy?

VIII. *Heretic*: Why is what is written about the cross not also written about the image? "The word of the cross—he says—is folly to those that are condemned, but to those that are saved, it is the power of God."[44] And he also adds, "Far be it from me to glory, except in the cross of Christ!"[45] and many other things are similarly celebrated by the verses of scripture. Where then will you find such a passage that concerns the icon, and by which authors?

Orthodox: Tell me, O you impudent man, which did he praise, or in which did he glory? In the cross, or in the representation of the cross? In the first, clearly; but the copy is not separated from the glory of the prototype, in the same way as shadow is not separated from light. And indeed, whatever is said about the cause, the same things can be said without exception of whatever is caused. In the former case, this will be said in the proper manner (*kyriōs*), because it is so by nature (*physei*); in the latter case, it will not be said in the proper manner (*kyriōs*), but rather by homonymy (*homōnymōs*). As Christ then had been announced from the beginning, talk about his image has followed accordingly (*schetikōs*); and you will find as many testimonies concerning Christ's image as you will find concerning Christ himself. In the same way concerning the type of the cross, you will find as many concerning the cross itself. Nowhere does scripture talk of type (*typos*) or image (*eikōn*), even if we allow that such terms mean the same thing. It is indeed utter silliness to look for such things, given that in the things that we see the effects share the power of the causes.[46] Is it not the case, after all, that every image is a kind of seal (*sphragis*) or imprint (*ektypōsis*), bearing in itself the very same form (*eidos*) from which it has its name? Indeed, we call "cross" the impressed mark (*aposphragisma*), because it is the cross; there are not two crosses. And we call the image of Christ "Christ," because it is also Christ, and not two Christs—since it is impossible to distinguish one from the other in virtue of the name (*homōnymia*), but only in virtue of the nature (*physei*); so the blessed Basil says that the image of the king is also called king, and there are not two kings;[47] neither is power divided, nor is the glory apportioned; and the honor of the represented images goes over (*diabainei*) to the prototype.[48]

IX. *Heretic*: It so happens that in virtue of the multiplicity of images, there are many who are called "Lords" or "Christs"; hence comes polytheism; but we have only one Lord and God who is honored by us.

Orthodox: So what? Is not the Father Lord? Or the Son? Or the Spirit? Is each of them not God? Of course they are. And does this mean that there are three Gods and three Lords? That would be impiety. There is one who is God and Lord. The same things must be understood about the images, my friend; even if the representations are many in terms of number (*tō arythmō*), yet there is only one Christ, not many, in the same way as Christ is one and not different individuals (*diaphoroi*).[49] For, just as in the former case the simplicity of the appellation "God and Lord" is appropriate to the nature that does not tolerate to be divided, so in the latter case the use of the same name brings the various types into one species (*eidos*).[50] Hence, your silly objection appears to be inane.

X. *Heretic*: Let it be conceded that Christ can be represented, yet this should be according to the sacred words of divine origin (*hē theoparadotos hierologia*): "Do this in memory of me,"[51] he said, clearly indicating that he could not be represented in any other manner than by way of commemoration;[52] only in the act of commemoration what is represented is truly present, and the act of representing is holy.

Orthodox: For your refutation, it is sufficient to point out that you are clearly contradicting yourself, as you are conceding that Christ can be circumscribed, while earlier on you denied the very same thing. But since it would not be appropriate to leave any of your claims unchallenged (*anepitimēton*),[53] let us proceed to refute them one by one. What have you to say about these things that are reverently pronounced (*hierologēthenta*) and sung by the priests? Do you call them image, or truth? If you call them image, what nonsense! You go from blasphemy to blasphemy, like people who step into some sort of mud and fall down with both feet into something even more slippery as they try to go further. Indeed, you did not hesitate to incur the label of atheism to make sure your claims would be strengthened; and instead you call them truth—which indeed they are; indeed, the very body and blood of Christ are acknowledged in the reception on the part of the faithful, according to the words of divine origin—why then do you talk nonsense taking as types (*typoi*) the sacraments (*mystēria*) of truth?[54] "Do this in memory of me" is what the word says, and rightly so; indeed, this mystery is the recapitulation (*synkephalaiōsis*) of the whole economy,[55] signifying the whole by means of a synecdoche (*synekdochikōs*) through the most important part.[56] And the fact that he said "Do this in memory of me" is not said for everyone, but only for those who received the sacred orders. Yet at the same time, he did not forbid us to celebrate the other mysteries; we do indeed celebrate memorials of Christmas and of the Theophany;[57] at a certain time we carry branches to commemorate his sitting upon an ass; and at another time we kiss one another as a sign of the resurrection. I will forego to mention the ascent to the temple and the temptation of the tempter, in imitation of which we undergo the abstinence (*enkrateia*) of forty days, as well as other practices that have the same significance (*theōria*).[58] The Word should be understood to have meant, "Do *all* these things in memory of me," including them through a sort of reticence under the heading of the most important mystery. And then, should we not understand the same thing concerning his manifestation in bodily form (*sōmatoeidous autou thea*) on a writing implement, such as in the case of the divinely imprinted Gospels? Nowhere, indeed, did he say that the "pointed word" (*ton syntetmēmenon logon*)[59] should be written down; and notwithstanding that it was written down by the apostles [and it was preserved] until the present day; and what there is accomplished by means of paper and ink, here on the icon is accomplished by means of colors of all sorts or by means of some other material. So the great Basil says, "The art of painting silently shows by imitation those things that the words of the story narrate."[60] For this reason we are taught that we should depict whatever falls under our perception by means of touch or of color, but also whatever we apprehend through reason (*dianoia*) by means of noetic contemplation (*theōria*). For this reason the custom has been handed down from antiquity not only to depict angels, but also to depict the future judgment, with those standing on the right or on the left having a sadder or more joyful countenance. There is only one thing that is utterly beyond circumscription, the Godhead, of which—so dictates its nature—there is no comprehensive concept or appropriate name; for this reason its circumscription is impossible. All the other things, however, that are defined through the comprehension of the mind, are circumscribed by hearing and by sight; their ratio is indeed identical.

XI. *Heretic*: What is it then that is shown? Is it the image of Christ or Christ? Certainly, it is not the two of them [together]. And how can one say that each is in the other, or that either one is in the other? The absurdity is manifest.

Orthodox: No one could go so mad as to assume that shadow and truth, nature and fiction (*thesis*), archetype and copy, cause and effect, will assume the same thing in terms of essence (*kat'ousian*), or as to say that each is in the other, or either one is in the other;[61] and this is what is implied when one presupposes or claims that Christ and his image are one in this respect (*kata touto*). Rather, according to nature (*kata physin*), Christ is one thing and his image is another, even as there is identity in virtue of the indivisibility of the appellation.[62] In fact, if you consider the nature (*physis*) of the image, you will say that you see neither Christ nor the image of Christ. It will be some sort of wood, or pigment, or gold, or silver, or some sort of different (*diaphorōn*) material from which it derives its name. And yet, when you consider the likeness to the original by means of a representation (*di'ektypōmatos*), you will see both Christ and the image of Christ. However, it will be Christ by virtue of homonymy (*kata to homōnymon*); it will be the image of Christ because of the relation (*kata to pros ti*). For the copy is a copy of the original, and so the name is the name of the one who is named. Here is the proof (*apodeixis*). Scripture says, "Josiah lifted his eyes toward the tomb of the man of God, who had spoken these words. He said: 'What is that protuberance (*skopelon*) that I see?' And the men of the city told him: 'It is the man of God who came from Judah.' And he said: 'Leave him. Let no man move his bones.'"[63] Do you get the sense of the scriptures? He called the protuberance—in other words, the tomb—"the man of God," calling the building after the body lying within it. How much more, then, should the prototype be named after the image? And in the same way God said to Moses, "Make for me two golden Cherubim," not "images of Cherubim." Mark, then, how in virtue of the homonymy the copy is called after the archetype, and cease to engage in insanity, or to go against what we are saying using unreasonable arguments (*asyllogista*).

XII. *Heretic*: How can you possibly say the divinity of Christ is in the icon? According to the nature (*physikōs*)? So then is it the object of joint veneration (*symproskyneitai*)?[64] Or not? And if it is in the image, then we have circumscription; if it is not, then the veneration is impious, because what is worshiped is what the icon is not, and not what the icon is called. However, the flesh (*sarx*) of Christ is eternally the object of joint veneration with Christ,[65] because the two are united without any separation; this is not the case with the icon.

Orthodox: You are still lingering in the same absurdities. Given that the archetype and the icon are not one thing, given that one is the truth and the other a shadow, why do you think that your argument is so wise? Indeed, in the body of the Lord, in virtue of the connection (*synapheia*) of the natures,[66] the divinity is jointly honored and glorified in a shared manner (*synaptikōs*), even as it is subject to the circumscription of the flesh. How else could it be, given that it is subject to touch, and apprehension, and sight, and in no way, in virtue of the union, does it take over the unsuitable properties (*ta anoikeia*) of the nature that is not subject to comprehension?[67] Given that, as it is said, the flesh suffered even if the impassible nature (*ousia*) did not share in the suffering.[68] In the case of the image, however, everything is completely different. Where indeed the nature (*physis*) of the flesh that is raised up as an image is not even present, much more will you profess the uncircumscribable divinity,[69] or will you be inclined to accept that the divinity is present, and it is venerated in the image to the extent that it abides in the shadow of the flesh to which it is united. Where is there a place, then, where the divinity is not present—in beings endowed with reason, and beings without reason? Or in beings endowed with souls, and beings without a soul? Divinity indeed shall be present to a greater or lesser extent, depending on the kind of natures (*physeōn*) that are actually receiving it. If anyone then will say that the divinity is present in the icon, he will not deviate from the truth; indeed, it is also present in the representation of the cross and in all other divine implements (*anathēmata*);[70] yet not by means of a natural union (*physikē enōsei*)[71]—indeed, they are not the flesh that is deified—but by virtue of a relational participation (*schetikē metalēpsei*), where the participation happens in terms of grace and honor.

XIII. *Heretic*: What does it mean, when they say, "It is not a good thing that the image should be displayed, and not venerated"? It is, in fact, much more advantageous; on the one hand, because this forces us to return to the things in question and to commemorate them in a way that is equal to hearing; on the other hand, because it induces us to flee from the lowliness (*to chamerpes*) of material depiction.[72] Scripture says, "The Spirit is God, and those who worship him must do so in spirit and in truth."[73]

Orthodox: If you concede that the capacity of the sense of sight and of the sense of hearing are equal, which is indeed the case, do show that you believe this; let the sacred book of the Gospel, despite the fact it should be worshiped, remain solely for hearing, and let it not be an object of veneration. But if this is folly, why should the other suggestion not be foolish too? Indeed, by you they are decreed to be equal. Why then do you not view both as venerable, but instead you claim that each conflicts with itself in giving both help and harm? So it appears that God is venerated in spirit and in truth in the image, and in the Gospel, and in the cross, and in any other consecrated object, as the materials have been subjugated by the elevation of the mind (*nous*) toward God. Nor does the mind rest in them, since it has not given them trust—this was the mistake of those who venerate idols; through them, in fact, the mind ascends to the prototypes, in line with the faith of those who are Orthodox (*tōn Orthodoxōn*).

XIV. *Heretic*: Is the letter[74] to be venerated or the icon of which it is the name? Is it only one of them? Not two? In what manner?

Orthodox: This is like asking: should one venerate the Gospel, or the name inscribed on it? The image of the cross, or the inscription on it? And I will add, as far as human beings are concerned, the individual, or the name? The same would go for Peter, and for Paul, and for each of the individuals of the same species. How is it possible not to say that this will be foolish (*anoēton*), if not ridiculous? Among the things that we see with our eyes, which one is there that does not have a name? And in what way can what has a name be distinguished from the glory of its own appellation, so that we can offer veneration to the one and withhold it from the other? These things indeed are relations (*pros ti*). Every name is indeed the appellation of something that is named and a sort of natural image of the thing of which it is said; in these things the unity of adoration is not divided.

XV. *Heretic*: Should the cross be venerated more than the icon? More, or less?

Orthodox: Given that there is a natural order in reality, you seem to me to be beating around the bush (*perittologein*). If by cross you mean the archetype, why not? On it the impassible Word suffered (*peponthen ho apathēs Logos*), and it is invested with such power that with the shadow it burns the demonic host and similarly drives it away from those that are thereby signed.[75] If instead you mean the representation, the question makes no sense (*ou syneton*). The honor that is ascribed to the effects is greater, the more the causes distinguish themselves, and whatever is received for the sake of something else is lower in honor than that for whose sake it is received; the same goes for the cross of Christ, which earlier on was an instrument of condemnation and later on is sanctified, being taken over for the purpose of the divine passion.

XVI. *Heretic*: There is no distinction (*diaphoron*) between idol and icon; indeed, they are identical in appellation. One comes from the term *eidos* ("form") in its general meaning—indeed, its chief significance is not "what is seen" (*to horōmenon*); the other comes from the term *eoikos* ("alike"), in its connotation of "likeness." Indeed, a likeness is merely what is not its prototype; in this the idol and the icon do not differ. In both cases, the term refers to the same. But to venerate an idol, thereby claiming to venerate Christ by means of circumscription, is an act of impiety. This is utterly forbidden by the word of truth.

Orthodox: From this claim (*ennoia*)—I mean, that the likenesses are not the divine, and that they illicitly usurp the truth in themselves—

there is no difference [between the idol and the icon]; because by the divine scripture it is equally forbidden not only to set up idols, but also inscriptions and simulacra, and so on. For scripture says, "You shall not make for yourselves any idols made by human hands (*cheiropoiēta*) or sculptures, nor shall you set up inscriptions; nor will you set up a prominent stone in your land so as to worship it; because I am the Lord your God."[76] And, in another passage, "Has not the workman made an image, or the goldsmith having melted gold coated the image in it, and turned it into a likeness (*omoiōma*)?" Indeed, the danger (*to epikyndynon*) of idolatry comes from both. Therefore, since from antiquity the term *phonē* ("icon") has been forbidden to us by God for a similitude that concerns his infinite nature (*kata physin apeiron*), therefore we cannot use it, and the same goes for similar terms (*ta systoicha*).[77] We should rather use the term *icon* to refer to the bodily form of Christ, as this was indicated at the beginning during the creation of the universe at the formation (*diaplasin*) of man. "Let us make man," scripture says, "according to our image and likeness (*kat'eikona hēmeteran kai homoiōsin*)";[78] and again, at the divine interrogation, "Whose image (*eikōn*) is this?";[79] because from these passages (*enteuthen*) we see [the legitimacy of] a transposed use (*paralēpsis*), by virtue of a catachresis of the terms *form* (*charaktēr*) and *likeness* (*homoiōma*), but nowhere of the term *idol*;[80] even if it carries the same connotation. The term *idol* is then applied solely to the ancient worshipers of creation (*ktismatolatrai*) and to any such as there might be nowadays, by whom the Trinity, which is undivided in nature and glory and power, is not worshiped, nor is the enfleshment (*sarkōsis*) of the Word acknowledged. The gods, however, who did not make the heavens and the earth, but were made of wood and of stone and of all sorts of other materials, and are divided among themselves not only in terms of nature but also in terms of will, glory, and worship, let them perish, as scripture says. And then they will bring out to us, as one brings out freed captives, the icons of Our Lady (*hē Despoinikē*) and of the whole host of saints.

XVII. *Heretic*: Some even claim that it is not appropriate to represent (*historeisthai*) and to venerate [the saints].[81] And why do they say that? Because it does not constitute honor to those who have entered the celestial glory to represent them using material images. Let us rather erect memorials through speech, which is more valuable than that in pigments, because it is more useful.

Orthodox: They also say the same thing about Christ, and the refutation (*ho elegchos*) is evident, lest we repeat ourselves. Hearing is indeed equal to sight, and it is impossible to prevent the two from being one. If you were to take away the one, you would then also have to take away the other completely; and if we are not mistaken, we would then have to eliminate wholly and completely the veneration of anyone who is venerated.

XVIII. *Heretic*: But not everyone who is portrayed in an image is worthy of being venerated; there are indeed many of them (*ho deina gar kai ho deina*), and it may happen that one is unimportant and not worthy of veneration.

Orthodox: In this case, however, we have some who are worthy of veneration and glory, because they have earned honor by way of the blood of martyrdom or a worthy life.

XIX. *Heretic*: From this it would then follow that veneration is of many types (*polyschidēs*). Yet, there is only one kind of veneration, not many.

Orthodox: Worship (*hē latreutikē*) is only of one type, and it belongs to God alone; to others belong, however, different types of honor. Kings and rulers are, for instance, the object of veneration among us, the masters among the slaves, the fathers among the children, but they are not worshiped as gods; even if the veneration is one in appearance, it differs according to the intention (*dia tēs dianoēseōs*), and this is because they are human beings, and they receive veneration in line with the honor that is due to them, whether by law, or by fear, or by persuasion. If, then, a person is cognizant of the difference (*diaphora*) in veneration, by means of which through the images the prototypes are venerated, he then has offered the veneration that is properly so called and that is properly offered to God alone; but to the other images, veneration is offered by analogy, to the Mother of God as to the Mother of God, and to the saints as to the saints.

There are sacred books that are put on public displays in all the churches of God to the eyes of all human beings, in the same way as their content is there for all to hear; they are venerated in the same manner, because they are invested with the same power; or perhaps those that are seen are more excellent in veneration because of the worthier quality of the perception. And in any case, what shall we do with the custom established from the beginning until the present day, as can be seen from all temples of God and all other liturgical tools? Did the choir of the confessor worship in an impious manner? Did the undefiled church engage in idolatrous activity? And when will the church be purified by the removal of the idols, and by whom?[82] Clearly this opposition is from the antichrist. And how will the paradigm of ancient customs and traditions that has been handed down from of old be overturned? Even if in this case the warning is unnecessary, the inspired fathers encourage us to stand firm even against a logical demonstration; indeed, they say: the simplicity of faith is stronger than sophisticated arguments. And elsewhere: Let the ancient customs be preserved. Indeed, you mindless one, having miscalled the church of God idolatrous because of the erection of the images, can't you see that you are bringing to completion the work of all the heresies? Stand back together with the opposing faction; listening to the voice that—so to speak—lapidates you, do not touch the mountain of the church, as a heretical beast.[83]

XX. If, then, anyone does not acknowledge that our Lord Jesus Christ—who has come in the flesh—is circumscribed in the flesh, even as the divine nature (*physis*) remains uncircumscribed, he is a heretic.[84]

If anyone argues that, because of the circumscription of the flesh of the Word, the divinity is co-circumscribed in a similar manner, failing to distinguish either nature in the one hypostasis according to the natural property—because neither absorbs (*anairountos*) the other in the undivided union—he is a heretic.

If anyone calls the circumscription of the bodily form of the Word neither the image of Christ nor Christ by homonymy (*homōnymōs*), but calls it an idol of deceit, he is a heretic.

If anyone dares to declare the relative (*schetikēn*) veneration of Christ in the image the veneration of idols and not of Christ himself, despite the fact that the great Basil claims that the glory of the prototype does not differ from that ascribed to the image,[85] he is a heretic.

If anyone says that the mere exposition of the image of Christ is sufficient, without honoring or dishonoring the image, thereby rejecting the veneration that is relative by honor, he is a heretic.

If anyone were to take over the scriptural injunctions against the idols, and were to apply them to the sacred image of Christ, hence calling the church of Christ an idolatrous shrine, he is a heretic.

If anyone were to say that, venerating the icon of Christ, he is venerating the divinity that is naturally (*physikōs*) in the image, when in fact [the icon] is the shadow of the flesh that is united to the divinity (and this is the case even if the Godhead is everywhere), he is a heretic.

If anyone were to compare to lowly devises the raising of the mind (*anagōgē*) to the prototypes by means of the holy icons, as if one were lifted without them by means of the sense of hearing to the contemplation (*autopsia*) of the prototypes, and were not to ascribe the same honor to the narration by means of words that are ascribed to the graphic depiction through silence (as the great Basil says),[86] he is a heretic.

If anyone does not agree that the image of Christ, no less than the symbol (*typos*) of the cross, should be everywhere represented and put on display for the salvation of the people of God, he is a heretic.

If anyone does not offer the adequate adoration to the image of the Mother of God and of all the saints, to the Mother of God as it is appropriate for her and to the saints as it is appropriate for them, respecting the difference (*to diaphoron*) in veneration between the Mother of God and her fellow servants (*homodouloi*), but were to call the salvific ornament of the church an idolatrous device (*epinoia*), he is anathema.

If anyone should not number among the other heresies the one that, in an insane manner, opposes the veneration of the blessed images, and that separates [the faithful] from God in the same manner as the others, but were actually to say that sharing the sacraments with these people is not unacceptable (*adiaphoron*), he is a heretic.

If anyone were to exaggerate (*hyperteinōn*) the honor that is due to the icon and were to say that he would not walk up to it, given that it would not benefit him until he is purified of all sin, he is a heretic.

SECOND REFUTATION OF THE ICONOCLASTS

As the word of truth (*tēs alētheias logos*) is undifferentiated (*monoeidēs*) and unshakeable in nature (*tēn physin*), it does not happen to be subject to differences of opinion (*gnōmikais diaresesin*)[1] or temporal modifications; indeed, it is always glorifying and asserting the same things, given that it is beyond the reach of any subtraction or addition. The myth of falsity (*tou pseudous mythos*), as it happens to be fragmented and characterized by a multiplicity of opinions (*myriognōmos*), constantly moving about from one thing to another, honors one thing at a moment and affirms the opposite at the next, and it never remains fixed at any point at all, being cast about by the passions of transformation and change. This is what happens with the howling of the iconoclasts; at a moment, they call the icon of our Lord Jesus Christ an idol of deceitful blasphemy; at another moment, they do not say so but claim that the depiction (*hē historia*)[2] is a good thing when its purpose is reflection on scripture (*exēgēsis*) and commemoration (*anamnēsis*), but it is not a good thing when its purpose is veneration; and for this reason they ascribe to it an elevated position, fearing that if it were placed in the lower places, providing an occasion for veneration, it would become a cause of idolatry to the same. Who would not be amazed at the lack of wisdom of those who fail to understand that the very fact that they are afraid of the lower position and of veneration is an indication of their obsession with idolatry (*eidōlikē emphasis*)?[3] And the mere removal of the lower icons will be insufficient for their mistaken opinion, if one were to leave the images that are above. After all, it is written in the Books of the Kings that no one pleased God except David, Hezekiah, and Josiah, who removed both the lower and the upper idols.[4] So if they sought to please God perfectly as much as it was in their power, or rather to commit perfect acts of impiety out of their misguided opinion, there would be no sacred buildings under the heaven that they would not despoil, and there would be no sacred items in them depicting the life of Christ and the saints[5] that they would not commit to the flames. However, enough has been said by me about these people, having tried as much as it is in my power with my limited intelligence (*tē oligonoia*) to oppose their absurd (*alogous*) claims and arguments. Now, having been forced to it by the evidence (*tois elenchois*), they are ready to acknowledge that Our Lord Jesus Christ can be portrayed, but they deny that one should venerate the image erected in his honor; then they seek to disturb the mind of the uneducated masses, claiming that in this act of veneration they worship the creation instead of the Creator. With the help of God then, even this present inadequate (*penichros*) treatise will deal with the same issue, so that through the opposition of two people, namely, an orthodox person and an iconoclast, the weight of their reciprocal arguments may be easier to grasp and to assess.

I. *Orthodox:*[6] Do you agree that, as the Son and the Word of God has become flesh, he is circumscribed by the flesh, yet he remains uncircumscribable as far as the nature of the divinity is concerned?

Heretic: I agree, and how could I do otherwise? Indeed our fathers, who truly were theologians, say so, with Gregory saying, "Circumscribed in body, uncircumscribed in spirit,"[7] and with Athanasios saying, "On the one hand, Christ was intellectually acknowledged as God and truly was such in an invisible manner; on the other hand, he was visibly touched as a human being (*anthrōpos*)[8] and truly in his manner he existed."[9]

II. *Orthodox:* Do you then object to recognize at the same time that this circumscription, namely, the image of Christ, should be acknowledged as worthy of veneration?

Heretic: Absolutely! None of the blessed fathers has said that. But I am going to ask you a question in return, and please respond to me. Where is it written in the Old or the New Testament that one should venerate an image?

III. *Orthodox:* Wherever it is written that we should venerate its prototype.

Heretic: "You will venerate the Lord your God, and you will worship him alone."[10] Thus it is written; we are not told to worship a prototype, or an image, as you say.

IV. *Orthodox*: The topic under discussion, most excellent man, is not theology; rather, it is the economy, where one can see the prototype and the image, if you acknowledge that Christ, having assumed flesh, has become like us.[11]

Heretic: But given that scripture says, "You shall venerate the Lord your God, and him only you shall worship," does not this passage command us to offer veneration to the Father and to the Son?[12]

V. *Orthodox*: Of course, but this law was not given to the men of old (*tois palai*) when God had not yet become incarnate; indeed, "no one has ever seen God," as the scripture says;[13] indeed, after he became flesh and entered circumscription, he who was not circumscribed could be seen, and he who could not be touched or seen became corporeally subject to sight and touch. And he is worshiped together with the Father, as someone who is equally God with him; he is also venerated in his own proper image, of which he is the prototype, having become man (*anthrōpos*) like us in all things except sin.

Heretic: In all the divinely inspired scripture, it is said most clearly of Christ that he is worthy of veneration; indeed, it is written, "Let all the angels of God venerate him."[14] Of prototype and image, however, we find no mention at all.

VI. *Orthodox*: When about Christ it is written, "Let all the angels of God venerate him," what else should be understood, but that the passage refers to the prototype? Indeed, he became man after being God (*meta tou einai Theos*),[15] in the same way as each human being is the prototype of his own image, and there cannot be a man for whom his own portrait would not be an image; in the same way, then, Christ, having become like us in all things, is the prototype of his own image, even if this is not written in these very terms (*tē lexei*). So, then, when you ask, where is it written that the icon of Christ should be venerated, then you should also hear the answer, which is, "Wherever it is written that Christ should be venerated," given that the copy is inseparable from the prototype.

Heretic: But given that it is not written that Christ is the prototype of his own image, this claim does not have to be accepted (*aparadektos*); indeed, it has not been included in our profession (*homologia*) of faith.[16]

VII. *Orthodox*: Many things that are not written explicitly (*lexesin autais*) have the same weight as the things that are written and have been announced by the holy fathers.[17] Indeed, the fact that the Son is consubstantial (*homoousios*) to the Father is not to be found in the divinely inspired scriptures but has been made clear by the fathers at a later stage; the same goes for the fact that the Holy Spirit is God, or that the Mother of the Lord is also the Mother of God, or many other doctrines that would be difficult to list; if these are not confessed, our truthful worship (*hē alēthinē latreia ēmōn*) is denied. These doctrines were confessed when the need arose to oppose the heresies that were rising up. Why, then, even if it is not written that Christ is the prototype of his own image, should it be at all surprising that now, as the timely moment has come, this claim should be made, in order to oppose the growing iconoclast heresy, as the truth now shines most clearly?

Heretic: While it is the case that Christ is both God and man, he is not a mere man, as if he were one of us; therefore, clearly, it is impious to claim that he is the prototype of his own image.[18]

VIII. *Orthodox*: When the fathers claimed that Christ is not a mere man, they did not do so to deny his circumscribability, but they intended to affirm that he subsisted simultaneously as both God and man—something that cannot be said of any one of us. In that respect, then, we can all be said to be mere human beings. Given, then, that he is circumscribed, he is the prototype of his own image; this is so as if he were one of us, and yet he is not for this reason a mere man.

Heretic: I can then accept that Christ is circumscribed, but not that he can be called prototype.[19]

IX. *Orthodox*: How could he be circumscribed without also being a prototype? Indeed, that which we call circumscribed is also what we call prototype. What can be circumscribed can also be taken as model for the image that is drawn.[20] If, then, you acknowledge that Christ can be circumscribed, you must then concede, whether you like it or not, that he subsists as the prototype of his own image, in the same way as you must accept that every human being is the prototype of his own representation (*indalma*). It is in this sense that the divine Basil says, "Let Christ, who is the presider over the struggles, be portrayed in the painting."[21] By saying that, he has firmly demonstrated that Christ is the prototype of his own icon; if, indeed, anyone who is depicted [lit. "written"] in a painting is modeled after the form of the prototype.

Heretic: What commonality of veneration is there between the prototype and the copy?

X. *Orthodox*: The same commonality that exists between the life-giving (*zōopoios*) cross and its own image.

Heretic: Where has this notion been taken from? I shall not accept you as a newly established dispenser of laws.

XI. *Orthodox*: From two who speak the dogma in a divine manner,[22] such as Denys the Aeropagite, who says, "What belongs to the truth is in the similitude, and what belongs to the archetype is in the image; indeed, each is in the other with the only difference of the essence (*para to tēs ousias diaphoron*)";[23] and the great Basil, who observes, "It is not the case that he, who in the public square looks at the portrait of the emperor, and calls the one in the image 'emperor,' thereby acknowledges two emperors, the portrait and the one whose portrait it is; nor, if, pointing at the one drawn in the portrait, he were to say 'This is the emperor,' he would not deprive the prototype of the denomination of emperor; rather, by his acknowledgment of this fact,[24] he further confirms the honor of the emperor. Indeed, if truly the portrait is the emperor, all the more it is obvious that the emperor should be the one who provides cause for the image."[25] And elsewhere Basil says, "In general, every image that is artificially created, taking after the prototype, has taken the likeness into matter, and participates in its character by means of the insight of the artist, and the impression of the hand; the same goes for the painter; and so it is that the sculptor, or the one who makes images out of gold or bronze, takes matter, considers the prototype, takes over the type of what has been observed, and presses it into the material as if it were a seal."[26]

Heretic: Yet, even if the fathers have said this, they have not said at all that the veneration for both should be identical.

XII. *Orthodox*: Given that the blessed Basil says that clearly the honor (*timē*) of the prototype should be ascribed in equal measure to the image, what else do you think this means, apart from the fact that the honor and the veneration that is due to both is the same?

Heretic: I agree as far as the honor is concerned, but not as far as the veneration; it is you, and not Basil, that uses this term interchangeably.[27]

XIII. *Orthodox*: You should then listen to what the blessed Athanasios says: "Indeed, on the one hand, in the image of the emperor, one can behold both the species (*to eidos*) and the form (*hē morphē*); and on the other hand, in the emperor, one can see the species of the image; so that the likeness of the king is expressed in the image without any discrepancy; so that, whoever sees the image, may see in it the king; and equally, whoever sees the king may acknowledge that he is the same as the one who is represented in the image. Moreover, given that in the two there is no difference at all, if anyone after having seen the image wishes to see the king, the image could then say: 'I and the king are one thing; in fact, I am in him and he is in me; and what you discern in me, you can discern the same thing in him; and what you will see in him, you will see also in me.' And he, then, who venerates the image, he also venerates the same king in it, given that the image is nothing except the very species and form of the king."[28] Therefore, if I may add anything of my own, whoever venerates the image (*typos*) of the cross venerates the true life-giving cross. The image is indeed the species (*idea*) and the description (*diagraphē*) of the latter.

Heretic: Cease then to talk about the cross here; the cross, indeed, is the unparalleled weapon (*tropaion*) against the devil.

XIV. *Orthodox*: You, then, should stop talking about the image of Christ. He is indeed the Savior of the world, through whom the cross, while before it was an instrument of punishment, has become a symbol of immortality, in virtue of the fact that he was crucified on it.[29]

Heretic: But this in no way brings it about, that the image of Christ should participate in his own veneration or that the image should also bear the name "Christ."

XV. *Orthodox*: And so, then, accept a parallel claim on my part: this in no way brings it about, that the image of the life-giving cross should participate in its own veneration or that it should bear the same name with the life-giving wood.

Heretic: Stop with these silly remarks (*tēs lērōdias*)! The veneration of the two is one, and it is shared; the image of the life-giving wood is called with the same name that is used for the reality. The cross, then, is both.

XVI. *Orthodox*: If you win, I will win too, because I will say the same. The adoration of Christ and the adoration of his figure (*ektypōma*) are one and the same, and the representation of Christ is called with the same name that is used for Christ himself. Christ, indeed, is both; in what manner this may be so is proved by the teachings of the blessed fathers quoted above. In the same way, all the things that are said of the prototype are necessarily also said of the copy, but in the case of the prototype, such things are said synonymously (*synōnymōs*), as they are present in an eminent manner (*kyriōs*); in the case of the image, on the contrary, they are said homonymously (*homōnymōs*), as they are not present in an eminent manner (*ou kyriōs*).

Heretic: What do you mean by that? I do not fully understand this.

XVII. *Orthodox*: I mean that the name "cross" is said of that on which Christ is lifted up, in virtue of the signification of the term, and in virtue of the nature (*tē physei*) of the life-giving wood. The imprint (*ektypōma*), on the contrary, is called "cross" in virtue of the signification of the term, and not in virtue of the nature of the life-giving wood, given that it is made of some sort of wood, or of gold, or of silver, or of stone, or of some other material designation (*diagraphē*). And it shares in the name of the prototype, in the same way as it shares in the honor and in the veneration; it is, however, distinct from the nature. Therefore, by whatever names the life-giving cross is called, by the same names the image is also called. If we call the cross "the pride of the inhabited world," in the same way its representation should be called "the pride of the inhabited world." And if we call the cross "light" and "life," similarly its representation is called "light" and "life." If we call it "torch of demons," similarly its representation is called "torch of demons." And so every name that is used for the prototype, by that name the image should also be called. This theoretical notion (*theōrēma*) also applies to Christ and to his image. Christ is indeed called God and man both because of the significance of the terms, and because of the nature of the divinity and of the humanity. His image, however, is called Christ because of the significance of the term, but not because of the nature of the divinity and the humanity. In terms of its manufacture, in fact, it is painted in various colors, or it is assembled with a variety of stones, or it is created from the artistry of the sculptor, or from gold, or from silver, or from some other configuration of materials. And it shares the name [of the prototype] as well as the honor and the veneration; however, it is distinct in terms of the nature. So every name that is used for Jesus Christ, so by that name his image should also be called. If we call Christ "the Lord of glory," then also his image should be called "Lord of glory."[30] If we then said that Christ is the power (*dynamis*) of God and the wisdom (*sophia*) of God, then in the same way his image should be called the power and the wisdom of God.[31] And if we said that Christ is the Son of man, then similarly his image is also called the Son of man. And in the same way, as the divine Word says, "I am the Light of the World," so the image can also be called by this inscription (*epigraphē*).[32] And so, when Christ says, "To me every knee shall bow, in the heavens, and on the earth, and under the earth," the image may also say this by its inscription.[33] And when Christ says, "I am the life and the resurrection,"[34] then the image may say this by the inscription. And by those names by which the divinely inspired scripture calls Christ, we must be able to call his image also.

Heretic: There is a lot of emphasis on identity [in what you say], and you almost seem to suggest that the copy is nothing but the prototype itself. For how did every knee bow, or how could every knee bow, in the heavens and on earth and under earth, to the icon of Christ?

XVIII. *Orthodox*: You should have listened to what is said by Athanasios, who fought many fights (*polyathlos*): "In the image of emperor, there is the appearance (*eidos*) and the form (*morphē*) of the emperor, and in the emperor there is the appearance of the image. And again, in theory the image could say the following: 'I and the emperor are one. Indeed, I am in him and he is in me, and what you discern in me, you will also discern in him, and what you will see in him, you will also see in me.' He, then, who venerates the image venerates the emperor in it, because the image itself is nothing else but the appearance and the form of the emperor."[35] In the *Thesauros*, then, St. Cyril says, "In the same way, if someone were to see a beautifully painted image and were full of wonder at the representation of the emperor, and if he had also the possibility to see these same things in the painting, which are manifest in him, he would also conceive the ardent desire to see the emperor for himself.[36] The painting could then rightly say to him: 'He who has seen me has seen the emperor.' And again, 'I and the emperor are one thing, as far as likeness and most exact representation are concerned.' And further, 'I am in the emperor and the emperor is in me, according to the imprint of the form (*kata tēs morphēs schēma*).' For the painting fully carries his appearance, and the appearance of the image is preserved in him."[37] [If you had listened to this], you would have understood that when Christ is venerated, his image is also venerated, because it is in Christ, and when his image is venerated, Christ is also venerated; indeed, he is venerated in it. And since now, incontrovertibly (*homologoumenōs*), every knee that is in the heavens, and on the earth, and under the earth bows down to Christ, in the same way, incontrovertibly, it is clear that every knee that is in the heavens, and on the earth, and under the earth should bow down to his image, as it is in Christ. So what is said applies only to the name, and to the identity of veneration, not to the material (*tēs hylēs*);[38] the latter cannot at all participate in the veneration, even if he who is depicted appears in it to be venerated.

To confirm most firmly what has been said, it is best to support our claims with the testimony of the fathers. The holy Sophronios, in his *Miracles of the Martyrs Cyros and John*, says the following: "Thus, when we entered a certain temple that had been completed, splendid and most beautiful to behold, touching the altitude of the very heavens, and having gone inside, we saw a huge and most beautiful icon,[39] having in the middle Christ the Lord (*ton Despotēn*)[40] painted [lit.

"written"] in colors; the Mother of Christ, our Lady, the Mother of God and ever-Virgin Mary, on the left; on the right instead, John, the Baptizer of the Lord and the Forerunner, who venerated him from the womb with his jumps, given that he could not be heard as he was speaking being inside. And beneath there were some of the choir of the apostles and of the prophets, and of the throng (*homēgyris*) of the martyrs. And with these there happened to be also the martyrs Cyril and John themselves; and standing in front of the icon they prostrated themselves before the Lord, bending their knees, and bringing their heads to the floor, begging for the healing of the youth." And shortly afterward, he says: "Standing not far from the icon, and coming closer, they said: 'Do you see how the Lord does not wish to grant you healing?'" And after a while, he says: "And coming to the icon for the third time, they used the words which they had used before; and after praying for a long while, they accomplished what they had been enjoined to do, and burst out: 'Christ has had pity (*splagchistheis*)[41] and has assented, as he is full of mercy, and has said "Minister to him before the icon."'"[42] Do you see, then, that the martyrs prostrated themselves in front of the icon, as if they were venerating Christ himself? And from the icon came out a voice as out of Christ himself, agreeing to their request; so then, what is venerated by the martyrs, it is clear that it may also be venerated by the angels.[43]

Heretic: What has been recounted is a vision (*theōria*), even if it is told by a saint, and as such it does not have the authority of a dogmatic claim.

XIX. *Orthodox*: That it is a vision, I do not deny; yet, if it were not true, it would not have been recorded by the saint. And the dogmatic claim has just been demonstrated; the vision has been brought in here by us by way of example (*paradeigmatikōs*). Examples are said to be the eyes of what is said, and indeed they are. Indeed, to this point the blessed Athanasios says something even more paradoxical: the copy shares so much with the prototype that the suffering (*to pathos*) of the icon of Christ appears to be the suffering of Christ himself, so to speak: "Lo, raise the eyes of your reason (*dianoia*), and behold this new sight. Once upon a time, having taken down the image of our Lord Jesus Christ, some Jews said: 'In the same way as once in the past our ancestors mocked him, let us also mock him in the same way.' Then those that had assembled there began to spit on the face of the icon of Christ, and hit it on the face on one side and on the other, saying; 'Whatever our fathers did to him, let us also do to his image.' And they go on saying: 'Since they mocked him, let us do the same as well.' And with boundless wantonness they mocked him; and what they actually said we do not dare to refer. And then they say: 'We have heard that they nailed his hands and feet; let us also do that to him.' Thus they transfixed the hands and feet of the icon of Christ with nails. And then they said in their insanity: 'We have heard that they gave him to drink vinegar and gall with a sponge. Let us do the same.' And they did so, pressing the sponge full with vinegar against the mouth of the image of the Lord. And then they said: 'We have been taught that our fathers struck his head with a reed; so let us do the same.' And taking a reed they hit the image of the Lord. Finally they said: 'As we learn with accuracy that they pierced his side with a spear, let us omit nothing, but let us add this too.' And after asking that a spear be brought, they made one of their number raise the spear and pierce it through the side of the icon of Christ. And when this was being done, lo, a great quantity of blood and water flew from it."[44] Do you see the power of the things that have been said? And I refrain from mentioning the healings from the outpouring of the side that benefited many.

Heretic: The miracle was seen by Jews; miracles are for unbelievers, not for those who believe.

XX. *Orthodox*: Of course I agree. But the point is that, even if nowadays such signs do not happen, the copy shares most fully in the same veneration as the prototype; and in reverse, the prototype shares the same veneration as the copy; and the veneration for both of them is one and the same, as it was said in the case of the life-giving cross and its representation. The recognition (*homologia*)[45] of the representation is also the recognition of the life-giving cross; and the same goes for the negation of the life-giving cross. The same will then be the case for the image of Christ and for Christ himself.

Heretic: This is all very well and sufficient for the holy cross and its representation, but not for Christ and his depiction. Indeed, your example is not appropriate; the icon should be compared to the icon, and the representation to the representation.

XXI. *Orthodox*: The accuracy of what has been said until now, Sir, is sufficient for the expression of agreement. Nonetheless, do accept from me a small question. Which is greater or more honorable, Christ or the cross?

Heretic: The former, obviously; it is indeed in Christ that the cross is sanctified.

XXII. *Orthodox*: Is, then, Christ's icon greater and more honorable than the representation of the cross?

Heretic: There is no doubt, even for those who have little skill in the art of syllogism, that the copies are distinguished according to the difference (*tēn diaphoran*) of the prototypes, given that the icon of Christ is more eminent than the symbol of the cross.

XXIII. *Orthodox*: If that which is inferior and lesser in honor is properly considered, only a foolish person would claim that that which is superior and greater in honor is not properly considered. For what closer comparison is there to the icon of Christ than the symbol (*typos*) of the cross, when the former and the latter bear the same relation [to the prototype]? Indeed, by way of a catachresis,[46] we even call the representation of the life-giving cross "icon"; and we talk of the representation of Christ when we mean his own icon; according to etymology, indeed, *icon* comes from *eoikos*, and *eoikos* means similar; the similarity is discerned (*nenoētai*),[47] and named, and beheld, both in the icon and in the representation of the cross.

Heretic: I can agree with this too; all the same, you must compare the icon with the icon and the representation with the representation, even if you think that the first and the second have equal worth (*isodynamein*).[48]

XXIV. *Orthodox*: If you have paid attention, [you will realize that] this has already been demonstrated earlier quite clearly from the writings of the holy fathers. If you have not, let us then listen to the words of St. Basil, who illumines our minds (*tas phrenas*): "The term 'emperor' is also used for the image of the emperor; but there are not two emperors; the power is not divided, and the glory is not apportioned.

In the same way as the principle (*archē*) and power (*exousia*) that rules over us is one, so also our glorification (*doxologia*) is one and not many. For this reason the honor of the icon ascends to the prototype."[49] What argument can deny that this example also applies to the image of Christ? In the same way, then, it must be said that even the icon of Christ is to be called Christ, and there are not two Christs; nor in this case is the power divided, nor the glory apportioned, and similarly the honor of the image ascends to the prototype.

Heretic: Actually, it was not correct on the part of the saint to compare the image of the emperor to the icon of Christ, but rather, [he should have applied it] to Christ the invisible (*aoratos*) image of God the Father.[50]

XXV. *Orthodox*: So this is what you find remarkable (*to thaumaston*)—that the artificial (*technētē*) image has been used by the saint to demonstrate the unparalleled identity of the Father and of the Son, but that this artificial image has been used by us not for the natural [image of the Father] but for the artificial icon of Christ. In the former instance, the artificial image is compared to the natural image; in the latter, the artificial image is compared to the artificial image. What a difference, and what a huge one! But given that the saint could not find any better example, he used that of the emperor. How much more can the image of any emperor be appropriately applied to the image of Christ the true emperor! [The image of the earthly emperor] approaches the image of Christ more closely, the more it is preeminent in the honor received by his subjects.[51] Indeed, even he who rules over the earth carries the image of Christ according to the title of dignity (*axia*). Scripture says indeed, "Power (*kratēsis*) was given to you (*hymin*) by the Lord, and dominion by the Most High; he will examine your works, and search your wills, because you were subject to his kingdom, and you did not judge correctly."[52]

Heretic: Even if the divine Basil said that the honor given to the image goes over to the prototype, he did not mean the artificial image, but rather the natural one, hence of the Son in relation to the Father; and he was right in saying so.

XXVI. *Orthodox*: Stop, my friend; he did not say, "The image of the invisible Father is also said to be God, and there are not two gods"—which is true—but to buttress the theological doctrine, he used the example of the emperor, saying that even the image of the emperor is said to be the emperor, and there are not two emperors; the conclusion (*symperasma*) is entailed by consequence.[53] For this reason when he says that the honor of the image goes over to the prototype, he adds, "What the image is here by imitation (*mymetikōs*), Christ is there by nature (*physikōs*)";[54] so in this way the relationship of the emperor to his own image has been taken as a prototype,[55] and not that of the Father toward the Son, or indeed he could have said the opposite. "In fact, what the Son is here by nature, the image is there by imitation." Moreover, the prototype and the copy appear to be things that belong to this world (*tōn kath'ēmas einai*), which can also be applied to Christ and to his icon. For we affirm that Christ has become a man in this world, even if he is also God. So it is possible to say in general about any emperor at all, "The honor given to the image goes over to the prototype."

Heretic: But honor is not at all understood by the saints as veneration; indeed, one thing is honor, and one thing is veneration.

XXVII. *Orthodox*: How will you admit that the power is not divided, and the glory is not fragmented, between the prototype and the example, when you do not understand that they are subject to the one and the same veneration? The power and the glory are indeed inseparable and undivided from the honor and the veneration; the things said are different because different terms are used (*tē heterolexia*), but they have the same power in terms of dignity (*tē axiōmati*).

Heretic: He said that the honor goes over but not the veneration. Even I, of course, honor the image of Christ, when it is placed in a high place, but I certainly do not venerate it, as I said.[56]

XXVIII. *Orthodox*: Before we discuss anything else (*prōton*), I have a question: Where do you get the idea that it is legitimate to honor the image of Christ when it is placed in a high place? Basil does not mention this but simply talks of honor without further qualifications. So your claim has already collapsed. In addition, how can anything be honored, whether placed in a higher or in a lower position, without also being venerated? In fact, we honor and we venerate the representation of the life-giving cross, whenever it is displayed in a high place or is seen in a low place. Similarly, even in the earthly sphere, we honor the emperor when he is sitting at a high place or he is seen in a lower place, and the same goes for the military leader, the prefect, the master, or the teacher. But let us transfer this claim (*to theōrēma*) to the divine scriptures. What do you think it means, when it says, "Worthy are you, Lord, our most holy God, to receive (*labein*) the glory and the honor and the power,"[57] and further, "Worthy is the Lamb that was slain to receive power and riches and wisdom and strength and honor and glory and blessing"?[58] And again, "To the One who sits upon the throne, and to the Lamb, blessing and honor and glory and strength for ever and ever. Amen"?[59] See, in all these passages, veneration is not mentioned anywhere. Should we then, given that it is not mentioned, abstain from giving veneration to the Lamb that was slain, who is our God and Savior? Or is it not clear that all these synonyms have the same meaning? For he, who is worthy of honor, is also worthy of veneration; and he, who is worthy of strength, is also worthy of power; and he who is worthy of blessing, is also worthy of glory and of all other qualities that are sung here in one way or another. If, then, you refuse veneration to the icon of the prototype, clearly you will also withdraw the honor and the power and the glory. And it is impossible that, if one of these qualities is present, the others should not be truly (*dynamei*) present as well.

And I will put forth yet another problem for you. Scripture says, "He who does not honor the Son does not honor the Father who has sent him."[60] What do you think? Does the honor given to the Father and to the Son exclude veneration? It would be foolish even to conceive (*ennoein*) of such a thing. Again, when the God of all says through the prophet Isaiah, "Behold I lay down in Zion a cornerstone worthy of honor,"[61] given that he does not add "and worthy of veneration," should we then deny that the Son of God is worthy of veneration? And again the scripture, "Honor your father and mother, that things may go well with you, and that you might be of many years upon the earth."[62] And again, "He who honors his father atones for his sins; and he who glorifies his mother is like one who accumulates treasures."[63] So God here does not order us to venerate the parents, but only to honor them? This would be of great foolishness. And again, the great Apostle says, "Fear God; honor the emperor."[64] Is it here commanded merely to honor him, or also to venerate him? Who out of those who have any sense at all would not understand this? I, for my part, when I hear the words of the priest, I understand that honor belongs to the same category (*homostoichos*)[65] and is invested with the same power (*homodynamos*) as veneration; for he says, "To you belong all the honor and glory and veneration."[66] Thus, when the divine Basil says, "The honor given to the image passes over to the prototype," he is implicitly (*kata to siōpōmenon*) affirming, echoing the blessed Athanasios, that the veneration of the image passes over to the prototype.[67]

Heretic: This claim should be demonstrated with testimonies from the blessed fathers, so that it may be more convincing to those who listen.

XXIX. *Orthodox*: The blessed John, from whose lips the golden speech flows, says this: "What therefore you have done for the names (*en onomasin*), you have also done for the image of that person. Indeed, in the settings of the rings, on chalices and bottles, and on the walls of bedchambers, and everywhere, many have imprinted that holy image in order not only to hear that name everywhere, but also to see everywhere the representation of his body, and thus have some sort of double consolation for his absence."[68]

Heretic: And whose should this image be?

XXX. *Orthodox*: The image of Meletios, the bishop of the Antiocheans.[69]

Heretic: [John] called the image holy but did not say that it is worthy of veneration; in fact, not everything that is holy is also venerable; for the holy Apostle indeed says somewhere, "The first tent had statues for worship (*latreia*) and an earthly sanctuary (*agion*). For a first tent was pitched, where there were the lamps, and the table, and the presentation of the loaves; and behind a second veil, there was a second tent, called the holy of holies, having a golden altar of incense, and the ark of the covenant all covered in gold; in it there was a golden urn containing the manna, and the rod of Aaron that blossomed, and the tables of the law; above it there were the Cherubim of glory overshadowing the set of mercy (*to hilastērion*); but of such matters it is not now the time to speak in detail."[70] While these things are called holy, the Apostle does not also call them venerable.

XXXI. *Orthodox*: As the Apostle has called these things holy, he also calls them worthy of veneration by way of a synecdoche (*kata synekdochēn*).[71] However, let the discussion of these matters wait a little, as it requires a more exhaustive explanation. In the meantime, answer one question for me. What do you think about the body and the blood of Our Lord Jesus Christ?

Heretic: That they are holy, of course; "Holy things are for the holy" is said by the celebrant.[72]

XXXII. *Orthodox*: Then do you recognize that these things are also worthy of veneration?

Heretic: Has anyone embraced the atheist position (*atheias phronēma*) so firmly that he would not acknowledge that these things are holy no less than worthy of veneration?

XXXIII. *Orthodox*: Then are you not contradicting yourself, having said earlier that what is holy is not necessarily worthy of veneration, and now you deny what you said before?

Heretic: But before I was not talking of these holy mysteries, about which everyone agrees.

XXXIV. *Orthodox*: What do you think of the gospel, which is called holy? Is it not also venerable? What about the representation of the life-giving cross, and all other sacred implements?

Heretic: They are holy and worthy of veneration. But the image of what is holy is far removed from their holiness. So even if the icon is called holy, it is by no means venerable.

XXXV. *Orthodox*: I also agree that, with respect to holiness, the latter is far removed from the former things; in fact, they are called Holy of Holies. It is also the case that whatever is holy is also worthy of veneration, even if one may happen to be inferior to another in terms of holiness and veneration; in fact, what is completely unworthy of veneration has no share at all in holiness. Show me, then, where anything could be called holy that would happen not to be worthy of veneration.

Heretic: I quoted the apostolic sayings (*rhēseis*) about the things that are said to be holy in the Law, to which you also promised to return.

XXXVI. *Orthodox*: First of all, I will say one thing, that whatever the Law says, it says it to those who are under the Law, nor should the things of old (*ta palai*) be in any way imposed on those who are under grace (*en chariti*). If this were the case, we would observe the Sabbath and be circumcised, and all sorts of contrary things would follow, but such things should only be understood as a foreshadowing (*en skiagraphia*).[73] Indeed, it is said by the Apostle that the Law has a shadow, but this shadow is not the image of the realities.[74] Second, it is necessary to show that even those things that in the Law[75] are said to be holy are also worthy of veneration. Now, if the Cherubim are glorified, and glory is related to honor, and honor is related to veneration, then, clearly, what has been glorified is holy and whatever is holy is also worthy of veneration, whether you want it or not.

Heretic: By juxtaposing things one next to the other (*akolouthia*), and by means of cunning, you have sophistically proved (*tetechnologētai*)[76] that what is holy is also worthy of veneration under the old dispensation, but you have not proved it from unimpeachable testimonies.

XXXVII. *Orthodox*: Let us, then, hear from the fathers, who are chief in leading the way (*koryphaiotatoi*):[77] in one of his orations, Gregory of Nazianzos says, "I know of Eli the priest, and slightly later Uzzah; the former had to undergo punishment because of the offense of his sons, which the latter committed against the sacrifices, taking the offerings [from the pot] before the appointed time (*pro kairou*); and this happened even if he did not approve of their impiety but actually repeatedly condemned them; the other [was punished] because having touched the ark when it was jostled by the ox, he managed to rescue it, but he was struck down nonetheless, as God was protecting the holiness of the ark."[78] And later, in the same work, he says, "No one dared to walk boldly into the Holy of Holies, which could be entered only by one person, and only once in the year. In the same way, hardly anyone dared to look or to touch the veil, or the mercy seat, or the ark, or the cherubim."[79] Second, Basil the Great says that around the ark of the holy covenant certain things happened that were unheard of before. So while, on the one hand, the ark could not be touched by the Israelites or by all their own priests, nor was it always appropriate to lay it down, yet, on the other hand, the ark, at different times and at different places, was carried off by impious hands, and instead of being laid down in holy places, it was placed in the temples of the idols.[80]

Heretic: That the holy things incite to piety (*sebasmia*), it is true, but the fathers do not say that they are worthy of veneration.

XXXVIII. *Orthodox*: How could they be holy and inspire to piety without also having part in veneration? The divine Apostle says, indeed, in the Book of Acts, "When I passed along and I beheld the monuments of your piety (*ta sebasmata*), I also found an altar (*bōmon*) where it had been written: 'To the Unknown God,'"[81] clearly saying of those things that inspire to piety that they are also worthy of veneration. Indeed, the emperor is called Augustus (*Sebastos*).[82] Scripture says, "As Paul had appealed to remain in custody until the decision of Augustus...."[83] And a little below, "I do not find him guilty of having done anything that is worthy of death; and as he himself had appealed to Augustus, I decided to send him."[84] Do you see, then, that what inspires to piety is also worthy of veneration? No sane person would ever dare to say that the emperor can inspire to piety but is not worthy of veneration.[85] In addition, the fact that it was forbidden to either see or touch the previously mentioned holy things, with the exception of the priest, indicates that according to the scriptures such things are very eminent in honor. And if the ark of God [performed] signs and wonders, and by means of them it struck Uzzah and his foreign kin who had captured it, how could it then not be full of every honor and glory and veneration, like the Cherubim, and all other things mentioned by the Apostle in conjunction with it (*kata synapheian*)?[86] In this way, then, echoing these concerns (*exeilēphotes*) in the very same canons that were issued later, even the fathers of the Sixth Holy Ecumenical Council say the following (*tade*): "In certain pictorial reproductions of the sacred mysteries (*tōn septōn*), the Lamb is depicted as the Forerunner points at it with his finger, and this representation (*hos*) was taken as a symbol of grace, prefiguring through the Law our true Lamb, Christ our God. Having acknowledged the old types and shadows as symbols and paradigms of the truth given to the church, we honor more eminently grace and truth, receiving the latter as the fullness of the Law.[87] So, then, that the ultimate perfection (*to teleion*) may be manifest in the eyes of all even by means of works of pictorial representation, we decree that from now on the [shape] of Christ our God the Lamb,[88] who has taken away the sin of the world, be represented (*anastēlousthai*) in icons according to his human shape instead of the old Lamb. Discerning through this the height of the humility (*tapeinōseōs*) of God the Word, we are led (*cheiragōgoumenoi*)[89] to commemorate his earthly life, as well as his passion and his salvific death, and the redemption (*apolytrōsis*)[90] of the universe that came henceforth."[91] You can see that they called the old symbols and the shadows worthy of veneration, by using the term "acknowledging" (*kataspazomenoi*). This is related to the verb "to embrace" (*aspazomai*), which means also to venerate and to welcome. In the same way, Theodore the archbishop of Antioch, in his synodical letter, says the same things, "Against those who oppose us in a heretical manner, and say that one should not venerate the images of the saints that are made by hand, calling them idols in their folly, or rather in their impiety; these people should know that the Cherubim and the mercy seat, the ark and the rod, which the divine Moses ordered to be made, were made by hand and were the object of veneration. Yet Holy Scripture condemns those who venerate graven images (*tois glyptois*)."[92]

Heretic: Why is it, then, that Hezekiah destroyed the bronze serpent? It is in fact written, "And he did what is good in the eyes of the Lord, in everything following what his father David had done. He destroyed the high places (*ta hypsela*), and he crashed all the statues, and he razed the sacred groves to the ground, and [destroyed] the serpent of bronze which Moses had made; because until those days the sons of Israel had burnt incense to it."[93]

XXXIX. *Orthodox*: Because the bronze serpent was not among the holy objects listed earlier by the Apostle. Concerning the serpent, Gregory the Theologian says, "The serpent of bronze was hung [as a defense] against the biting serpents. [It should be understood] not as a type of him who suffered for us, but rather as an antitype; and this, we believe, does not happen because it is alive, but because it is dead and in its death he also puts to death (*synnekroi*) those powers that are underneath it, as he is worthy of that. And which appropriate epitaph should he receive from us? 'Where is your sting, O death? Where is your victory, O hell?' You were wounded by the cross; you were put to death by the giver of life; bereft of soul, dead, lacking in movement and energy, even if, raised up on high, you preserve the form of a serpent."[94] And rightly was it destroyed, when the Israelites were offering incense to it; in fact, if the prototype is not worthy of adoration (*latreuteon*), the copy should also be spurned.[95] Indeed, the God-bearing Cyril shows that all the objects in the tent were prefigurations of the worship (*latreia*) in spirit.[96]

Heretic: I concede that this citation is appropriate, but since those cited previously are recent, they cannot be accepted as testimony.

XL. *Orthodox*: If what is said by them does not follow Basil or the other inspired fathers, I do not believe them, nor does anyone who follows the right faith (*tis tōn eusebountōn*). If, however, there is agreement and equivalence, not only those who are commemorated because they spoke two hundred years ago, but also those who live at the present time, if he were to say the same thing, should be accepted by the church of God, and in virtue of the dogma of truth, should be numbered among the holy apostles themselves, and not just with the later god-bearers. To this end, listen to the *Acts* (*ta praktika*) of the holy and much-tried (*polyathlos*) Maximos, where he says, "Masters, since it seemed appropriate [to you] that it should be so, may what you have decided be accomplished; and wherever you command, I follow you. At these words, everyone arose with joy and tears, and they bowed (*metanoian*) to each other and recited a prayer. And each of them embraced (*ēspasanto*) the Holy Gospels, the honorable cross, the icon of our God and Savior Jesus Christ, and that of Our Lady the most holy Mother of God, who gave him birth, having extended their own hands in testimony of what had been said."[97] And I forego to say more because of the superabundance (*proskores*) of my speech, despite the fact that there is a great swarm of texts, both ancient and modern, that deal with the blessed icons, if only we were so inclined to unroll them (*anelittesthai*).

Heretic: I also have a great swarm of texts from ancient and modern authorities, yet they are opposed to the erection and the veneration of icons.

XLI. *Orthodox*: If this opposition were directed to the erection and the veneration of the icon of Our Lord Jesus Christ, you could indeed bring forth such authorities; but since you accepted the depiction (*historian*),[98] making only an exception for the veneration, why then do you move back and forth from one position to another, which is typical of liars?

Heretic: Even if it is agreed that our Lord Jesus Christ is circumscribed, [this is the case] only until the passion, not after the resurrection; in fact, the Apostle says somewhere, "Even if we knew Christ according to the flesh, now however we no longer know him in that manner."[99] And in the same way, Gregory the Theologian says, "He is perfect not only in virtue of the divinity, than which nothing is more perfect, but also in virtue of [the flesh], which was assumed and anointed by the divinity, and which has become that which anoints,[100] and, I dare to say, equal to God (*homotheon*)."[101] If the flesh that has been assumed is equal to God, how could it be circumscribed as it was mingled with the incorruptibility of the divinity?

XLII. *Orthodox*: Nonetheless, you conceded that Christ was circumscribed before the passion and is venerated in the circumscription of such an icon.

Heretic: And even if I concede that and do not raise up in opposition, where would such an argument lead?

XLIII. *Orthodox*: In fact, the authorities that you began to introduce earlier do not appear to show that Christ was circumscribed either before the passion or after the resurrection; nor do they say that, even if he was circumscribed, his icon should be placed in a high place and should not be venerated. Why do you embrace as supporters those who oppose you in half your arguments? It is high time for you to find other authorities that support your whole argument. And yet even after the resurrection, Christ is circumscribed. Listen, then, to him saying to his own disciples, when after the resurrection they thought they were seeing him as a ghost (*pneuma*): "See then my hands and my feet—it is I."[102] If, then, he said that he who was talking with them before the passion was the same as the one whom they saw after the resurrection, clearly as he was circumscribed before the resurrection, then after the resurrection he was limited by circumscription, as he had not lost the properties (*ta idiōmata*) of the human nature. Which hands and feet did he then show them, O best of man? How then did he ask to be touched, as someone who has flesh and bones? In what way, then, was he able to take nourishment? Is there not a necessity, then, that someone having these characteristics should be circumscribed, or, if he does not have such characteristics, he should be a spirit, as he was esteemed to be by the apostles?

Heretic: But even if Christ is said to have these properties, he did not have them as we do; for that reason, he is said not to be circumscribed.

XLIV. *Orthodox*: If, then, he does not have these properties like us, he is also not believed to have become like us. If, instead, the second is true, how can the first one not be believed? Or perhaps it seems to you that in Christ those things that in him are called members are used to indicate some sort of operations (*energeiai*) and not the actual truth of material realities (*pragmatōn*)?[103] For instance, the divine Basil says, "Many anthropomorphic expressions are used, but for that reason we do not understand God to be a man." And then, "Having heard 'the hands of God,' think of the creative power of God; having heard, 'ears,' think of his acoustic power; 'eyes,' his visual power; 'wings,' his power of protection; and all other terms similarly."[104] If you think in this manner, it is necessary to come to the conclusion that you did not believe that Our Lord Jesus Christ became man. If he became man, as is indeed the case, you must also believe that he truly had flesh and bones, even after the resurrection.

Heretic: Using the strategy of condescension, the Lord showed himself to the apostles after the resurrection, having the properties of the body but not in thickness (*pachytēs*)[105] or in circumscription (*perigraphē*); in fact, even if the doors were closed, he appeared in their midst; again, he was taken from their sight.

XLV: *Orthodox*: If, then, you assert that Christ is not circumscribed because he is beyond thickness after the resurrection, you must also claim that he is not seen by the apostles. If, instead, he is seen, he is not circumscribed. Everything, indeed, that is subject to sight is also subject to circumscription; the more so, then, that which has hands and feet, flesh and bones, that which is touched and can take nourishment.

Heretic: The apostles can see the Lord as their eyes have been purified (*kekatharmenois*),[106] whereas it is not given to us to see in such manner.

XLVI. *Orthodox*: But what does Christ then say to Thomas? "Because you have seen me, you have believed. Blessed are those who did not see, and believe."[107] Therefore, as the apostles saw and handed down, both before and after the resurrection, so do we accept, and so do we circumscribe Christ. For it was not said by them that Christ could not be seen by us with the same eyes as those with which they saw him;[108] in fact, even before the passion, when they were starting to drown in the boat, all of a sudden Christ was seen to walk on the water; in fact, as the divine Denys says, it is not proper of the human nature that the unstable water, carrying the weight of material and earthly feet, did not give way, rather holding together against the dissolution by a supernatural power.[109] But similarly, before the passion, he revealed the things that were above nature (*ta hyper physin*). What power, then, was not at his disposal, if only he had wished? So, then, after the resurrection, even if he was beyond the reach of thickness, if he wished he could show properties as if he were in thickness,[110] and he was seen, and he was touched, and he could take food; these are properties of evident circumscription.

Heretic: How then could we understand the apostolic saying (*rhēsis*), "Even if we have known Christ in the flesh, now we no longer know him so"?[111]

XLVII. *Orthodox*: In the first place, we learn from the Apostle himself that we are members (*syssōmous*) and partakers (*symmetochous*) of Christ;[112] it is certainly not the case that we cease to be subject to circumscription because we are considered worthy of this grace. If, as you say, Christ were to be uncircumscribed after the resurrection, then we also should be uncircumscribed, because we are one body with him. In the same way as the concept of identity with God (*to homotheon*), the concept of shared corporeality [with Christ] (*to syssōmon*) must be understood in terms of a relationship (*kata synapheian*).[113] And hence, it does not follow that Christ should be uncircumscribed, or that we should be uncircumscribed in virtue of the fact that we share a body with him. In addition, listen to what Gregory the Theologian says, "'For there is one God and one mediator between God and men, the man Jesus Christ.'[114] Even now he intercedes as man for our salvation, for he is still with the body which he assumed, so as to make me God by the power of his hominization (*enanthrōpēsis*); and this is the case even if he is no longer known according to the flesh—by which I mean the passions of the flesh with the exception of sin."[115] Do you not see, then, that Christ is now with the body that he assumed? And that as far as being known according to the flesh is concerned, [do you not see that] it meant the passions of the flesh, except for sin, and that this does not entail uncircumscribability, as you say? He himself says, "Circumscribable in the body, uncircumscribable in the spirit,"[116] without referring to a limited time, but referring to all eternity without any limitation. And in another place, he says the following: "How then could he be touched after the resurrection, and how will he be seen by those who have pierced him? In itself, in fact, the Godhead is invisible. But he will come with the body, as I say; but such then as he was seen by the apostles on the mountain, or as he was revealed with his divinity triumphing over the carnal element, as the latter had already been revealed as such."[117]

Heretic: What, then, if I bring forth a variety of citations from the holy fathers? And how will you be able to object to them, when they completely forbid the erection of images of Christ, or the Mother of God, or any of the saints?

XLVIII. *Orthodox*: The citations are not from saints but from interpolators and heretics; otherwise, they would agree with the truth and with the holy fathers.

Heretic: Epiphanios is one of them, who is preeminent and illustrious among the saints.

Orthodox: We know that Epiphanios is a saint and is great in the art of performing miracles; his temple after his repose was erected by Sabinos, his servant and disciple, and was decorated with the whole story of the gospel, and he would not have done this if he had not been following his own teacher. But even the divine Leontios, the interpreter of the words of Epiphanios, bishop of the church of Neapolis in the very same Cyprus—his speech about Epiphanios explains most clearly how adamant the latter was in support of the blessed images, abstaining from saying anything negative about the blessed Epiphanios. Thus, the treatise against the icons is inauthentic and cannot at all be ascribed to the divine Epiphanios.[118] In addition, then, listen to what the great Basil has to say to this purpose, "As far as I am concerned—he said—if anyone receives a letter from men and were to glory in it, I would in no way agree to change my mind. And even if the letter were to come from heaven itself but were not in agreement with the healing (*hygiainonti*) word of faith, I would not be able to conclude that it has a share with the saints."[119] And listen to [John] Chrysostom, who says that the divine Paul does not respect the dignity of people when the truth is at stake.[120] Or rather, let us listen to Paul himself, who at a certain point says, "But let us say that, even if we or an angel were to announce to you a gospel different from the one that you received, let him be anathema."[121] And again, "If anyone will preach to you a gospel that differs from what you have received, let him be anathema." Finally, so as to show that we have received from the apostles themselves and have preserved up to the present the tradition of erecting the icon of our Lord Jesus Christ, or of the Mother of God, or of any of the saints, raise your eyes around you and look under the heavens, throughout the various sacred temples and the monuments that are in them, at all these images (*anistorēmenas*) that are also necessarily venerated in the places where they are to be found. And even if there were no doctrinal reason or no opinions from the holy fathers in support of the erection or veneration [of the icons], the ancient tradition that is in force should be sufficient in support of the truth. And who can presume to oppose such things? For this reason he would fall away both from God and from the flock of Christ, being of the same opinion of the Manicheans and the Valentinians, who foolishly assert in a heretical manner that God appeared to those on earth in appearance and phantasy.[122]

THIRD REFUTATION OF THE ICONOCLASTS

David, the composer of the psalms, is celebrated for having cast down the foreigner Goliath with the throw of a stone from his sling.[1] I am not an expert in war; yet, casting this third throw of verbal stone to complement the previous two,[2] I hope to destroy the foreign opinion (*noun*) of the iconoclasts, even if the attempt might be beyond my strength. To support my argument, I will resort to a number of syllogisms that lack the artful and cunning Aristotelian sophistry (*technologia*),[3] not to say foolishness; rather, [my syllogisms will resort to] a plain form of expression, relying on the strength of the truth. And perhaps this effort will not be fruitless to those who use it, and perhaps for those who are wise, it will be a starting point for a more informed evaluation, and for those who are not learned, it will be a sort of support in aid of a correct understanding that now labors under the attack of the iconoclast heresy. And since a clear distinction into categories (*to eukrines*)[4] is helpful to the readers, I will divide the treatise into four headings. Under each heading, I will collect all the arguments that pertain to the same goal.

1. The portrayal (*eikonographia*) of Christ in the body.
2. As Christ is circumscribed, he has an artificial image wherein he is contemplated, and in the same way the image is also in him.
3. That the veneration ascribed to Christ and to his image is one and indivisible.
4. As Christ is the prototype of his own image, he has one relation (*emphereian*) to it,[5] in the same way as he has one veneration with it.

PART 1

On the portrayal of Christ in the body

1. One may define common notions (*koinai ennoiai*) as those that are equally acceptable to all; for instance, it is a common notion to assert that it is day and not night when the sun is above the earth; or to claim that something living that is endowed with reason (*logikon*), mortal, and capable of discernment and understanding is a human being (*anthrōpos*).[6] And similarly, each body that has three dimensions, is characterized by solidity, and is subject to sight and touch can be said to be circumscribed. So what do you think, O excellent among men? Do you believe that this was the kind of body taken by the Word of God when he became man? If they agree, then they must entirely concur that this body was circumscribed. But if they disagree, this is no different from claiming that it is not day, but night, when the sun is above the earth; and that when something living is endowed with reason and it is mortal and it is capable of thought and discernment, it is not a human being. It is typical of foolish men to think and speak in this way. And it is unreasonable to debate with fools. Thus we engage in conversation not with people who voluntarily choose to be deaf, but rather with those who have ears to hear.

Further:

2. Sight precedes hearing, as far as both the location of its organ and the sensory perception are concerned. Indeed, one sees something first, and then one transmits the sight to the sense of hearing. For instance, Isaiah saw the Lord sitting on a throne of glory, surrounded and praised by the seraphim that have six wings.[7] In the same way, Ezekiel saw the chariot of God and the cherubim.[8] In the same way, as far as the disciples of the Lord were concerned, first they saw the Lord, and then they committed his message to writing. If, therefore, this is how things are, and no matter how far back you go, you will always find that the written text (*logographia*) goes back to direct inspection (*istoria*) and it rests in the latter; similarly, it is undoubtedly necessary that if the sight of Christ is removed, everything that is written of him ought to be removed, and if the visual image of Christ is outlined, then the written report must be laid down first.

Further:

3. If it pertains to the divine essence to be uncircumscribed, while it pertains to the human essence (*ousia*) to be circumscribed, and if Christ is from both, then he is known (*gnōrizomenos*) from both sets of properties (*idiōmatōn*) as they pertain to both natures (*physeōn*).[9] How, then, could it not be blasphemous to claim that he is uncircumscribed both in body and in spirit, given that through the elimination of circumscription his very humanity would also be eliminated?

Further:

4. If the properties are different, then the essences are also different (*diaphoroi*).[10] Uncircumscribability, bodilessness, and formlessness are properties of the divinity. On the contrary, however, circumscribability, tangibility, and three-dimensionality are characteristics of humanity. If therefore Christ is of both essences, he must be both uncircumscribable and circumscribable. If he is only either of the two, then he must be of only the one nature, of which he has the property—which is heretical.

Further:

5. If the circumscribability is eliminated by the uncircumscribability, as if it were not possible that both should be in Christ, then it would necessarily follow that the tangibility would also be eliminated by the intangibility, and the same would apply to all opposing properties that belong to the two natures. And if this is heretical, it would also be heretical to conclude that he is not circumscribed with respect to the incarnation.

Further:

6. If Christ cannot be circumscribed, he cannot suffer, because to be uncircumscribable is identical to being impassible. But he is able to suffer, because this is what scripture says; as such, he is uncircumscribable.

Further:

7. *[Scripture says,] "The Lord created me at the beginning of His ways, the first of His acts of old,"*[11] *[and] "Before all the hills, He generates me."*[12] *This is proof of the two natures of Christ, the circumscribable and the uncircumscribable.*

If the first verse, "The Lord created me at the beginning of His ways, the first of His acts of old," pertains to the humanity, whereas the second verse, "Before all the hills, He generates me," pertains to the divinity, then it is necessary that the one who speaks such things be subject to circumscription inasmuch as he is created (*ōs ktiston*), but equally he is not subject to circumscription inasmuch as he is uncreated (*ōs di'aktiston*).[13] If, however, circumscribability in one nature entails circumscribability in the other nature too, as is the case with the uncreated nature with regard to the created, then it necessarily follows that the one should change from uncircumscribable to circumscribed, and the other should change from circumscribed to uncircumscribable. Each nature must then exchange with the other what is proper to itself and forego what is proper to itself and the characteristic that is not shared; thus neither remains truly what it is, because of the inane alteration—which is most absurd.

Further, but what of "deductio (apagōgē) ad absurdum"?[14]

8. If by the saying, "The Lord created me at the beginning of His ways," we understand not that the Word has permanently changed into flesh in virtue of the mingling of humanity and divinity in him, but rather that the Word has transformed itself into flesh while remaining on the pinnacle of divinity; in the same manner, when we say that he is also circumscribed, we do not believe that he is transformed into circumscription, inasmuch as he is God, but rather that he is seen to be like us inasmuch as he has become man. Yet, if in being circumscribed the uncircumscribability is transformed, it would then follow that the nature of the divinity would also be transformed through becoming flesh—which is absurd.

Further:

9. It is the same to say, "The Lord created me" and "The Lord circumscribed me." Indeed, if it is impossible to say—because it is not written that "the Lord made me" or "the Lord clothed me with a body"—that these things did not happen to him, it follows that, given that it is written that "the Lord created me," it is possible, then, for those who desire to think correctly to conclude that "the Lord circumscribed me." Indeed, creation is a characteristic (*idiōma*) of circumscription, as it is clear even to those with little understanding.

Further:

10. If Christ is uncircumscribable, as you claim, not only according to the divinity, but also according to the humanity, then it follows that his humanity is also divinity. Indeed, if two things share the characteristics, one is their nature (*physis*). But if he is of two natures, he, then, is also invested with two sets of properties; otherwise, in virtue of the removal of circumscription, the nature of humanity would also be removed.

Further:

11. If every image encompasses form, shape, appearance, and color, Christ, then, must be in all of these; according to the scripture indeed, "he took the form of a servant, and he was seen to have the shape of man,"[15] and he had a dishonorable and lowly appearance,[16] which indicates the bodily condition; as such he is portrayed in the very circumscription of his likeness.

Further:

12. Just as uncircumscribability, intangibility, and formlessness belong to the same category (*homostoicha*), so do circumscribability, tangibility, the characteristic of having a shape, and whatever other characteristics are opposed to each other. If, therefore, Christ is uncircumscribable as a man, one would have to say that he is intangible and lacking in shape; both assertions are analogous. But if this makes no sense, and neither property tolerates being separated from the other—in the same way as uncircumscribability may not be separated from intangibility and formlessness—it necessarily follows that if he is tangible he must also be circumscribable, so as not to conclude that he is also intangible in virtue of his uncircumscribability—which is impious.

Further:

13. There are all sorts of circumscription: comprehension, quantity, quality, position, space, time, form, embodiment; all of these are denied when one talks of God, as the divinity is not subject to any of them. Christ, however, having become man, is manifest within all of these. He who cannot be contained is now contained in the womb of the Virgin; he who is beyond measure is now three cubits tall; he who is beyond quality is conformed to a certain quality; he who is beyond location stands up and sits down and lies down; he who is beyond the boundaries of place is laid down in the manger; he who is before time becomes twelve years old by increasing in age; he who is without form appears in the form of man; he who is without body, having taken a body, says to his disciples, "Take and eat, this is my body."[17] As such, the same one is circumscribed and uncircumscribed, the latter according to his divinity, the former according to his humanity—even if this is against the will of the most impious iconoclasts.

Further, by means of a gospel comparison:

14. If "no one has ever seen God, but as the only-begotten Son of the Father, being himself God, has made Him know,"[18] how can he, then, say to the blind man who has recovered his sight, "You have seen

him, and he who is talking to you is he"?[19] Thus, we must conclude that the same one is both visible and invisible; he is invisible according to his uncircumscribable nature, for what may not be circumscribed is indeed invisible, and he is visible according to his circumscribable humanity, for what may be circumscribed is visible. And what has been said here is true.

An objection on the part of the iconoclasts:

15. "If Christ truly assumed flesh in a miraculous manner in his own hypostasis, and yet this flesh was lacking in characteristics, as it did not indicate any individual in particular but rather man in general (*ton katholou anthrōpon*); how, then, is it possible that this flesh be found to be sensible to the touch and even be portrayed in a variety of colors? This notion is foolish, and the idea is deceitful."

A response to the objection:

If Christ truly assumed flesh in his own hypostasis in a miraculous manner (*paradoxōs*), and yet, as you say, this flesh lacked defining characteristics as it did not denote a specific individual, but rather man in general, how could he subsist (*hypestē*) in it?[20] Generalities (*ta katholou*) have their existence in particulars (*en atomois*); in this way, for instance, humanity is seen in Peter and in Paul and in all other members of the same species. If individual members did not exist, humanity in general would also not exist. Therefore, humanity cannot be in Christ if it does not subsist within an individual; and, in that case, we would have to say that Christ became incarnate in imagination (*phantasia*) and could not be touched or circumscribed by means of a variety of colors. Yet this is the notion of the Manicheans.[21]

Further:

16. Generalities are seen by intuition and by reason (*nous kai dianoia*);[22] it is with the eyes, however, that particularities are seen, as the latter come under the purview of the senses. If, then, Christ assumed our nature in general, and not in a manner that is contemplated in an individual manner (*en atomō theōroumenēn*), he can be contemplated only by the mind and only be touched by thought.[23] And yet he says to Thomas, "As you have seen me, you have believed; yet blessed are those who have not seen, and believe."[24] And he also says, "Place your finger here, and look at my hands; and put out your hand, and place it in my side";[25] thus he associates sensible things with [other] sensible things (*aisthēta*). So Christ can be perceived and touched, and he can be seen by bodily eyes, and therefore he is circumscribable.

Further:

17. When I say "man" (*anthrōpos*), I indicate the common essence (*ousia*). When I add "a particular man" (*tis*), I indicate the hypostasis, or in other words, the independently subsisting existence (*hyparxis*) of that which is signified, and (so to speak) the circumscription that is denoted by certain properties, whereby those who share the same nature (*physis*) are distinct one from the other, as, for instance, Peter and Paul. As Christ, then, said to the Jews, "Now you are trying to kill me," if he had merely said "man," he might have intended to signify "man" in general. And yet, when he added "Who has told you the truth," he indicated his own hypostasis or person (*prosōpon*). Indeed, the pronoun "who" (*Hos*) is effectively equivalent to the term "one" (*tis*). Thus, even if human nature was assumed in general, yet he assumed it so that it was contemplated in an individual manner; for this reason the possibility of circumscription exists.

Further:

18. The general term "man" (*anthrōpos*) is a common noun (*prosēgorikon onoma*), but "Peter" and "Paul," to give an example, are instances of a proper (*kyrion*) noun. So the particular individual can be called by the common name as well as by his own proper name. For instance, Paul is also called "man." In consideration of what he shares with other individuals of the same species (*homoeidesin*), he is called man; but with regard to his own hypostasis, he is called Paul. If, therefore, the incarnate Christ were called merely God or man by scripture, then he would merely have assumed our nature in general; and, as we demonstrated previously, our nature cannot subsist unless it is contemplated in an individual manner. However, Gabriel said to the Virgin, "Behold, you will conceive in your womb, and bear a son, and you will call his name Jesus."[26] Thus, Christ is called not only by a common name, but also by a proper name, and this distinguishes him from all other men in virtue of his hypostatic properties, and because of this he is circumscribable.[27]

Further:

19. If "Christ" does not denote an individual, as you say, but "man" in general, how then can he say to his disciple, "Who do men say that I, the Son of Man, am?"[28] Thus, he is one like us, even if, as God, he is also one of the Trinity. Therefore, just as he is distinguished from the Father and the Spirit by the property of sonship (*tō hyikō idiōmati*), so he is differentiated from all other men in virtue of the hypostatic properties; for this reason he is circumscribed.

Further:

20. If Christ does not represent an individual, as you say, but a universal man, how then can he say to the Jews, "'Whom do you seek?' And they answered him, 'Jesus of Nazareth,' and he said to them, 'I am he.'"[29] Therefore, Christ is an individual, as he is called by his proper name, Jesus of Nazareth. Thus, if he is an individual, he is also circumscribed, as he is characterized by his hypostatic properties.

Further:

21. Those that are members of the same species (*homoeidē*) are one according to the nature (*kat'ousian*). Yet hypostatically they are distinct one from the other; one is here, and one is there. If Christ, then, does not represent an individual but man in general, as you say, he could not be distinguished from other people (*prosōpon*). As such, how can he say to Peter, "Thus the sons are free. Yet, so as not to cause scandal, go to the sea and cast a hook, and take the first fish that comes up, and when you open its mouth, you shall find a statera; take that and give it to them for me and for yourself."[30] Thus, as he is distinguished from Peter, and equally with Peter he pays the tithe, so equally with him he is circumscribed, as someone who represents an individual, even as he has assumed human nature in general.

Objection from the iconoclasts:

22. "If the Word assumed human nature in his hypostasis, since this nature is invisible and lacking in shape, if it were given shape by circumscription, a second person (*prosōpon*) would be incorporated into the hypostasis of Christ; but this is absurd, and indeed, it is similar to the heresy of Nestorius, since it would attest a duality of persons (*prosōpon*) in Christ."[31]

Response to the latter:

If we say that the flesh assumed by the Word is invested with its own hypostasis, what you say would make sense. However, given that according to the consensus of the church (*kata tēn ekklēsiastikēn doxan*), we confess that the hypostasis of the Word has become the shared hypostasis of the two natures, and that it endows with a hypostasis the human nature that rests in it, together with the properties that differentiate it from the others belonging to the same species, we may then reasonably claim that the very same hypostasis is uncircumscribed according to the nature of the divinity, and that instead it is circumscribed according to the nature that it shares with us; this human nature does not have its own subsistence (*hyparxin*) in a person (*prosōpon*) that is self-subsistent and self-circumscribed outside the hypostasis of the Word, but in this very hypostasis—since there cannot be a nature that lacks a hypostasis (*anhypostatos*)[32]—and it is contemplated and circumscribed in an individual manner.

Further:

23. If, given that a second person cannot be admitted into the hypostasis of Christ, they were to say that the hypostasis is uncircumscribed with respect to the humanity, they must necessarily say that there is one nature of the Word that is composed (*synkratheisan*) of two natures, and therefore it cannot be circumscribed, since neither of the set of properties has been eliminated; this is related to the belief of the Akephaloi, and of the Apollinarians.[33]

Further:

24. If, because a second person is not admitted into the hypostasis of Christ, they were to say that the hypostasis is uncircumscribable with respect to the humanity, [this would entail] that he did not really assume the latter, but only the appearance and form of the flesh, as claimed by the Montanists.[34] But if he did so in truth, as indeed we confess, the hypostasis of Christ is circumscribed, not according to the divinity, which no one ever saw, but according to the humanity, which in it is contemplated in an individual manner; how could one be the mediator (*mesitēs*) between God and humanity without preserving in an intact manner the properties of the two natures wherein he subsists?

Further:

25. Where (*Pou*) signifies the location by which a body is contained. Thus not only is the body circumscribed, but also the place that contains it, and only that which is outside location is uncircumscribed, as it lacks in limits. If, therefore, the Christ is not circumscribed, not only is he not a body, but also he is without location; how, then, can he say, "The bread I give you, this is my flesh"?[35] And similarly, he answered, "Come and see," to Andrew and the other disciple who asked, "Where do you live?" and [scripture] says, "They came, and saw where he lives." Thus he is circumscribed, as someone who has assumed a body, independently of whether he stays, or he leaves, or he returns home.

Further:

26. A seeming contradiction (*enantiotēs*) suggests that Christ is not circumscribed, as scripture says, "You have heard the sound of the words, but you saw no form; there was only a voice."[36]

If Moses, speaking of the God of all, says, "You have heard the sound of the words, but saw no form," and yet Isaiah says, "We saw Him, and He had no shape or beauty, His appearance was dishonorable, and inferior to that of all sons of men,"[37] how can such claims come to terms with each other, if indeed one does not conflict with the other? Clearly, both are speaking about the same thing; one is talking against the possibility of the Godhead being present in a likeness, since divinity cannot be seen; the other is talking of the fact that the very same Lord was seen in our form, after having assumed the shape of a servant. Hence, Christ is circumscribed in body, even if he remains uncircumscribed in terms of his divinity.

Further, asking a question by way of a deductio ad absurdum*:*

27. If Christ is uncircumscribable, and Isaiah says of him, "A man who received blows, and acquainted with the bearing of sickness,"[38] I will ask whether what receives blows is a body, or is lacking in corporeality. If it is incorporeal, it has the appearance of a ghost, but if it is a body, how can it possibly not be circumscribed, characterized by three dimensions, and by hardness (*antitypia*),[39] so that it can naturally be wounded?

Further:

28. If Christ is not circumscribed, how can he say, "I gave over my back to the whips, and my cheeks to those who pulled out my beard; I did not turn away my face from the shame of spits"?[40] These are truly properties of circumscription: a back being whipped, a beard being pulled out, a face (*prosōpon*) being spit upon. Thus, if it is true that he suffered, he lies who says that he was not circumscribed.

Further:

29. If Christ is uncircumscribable, how can he himself say, "They have pierced my hands and my feet; they counted all my bones"?[41] Indeed, that which is uncircumscribable does not have a nature to be pierced, or to have its bones counted. And instead, the hands were pierced, and the bones were said to be counted; affirming these things is a confirmation of circumscription.

*Further, resorting to philosophical speculation (*theōria*):*

30. A line is a length devoid of width, comprised by two points; a drawing (*epigraphē*) has its beginning in a line.[42] A figure (*schēma*) is something that is composed of at least three lines; and from the figure begins the body, which is made up of different (*diaphorōn*) figures, and it is circumscribed by place. What is uncircumscribable, however, is dissimilar to these; it is certainly not bound by a line or by a form or a place

or a body. If Christ, then, is uncircumscribable, he will be found neither as having taken over a form, nor in a place, and certainly not in a body. Yet, he was found in a figure, as a man (*anthrōpos*), according to the scripture; and he was circumscribed by a place, living in Nazareth, and he became flesh, as the Evangelist says; hence he is also circumscribed.[43]

Further, according to an evangelical comparison:

31. If Christ is uncircumscribable, how can the Forerunner (*ho Prodromos*) say, "See the Lamb of God, who takes away the sins of the world"?[44] What is seen cannot be uncircumscribable, and this is even more the case for things that are pointed out with the finger (*to daktylodeiknoumenon*). If, instead, something is perceived in this way, then it would be within circumscription, and it would be marked by the finger. Hence, Christ is circumscribed.

Further, putting forth a doubt:

32. If Christ is uncircumscribable, he is not of two natures—the divine and the human—because he does not have the properties of each. For circumscription is characteristic of humanity. But if he is of two [natures], how can he possibly fail to have the properties of the natures that he has?[45]

Further, through a comparison of the thesis of the Theopaschites:

33. If it is heretical to say, as the Theopaschites do, that because Christ was crucified in the flesh, the Godhead (*to theion*) also suffers, then in the same way, it is heretical to say that, because he is circumscribed by the flesh, the Godhead is also circumscribed (which is the teaching of the iconoclasts); and this is the most impious claim of all, all the more so as the flesh is conjoined to the divinity through a union of natures, while the image [lit. "the shadow"] that is depicted is united to the flesh by a union of relation (*schetikōs*).[46]

An objection from the iconoclasts:

34. "If Christ is of two natures, why is it that, when you claim to portray him, you do not portray both natures from which and in which he is, if what you say is true?[47] But given that one of the two is falsified, given that it does not contain the uncircumscribability of the divine nature in the human circumscription, it is then heretical to circumscribe Christ."

Solution of the above:

When anyone is depicted, it is not the nature but the hypostasis that is depicted; how, then, could a nature be portrayed if it were not contemplated in a hypostasis? For instance, Peter is not portrayed inasmuch as he is a rational and mortal animal, endowed with intuition and reason; this, in fact, does not define just Peter, but also Paul and John and all those who belong to the same species (*eidos*). But inasmuch as he adds to the common definition (*oros*) a set of specific properties, such as a crooked or a simian nose, curly hair, a good complexion, or beautiful eyes, or whatever else characterizes his particular appearance (*idea*), he is distinguished from the other individuals that belong to the same species. In addition, even if he consists of body and soul, he does not show the property of the soul in the appearance of his form; how could that be, given that the soul is invisible? The same applies to the case of Christ. It is not because of the fact that Christ, alongside being divine, is also a human being, that Christ can be portrayed, but rather because he is differentiated by his hypostatic properties from all the other members of his species: he is crucified and has a certain appearance. Thus, Christ is circumscribed with respect to his hypostasis, but he is uncircumscribed with respect to his divinity, or with respect to the two natures of which he is composed.[48]

Further:

35. If Christ is not circumscribed, as you say, lest he may be diminished in glory, then he was not conceived in the womb of the Virgin, so as not to undergo humiliation. And yet, if he was conceived in utter humility (*anhybristōs*), all the more so as he became an infant, then he is circumscribed without indignity (*anepaiscuntōs*).

Further, as a deductio ad absurdum*:*

36. Everything that moves is not the species that can be defined according to a general principle—indeed this is invisible, and lacking in form and shape, and thereby uncircumscribable—but is rather the individual, which it is natural should consist of properties; and this is seen and moves and speaks, and for this reason is circumscribed, as for instance, James and John. If, therefore, Christ is uncircumscribable, he is not seen, he does not move, nor does he speak with a clear voice, not having a tongue or lips; nor would he eat or drink, nor would he sleep or wake up, nor do any of the things that one can do or endure. But if he is confessed to have done these things, how can he not be circumscribed, unless the mystery of the divine dispensation (*oikonomia*) is sheer phantasy?

Further:

37. If things that are of a different kind (*eterogenōn*) and are not of the same essence (*ouch homoousiōn*) have properties that correspond

to their essences, such as, the divinity and the humanity, how is it then that Christ, who is from both, is not in both, if indeed every essence is distinguished from all others in virtue of its own property? And yet, if he is in both, he is circumscribed, in the same way as he is uncircumscribed.

Further:

38. The true (*alēthōs*) properties of the essences are indicative of the essences of which they are the properties; for instance, uncircumscribability makes divinity known, and circumscribability makes humanity known. If Christ is then from both, he is circumscribed in the same way as he is uncircumscribed. But if he is not circumscribed, then he is not truly man, in the same way as he is truly God. But if he is truly man, then he is truly circumscribed.

An objection from a member of the iconoclast group:

39. "If the Son is an exact (*aparallaktos*) image of the Father, so that the Father appears in him, as it is said in scripture, 'He who has seen me, has also seen the Father,'[49] it is necessary that we should say that he who comes from the uncircumscribable Father is also uncircumscribed. For how is it possible that that which is uncircumscribed should be seen in what is circumscribed? Therefore Christ is uncircumscribable."

A response to the above, following a similar argument:

If he who comes from the uncircumscribable Father is also uncircumscribed, then clearly he who comes from a circumscribed mother will also be circumscribed; unless perhaps it is the case that the former is true and the latter is false. But if both things are true in the one Christ, then he has also acquired the properties of both origins, and he is simultaneously uncircumscribable and circumscribed.

Further, by deductio ad absurdum*:*

40. If the archetype (*to archetypon*) appears in the image, let us suppose that the latter is in all respects like the former. But Christ is endowed with a body (*ensōmatos*). Then the Father should also be endowed with a body, given that the image is modeled after him. But if this is absurd, let us say that Christ is uncircumscribed, inasmuch as he is the image of the Father; indeed the Father, as he is incorporeal, is uncircumscribed. Yet, according to what he himself said—and do not consider this strange—he is also the Son of man, and as such he is circumscribed; indeed, each human being is circumscribed, because each is endowed with a body, and this is the truth.

Further:

41. If, as you say, it was in reference to his corporeal appearance (*idea*) that Christ said, "He who has seen me, has seen the Father," then it is necessary that he should be invested with the same properties that belong to the Father according to the nature (*kata physin*); in this way, the imprint (*ho charaktēr*) is accurate (*akribēs*). And yet the Father has no form, or shape, or circumscription [or comprehension]. These properties also belong to Christ. For how could formlessness (*to aneideon*) appear in someone who has been endowed with a form, or shapelessness in one who has been invested with a shape, or uncircumscribability in one who has been circumscribed? But if this is heretical, then it would also be heretical to claim that Christ is talking of his corporeal appearance when he says, "He who sees me, also sees the Father." The only possible alternative is to say (*leipetai dē legein*) that he is speaking of the form of divinity; and this is the truth.

An objection from the iconoclasts:

42. "If Christ were a mere human being (*psilos anthrōpos*)," they say, "he would also be circumscribed, because circumscription is a characteristic of a mere man; but since he is not a mere man—given that he is God no less than a human being—he is not circumscribed."

A solution to the above:

If, in denying that Christ is a mere human being,[50] they were to say that he is uncircumscribable, they would also have to say that he is bodiless. This is because a thing is recognizable as corporeal if it is circumscribed and has a form. If these qualities are not there, however, then it is also necessary to deny that to which they belong. But Christ is in a body and in a form; hence, he also has circumscription.

Further:

43. If, because of the fact that Christ is not a simple man, they should say that he is uncircumscribable according to the humanity, given that this is a property of the divine nature, things would be mingled that cannot be mingled (*emichthē ta amikta*), or in other words, circumscription [is mingled] in uncircumscribability. And if properties of things are mixed, the same also happens with the natures. And if to say or think such a thing is impious, then Christ is not a mere man even as he is circumscribed in the body, since otherwise, in virtue of the circumscription, things that cannot be mingled would be mingled.[51]

Further:

44. That which is uncircumscribed is simple and not composed (*asynthetos*), since it is utterly exempt from all position (*theseōs*). Christ, however, being double and composite (*diplous kai synthetos*),[52] if he were not circumscribable, would lose the form and the use of duality and composition. However, we confess that he is double and composite; thus he is circumscribed, which is the truth.

Further:

45. The male and the female gender are to be sought merely in the forms of bodies, since none of the difference that characterizes the two can be seen in incorporeal realities. Thus, if Christ is uncircumscribable, as being without a body, he would also be beyond the difference that we just mentioned. But, as Isaiah says, "He was born male (*arsēn techtheis*) from the prophetess";[53] thus he is circumscribed.

Further:

46. Some bodies may only be divided in thought; for instance, some cannot be touched, and as such are uncircumscribable; other bodies, instead, can be cut in actuality; for instance, some are solid (*pachymerē*), because they can be touched, and as such they can be circumscribed. If, then, Christ assumed a body that cannot be cut (*atmēton sōma*), then this body is also uncircumscribable. But Christ's body can be cut (*tmēton*); indeed, Luke of blessed speech says, "And when the eight days were passed of his circumcision (*peritemein*)."[54] And if he was circumcised, then he was circumscribed—and this is the truth.

An objection from the iconoclasts:

47. "If whatever bodies cannot be cut or touched are also uncircumscribable, then, given that the angels are incorporeal, how is it possible that they be subject to circumscription? Hence, if they are circumscribed, they are also corporeal. And if they are incorporeal, then they are not circumscribable."

A solution to the above:

In comparison to a thick body, the nature of the angels is incorporeal; but if considered next to the divinity, it is neither incorporeal, nor is it uncircumscribed.[55] For this reason the Apostle says, "There are celestial bodies, and there are terrestrial bodies."[56] That which is truly (*kyriōs*) incorporeal is limitless and uncircumscribable; this applies exclusively to the divine nature; an angel, however, is bound by place and therefore is circumscribable. Indeed, when [the angel Gabriel] went to Nazareth and said to the Virgin, "Rejoice!" he was not somewhere else.[57] But the Word of the Father, having been conceived in the womb of the Mother of God, was there, and at the same time, he was everywhere else. And for this reason he is God, uncircumscribable no less than boundless; although as a man, because he was born of the Virgin, he is circumscribed.

Further:

48. If he who was in the form of God and took the form of a servant is not circumscribed,[58] this latter form would be nothing but the divine form. This is because uncircumscribability characterizes the divine form. And yet, if the form of a servant is different and is consubstantial (*homoousios*) with us, how could he possibly have taken the form without having taken its property? Given that we whose form he took are circumscribed, Christ is circumscribed as well.

Further:

49. If the fact that Christ is circumscribed as a human being weakens those properties in virtue of which he, as God, is not circumscribed, it is then also necessary that the things that he is seen to do and say as man would weaken those properties by which he is revealed to be God, preaching and working miracles. If, instead, one thing is not violated by the other, and each of the two remains within its limits in the one Christ that is made of the two, then it is not the case that circumscription is not eliminated by uncircumscribability.

Further, from a comparison in the inspired scriptures:

50. Talking to the Jews, the Savior said, "Before Abraham was, I am."[59] And yet the evangelist [Matthew] says, "This is the book of the genealogy of Jesus Christ, son of David, son of Abraham." In what way, then, can he who was before Abraham be the son of Abraham? Is it not clear, then, that we should understand that one statement is appropriate to divinity, and one is appropriate to humanity? And the same should be thought concerning circumscribability and uncircumscribability; indeed, one will not take away from the other in the single Christ who is acknowledged to be from both.

Further:

51. If every mediator (*mesitēs*) mediates between two persons who are in opposition to each other, distributing within himself in an equal manner the rights of either part, it is, then, necessary that Christ, who is the mediator between God and humanity, and who, by a right judgment, unites the extremes as it were into a natural union (*eis enotēta physikēn*), must be uncircumscribable in spirit but circumscrib-

able in body.[60] If he were to favor one—namely, uncircumscribability—and he were not to preserve unharmed the circumscribability, he would fall short from being a just mediator.

Further:

52. If Christ died as a man, and no injury was inflicted to him as a God, it would be no disgrace to him to be circumscribed in any way. But if circumscription is demeaning, then to be put to death (*hē thnēsis*) is even more so.

An objection from the iconoclasts:

53. "Circumscribing Christ is somewhat incompatible with, and abhorrent to, the divinely inspired scripture. Indeed, scripture says, 'And the Lord spoke to you on the mountain from the midst of fire, and you heard the sound of the words, but you did not see a likeness, but only a voice.'"[61] Thus, to erect an image of Christ is incompatible with the divine commands.

A solution to the above:

Those who speak in this manner make themselves deaf deliberately, as they do not recognize for what reason Holy Scripture would bar a shape or a likeness, or why there is a prohibition of any other representation used as an idol; the reason is that scripture is talking of the divine nature—the Godhead (*to theion*) is indeed without quantity and form (*aposon te esti kai aschēmatiston*)[62]—and not of the Word that has been ontologically transformed according to our form. In fact, if the latter were the case, how could the evangelist then say, "And as he was praying, the appearance of his face was transformed, and his garment became white and resplendent"?[63] See here how the one who had no appearance (*ho aneideos*) had an appearance, or indeed a likeness; the one who had no form was given a form; and the one who had no quantity became subject to quantity. And since his countenance was characterized by certain particular properties, Christ is thus circumscribed with respect to his corporeal appearance, in the same way as he is circumscribed with respect to his invisible essence.

Further, by a deductio ad absurdum*:*

54. If it is necessary that whatever is born should come from the same type of being as the one belonging to the one who gives birth—and the mother of Christ is circumscribed—thus even Christ will be circumscribed, since he is her son, even if he is God by nature. Therefore, if he is not circumscribed, he would not be consubstantial

to his mother; hence, it would follow that his mother is not his mother, which is absurd.

An objection from the iconoclasts, by way of an apostolic comparison:

55. "Everyone will understand that the practice of depicting Christ is an invention reflecting an idolatrous frame of mind (*epinoia*). Indeed, the Apostle says somewhere, 'And they exchanged the glory of the immortal God into the likeness of the image of a mortal human being, and they prostrated themselves, and offered adoration to the creation instead of the Creator.'"[64]

A response to the latter:

To speak in an apostolic manner, it is true (*tō onti*) that the iconoclasts have fallen into a degenerate state of mind (*adokimon noun*): "Their foolish heart is obscured; and claiming to be wise, they became unwise."[65] "They understand neither what they are saying, nor what they are talking about."[66] Indeed, if it is to prohibit the practice of portraying Christ that the Apostle says, "They exchanged the glory of the incorruptible God for the likeness of the image of the corruptible human being," he has not yet confessed that he has become man.[67] How, then, can he say elsewhere, "Who being in the form of God, did not consider that equality to God was a thing to be grasped; rather, he emptied himself (*eauton ekenōse*), taking the form of a servant, being born in the likeness of human beings, and being found in the form of man. He humbled himself, being made obedient unto death, and a death on the cross"?[68] Thus it would seem that he contradicts himself, denying at one point that God has been made equal to human beings, and saying at another point that he was born in the likeness of men. But let go of this foolishness! The first passage is applied to those who engage in idolatry, who "exchanged the glory of the immortal God into the likeness of the image of a corruptible man, and of birds, and of quadrupeds, and of serpents";[69] "who exchanged the truth of God into a lie, and venerated and served the creature instead of the Creator."[70] The second passage is instead meant for the faithful, who believe that the Word of God, while remaining in the form of God, was also made similar [to us], not by being equal to God, but by emptying himself and assuming the form of a servant, so that he was found in a form that is similar to that of man; and all such things are characteristics of circumscription.

Further:

56. If we are the body of Christ, and we are all his members and Christ is our head,[71] then it is quite certain that the head should be

circumscribed in the same way as the members. If, instead, he were uncircumscribable, we would have ceased to be members of Christ, as we are subject to the form of circumscription. And how is this not of the ultimate absurdity (*euētheia*)?

Further, regarding the passage "I am the vine":

57. If, as scripture says, the Savior is the vine, and we are the branches, then clearly the branches do not have a different nature (*heterophyē*) from the vine. But if this is true, given that the branches are circumscribed, how can the vine not be circumscribed? For the vine is recognized by the branches.

Further:

58. It is impossible that things that belong to different species (*heterogenē*) or to different natures (*heterophyē*) should have the same properties (*idiotēta*); no one, indeed, would say that fire moves downward, whereas water moves upward; but in the same way as they have a distinct principle of being (*tēs ousias logon*), so they should have a distinct mode of property (*tēs idiotētos tropon*).[72] Since Christ belongs to two different natures that are not consubstantial (*ouch homoousiōn*)—meaning the divinity and the humanity[73]—he will also be known by two sets of properties. One then will not be circumscribed, and the other will be circumscribed. In fact, through the elimination of the property, that essence that is characterized by that property is also eliminated.

PART 2

Since Christ is circumscribed, he also has an artificial image (technētēn eikona) *in which he is contemplated, because the image is itself in Christ*

Whatever is artificial is creation in imitation of what is natural; for, in fact, nothing would be called artificial if it were not preceded by something that is natural. Thus, there is an artificial image of Christ, as he is himself the natural image of his mother, who gave birth to him. If the latter were true, but the former false, he would not be the natural image of his mother because he would not have an artificial image as she does—which is absurd.[74]

Further:

Every image has a relationship (*emphereia*) to its archetype, but the natural image has a natural relationship, whereas the artificial image has an artificial relationship. The former is identical both in essence and in likeness with that of which it is the imprint (*aposphragisma*)[75]; thus Christ, according to his divinity, is identical to his own Father and, according to his humanity, is identical to his own mother. The latter, however, while being identical in likeness, is distinct from the essence of the archetype; this is how the image of Christ relates to Christ himself. Therefore, there is an artificial image of Christ to whom [the image] has a relationship.

An objection as from the iconoclasts:

"If Christ has an artificial image insofar as he is the natural image of his mother, then, in order that there should be no discrepancy at all from the relationship, he would also have an artificial image inasmuch as he is the image of the invisible Father. But if this is the case, the divine would not be outside circumscription—which is heretical."

A response to the above:

Out of their utter foolishness, the iconoclasts mingle things that cannot be mixed, nor do they understand how each origin (*gennēsis*) is endowed with its own properties, by which Christ is uncircumscribed but is also circumscribed. With respect to the fact that he proceeds from the uncircumscribable Father, and is therefore uncircumscribable, he would not have an artificial image; to what simulacrum could the Godhead be compared, regarding which there is utter absence (*apophasis*) of description in the inspired scriptures? With respect to the fact that he is born out of the circumscribed mother, it is most appropriate that he should have an image, corresponding to the appearance of the mother. But if he did not have one, he would not be from the circumscribed mother, and he would then be from only one generation, namely that from the Father—which fact is incompatible with the divine plan (*oikonomia*).

If what is displayed in the image shows a relationship (*emphereia*) to the prototype, and it is impossible that there should be a prototype and there should not be an image—according to the Lord's saying, "Whose image is this, and whose inscription?"[76] and to what he subsequently says to his questioners, "Render to Caesar what is of Caesar, and to God what is of God"[77]—then Christ, having become like us (*gegonōs*),[78] has an artificial image, which is related to him through a relationship of likeness. And if he does not have an artificial image, then he is not what is called the Christ.[79] But Christ is, and is called, the truth itself (*autoalētheia*).[80] Therefore, he has an image, and as the relationship of veneration of this image goes over to him, there is no distinction in glory that separates the two.

Further, based on the statement, "Let us make man in our image and likeness":[81]

The fact that man is made in the image and likeness of God shows that to undertake the work of iconography (*eikonourgia*) is a divine activity. But since an image can be copied (*metagraphetai*) from an image, given that he is man while also being God, Christ can be portrayed in an image, not in spirit but in body. But if he is portrayed under one of the two natures, then clearly he must have an image exactly resembling him, so as to display the shared likeness.

Further:

If Adam, the first man, is circumscribed by [his] form (*tō eidei*), then Christ, who is the second Adam, since he is both God and man, can similarly be represented in his bodily form. If, then, "as the son of the earth was, so are those who are earthly; and as the son of heaven was, so are those who are heavenly," and if we who are of heaven can be represented, then Christ, who is the one who laid the foundation (*archēgos*) of the salvation of all, is also the archetype of his own image.

Further:

If God is not in need of any help, or subject to any suffering of any kind, how is it that the Apostle says about him, "In the days of his flesh, he offered up prayers and supplications to the one who could free him from death, with great shouting and tears, and he was heard because of his obedience (*eulabeia*)"?[82] Is it not clear that the one without flesh who assumed flesh is unable to suffer and is immune to suffering, and yet he suffers, in the same way as he is uncircumscribed and he is circumscribed? And if he is circumscribed, he also has an image that resembles him and that reveals the mutual likeness.

PART 3

The veneration of Christ and of his image is one and indivisible

An objection coming from the iconoclasts:

1. If everything that is made in the likeness of something else inevitably falls short of equality with its prototype, and is second to it in terms of glory, then clearly, in terms of veneration, Christ is not the same as his portrait. And if these things are different, the veneration that is introduced is also different. This, then, is the cause of idolatrous adoration.

A solution to the above:

The prototype is not in the image according to the essence; if this were the case, the image would also be called prototype, and conversely, the prototype would be called image. This is inappropriate, because the nature (*physis*) of each has its own definition. Rather, [the prototype is in the image] by the similarity of the hypostasis, for which there is no different principle of definition (*logos tēs dioriseōs*).[83] Thus, the fact that the image does not equal the prototype and is inferior to its glory is not understood in terms of the hypostasis, but rather in terms of the difference in essence. The nature of the image is not worthy of veneration, and yet he who is represented in it is seen so that he may be venerated. Thus, there is no introduction of a different kind of veneration, but the image has the same veneration [as the prototype], according to the identity of the likeness.

Further:

2. It is not the essence of the image that we venerate, but the imprint (*charaktēr*) of the prototype that is inscribed in it, given that the essence of the image is not susceptible of veneration (*aproskynētos*). Nor is it the material (*hē hylē*) that is worthy of veneration, but rather the prototype together with the imprint, and not the essence. If, then, the image [is venerated], the veneration is one with the prototype, in the same way as the likeness (*homoiōsis*) is the same.[84] Thus, whenever the icon is venerated, there is no introduction of another veneration beyond the veneration of the prototype.

Further:

3. Those realities that do not have the same imprint, have different venerations; likewise, those realities that do have the same

imprint, have the same veneration. But the imprint of the icon with regard to the prototype is one; thus, the veneration is also one.

Further:

4. Everything that is unequal is different from that which is equal; thus, everything that takes second place with regard to glory is distinct from what takes first place. They are two different things, and not one. Wherever there is equality, inequality is erased. And wherever there is identity, the distinction between first and second is eliminated. Now, the image of the emperor is also called image, and not two emperors. Indeed, as it is written, the power is not scattered, nor is the glory fragmented.[85] Thus, there is one glory, and there is no introduction of a second veneration, as the image of Christ is venerated because of Christ. Clearly, however, [the icon] is inferior and takes second place in terms of glory according to the principle of the essence.

Further:

5. Even if we grant that the image lacks resemblance (*hisotypon*) from the prototype because of lack of technical ability (*ex atechnias*), yet even in this case our claim would not be inappropriate. Indeed, the veneration is given in virtue of what is identical, and not in virtue of what is inferior in terms of the relationship. In this respect, the icon is identical to the prototype, and there are not two objects of veneration, but one and the same, the prototype in the image; the same goes for the symbol (*typon*) of the cross in relation to the life-giving (*zoōpoion*) cross itself, given that, in this case, the iconic representation is not identical to the archetype in terms of length or width or any other characteristic, because it is represented in different ways. One can see a cross that is small and large, wider and narrower, having blunt and sharp ends, with inscription and without inscription. And this is to pass under silence the varieties of decorations underneath and on top, and the variety of skills. But nevertheless, in the presence of all these differences, there is one veneration of the symbol and of the prototype; the same identity is clearly discerned in both.

Further, by way of example:

6. If the life-giving cross is venerated in its own symbol, and there are not two venerations, because there is not another veneration from the essence of the symbol, it is then necessary that, as Christ is venerated in his own proper image, there are not two venerations; since there is no veneration of the essence of the image, but one and the same veneration ascribed to Christ and to the icon.

Further:

7. If despite the fact that the Son differs in some ways from the Father—albeit the difference is merely in terms of the property of sonship—nothing prevents him from having the same substance and the same veneration as the Father; in a similar way, the fact that the image differs in some way from the prototype, and the difference is in terms of the principle of the essence, does in no way prevent it from having the same likeness and veneration as the prototype. In the same way as Christ is distinguished from the Father by his hypostasis, so is he distinguished from his image by his essence.

Further:

8. If the image is the object of a distinct veneration (*eteroproskynētos*) from its own prototype, in what way is the latter seen in it, and in its turn how is it seen in the prototype? Clearly, so to speak, we do not contemplate the form of Peter in Paul; similarly, no one can discern the form of Paul in the form of Peter. This is because "like" appears in "like," whereas things that are reciprocally distinct in likeness could never appear in each other; so the image of Peter appears in Peter, and Peter appears in his own image. Thus, the image of Christ is not venerated differently from Christ himself but is the object of the same veneration (*homoproskynētos*), as it bears a relationship and a similarity to it.

An objection from the iconoclasts:

9. If veneration from us and from the angels is only due to God, how can there be a single veneration of the icon of Christ? Indeed, we profess that the image is venerated by relationship, whereas Christ is venerated by nature. Thus, there are two kinds of veneration in Christ, because of the veneration of the image, which is impious.

An answer to the above:

If it is the case that, because we offer veneration only to God, we should not venerate the image of Christ, on the ground that we would be introducing two kinds of veneration instead of the one and only adoration (*latreutēn*), in accordance with the distinction between image and prototype, then the veneration to the Father and to the Son should also be dual, because of the distinction between the two hypostases. But this is impious to say; one indeed and the same [is the veneration] according to the obvious oneness (*to monadikon*) of the divine nature, and so one is also veneration of Christ and that toward his own image, in virtue of the oneness of the hypostatic similarity, and not because of the diversity of the natures.

Further:

10. One talks of a relation inasmuch as the copy (*to paragōgon*) is in the prototype; one is not separated from the other because of this, but only because of the distinction in essence. Thus, since the image of Christ is said to have in its own linear structure (*epigraphē*) the very form of Christ, then similarly the veneration is one with Christ and not distinct.

A claim from the iconoclasts:

11. "How could it ever be possible that the identity of veneration were preserved in the case of Christ and his image, if indeed Christ is venerable by nature (*physei*), whereas the image is venerable by position (*thesei*)?[86] It is, in fact, absolutely necessary to say that what is in a certain way by nature can in no way change. If this is the case, nothing prevents us from saying that the icon [can be venerated] by nature, and Christ by position; and everything gets confused."

*The solution to the above, by way of a mutual interrogation (*anterōtēmatōs*):*

But how, O excellent men, could it ever be possible that the identity of veneration were not preserved in the case of Christ and his own image, if the image is the likeness of Christ, and the image reveals Christ in itself? It is indeed clearly known, and it must be acknowledged by all, that no one can see the appearance of one, let us say Luke, in the appearance of the other, let us say Thomas. Indeed, the appearance of the likeness takes place in things that have a relationship of identity (*en tois tautempheresin*) and not in things that differ from each other in terms of their defining characteristic. If therefore this is true, and he who has seen the image of Christ has seen Christ in it, it is absolutely necessary to say of the image that in the same way as there is one likeness, so the veneration of the image of Christ is the same as the veneration addressed to Christ.

Further:

12. That which is similar in some degree (*kata ti*) [to something else] shares the same veneration to the degree in which it is similar. That, on the other hand, which is similar in all respects should share the veneration in all respects. But the Son is similar in all respects to the Father, given that he is consubstantial; thus, he is also worthy of the same veneration. The image of Christ, however, is related (*emphērēs*)

solely according to the similarity of his hypostasis; therefore, only in this respect could it share its veneration.

Further:

13. If one who has seen the image sees in it also the likeness of the prototype, there is an absolute necessity that he who venerates the image should venerate in it the form (*to eidos*) of the prototype as well. But since the likeness is one, one is also the veneration of both.

An objection from the iconoclasts:

14. "If the image that is patterned after Christ shares in his veneration, how can Christ himself say 'My glory I do not give to anyone else?'[87] Thus [the image] does not share [in the veneration]. But if it does not share in the veneration, then it must be conceded that it is venerated idolatrously, since a second type of veneration is thereby introduced."

The solution to the above:

The image of Christ is nothing else but Christ, with the exception obviously of the substance, as has been indicated many times. Thus, it is the case that the veneration of the image is the same as the veneration of Christ; of course, the material of the image is not venerated, but rather only Christ who is expressed in likeness in the image. Indeed, it is clear that things that share the same substance also share the same veneration. Thus, in his own icon, Christ does not give his own glory to anyone else, but rather he appropriates this glory for himself in the image, because the material is different from the likeness. Indeed, even if they are made with different materials, the same imprint is in all [images]. And the form would not remain unchanged in the different materials, were it not for the fact that it does not have anything in common with them; rather, it is conceptually (*tē epinoia*) distinct from the materials in which it inheres.

An objection on the part of the iconoclasts:

15. If God is spirit, as scripture says, and it behooves those who adore him to do so in spirit and in truth, how is it then possible not to introduce a display of idolatry in the icon, when you say that Christ, inasmuch as he is God, should be venerated in spirit?

Answer to the above:

Who is not aghast at seeing how full of insanity the iconoclasts are, as they do not distinguish how different the mystery of the economy is from that of theology, under which purview one should consider the saying "One must venerate in spirit and in truth"? As then

God the Father is also spirit, he is understood to be venerated in the Holy Spirit and in the Truth, which is his only begotten Son.[88] But the veneration of Christ in the image belongs to the rationale (*logos*) of the economy. Even if Christ is spirit inasmuch as he is God, yet he is also flesh inasmuch as he is also a human being. And even if his image in the form of a body (*sōmatoeidēs*) is given a likeness in a material, yet it is inseparable from Christ, as a shadow is inseparable from its own body. It is not the material of the image that is venerated, but rather the Christ that is portrayed in it—Christ in whom the Father is venerated, and the Holy Spirit.

Part 4

Since Christ is the prototype of his own image, he has one relationship as well as one veneration with it

1. The prototype and the image are one thing in terms of the hypostatic likeness, and two separate things in terms of the nature; not in the manner of one thing that is divided into two likenesses, so that afterward they no longer have anything in common or any relationship with each other; nor is it the case that the one and same entity is called by two different names, so that at one time the prototype is called image, and at another time the image is called prototype. This is because the prototype would always be called prototype, and the image would be called image, never changing into each other. Even if this is the way things stand, and even if we are talking of two different things, both have one likeness and one way of addressing them (*prosēgoria*) in accordance to the likeness; so that, for instance, we talk of the king and of the image of the king, and not of two kings. And if this is the case, there is only one veneration of the image of Christ with Christ who is its prototype.

An objection from the iconoclasts:

2. If Christ, being invested with the principle (*logon*) of the prototype with respect to his own icon, is said to exist by nature, whereas his icon exists by position,[89] how can it be that the natural and the artificial exist at the same time? It is, in fact, not true that as soon as Christ was seen, his image was seen drawn beside him. Thus, since the two are

not simultaneous, they cannot have the same veneration, since there is an interval of time after which the image was produced after Christ.

A solution to the above:

If every shadow inseparably follows its own body, and no one in his right mind could ever say that a body lacks its own shadow, but rather it is possible to see (*idein*) in the body the shadow that follows, and in the shadow the body that precedes, thus no one could say that Christ cannot be portrayed, if indeed in him there is a body that is defined by characteristics. Rather, we can see his image subsist (*hyphestōsan*) in Christ, while Christ can be seen in the image as prototype. From the fact that the two exist at the same time, it follows then that when Christ is seen, his image is also seen in potency (*dynamei*), and from him the image can be transposed and delineated in any material whatsoever.

Further:

3. Even if what exists in nature does not exist at the same time as what exists by position, as is the case instead with Christ and his own image, nevertheless, by way of the image's potential existence before it is produced artistically, it is always possible to see the image in Christ; just as, so to speak, it is always possible to see the image subsist in the body, even if the image is not given form by a radiation of light; therefore, it is not beyond reason to claim that Christ and his image exist simultaneously.

Further:

4. The prototype and the icon belong to the category of things that are related to each other (*tōn pros ti*), as what is double and what is half. The prototype, in fact, always implicitly carries with itself (*syneispherei*) its own image, of which it is the prototype; the double always implicitly carries with itself the half, with respect to which it is called double; if there were no prototype, there would be no image, and if there were no double, nothing would be thought to be half. But since these things exist at the same time, they are understood and they subsist at the same time. Since, then, no interval of time intervenes between the image and the prototype, the veneration of each is not distinct, but rather it is one and the same.[90]

Further:

5. The prototype and the image have their being, so to speak, in each other. When one is taken away, the other is taken away too; in the same way as when the double is removed, the half is removed as well.

If Christ, then, cannot exist unless his own image also exists in potency (*kata to dynamei*), even before being artistically produced, the image always subsists in the prototype; then the veneration of Christ is taken away by anyone who does not acknowledge that his own icon is also venerated in him at the same time (*symproskyneisthai*).

An objection from the iconoclasts:

6. "That which is similar in some respect may, however, not be similar in some other respect; thus, the image is similar to the prototype according to the likeness, but according to the nature it is not similar. Thus, the image is not wholly (*holon*) what the prototype is. But since this is the way things are, the veneration cannot be the whole and the same in both. If the veneration is not whole, it is foolish (*eōlon*) to claim that the veneration of both is the same."

A solution to the above:

Insofar as the image has a relationship to the prototype, according to the latter it also shares its own veneration according to the likeness, without bringing along to veneration the material in which it appears; this is indeed the nature of the image, that it should be identified (*tautizesthai*) according to the likeness of the prototype, but also that it should be distinguished according to the principle of the essence, from which also derives the fact that the same name is used for both (*homōnymia*). If, instead, it were wholly similar, our argument would fall through, and the image would be simply the prototype. However, it resembles the prototype according to the whole of its likeness but not according to the nature. Therefore, both are entitled to the same veneration based on the likeness (*homoiōtikē*).

Further, from a theological example:

7. Even if according to the essence the Son is equal to the Father, yet what is begotten is not equal to what is unbegotten, nor is that which is spirated (*to ekporeuton*); these properties that are contemplated with regard to the divine nature are distinct from what they share (*koinōnias*) with one another. But the divinity is one in the three Persons (*en tois trisi charaktērsin*),[91] as the veneration is one, and the latter in no way deflects from identity of nature because of the diversity in characteristics (*tē tōn idiotētōn eterotēti*). And the same goes for the image of the prototype, because, if in virtue of the difference of essence there is not the same veneration for both—as it is not the nature of the icon that is venerated, but the one who is seen to be represented in it—nonetheless, with respect to the identity of the hypo-

static likeness, the veneration is carried out in an identical manner (*tautizomenē*) on the basis on the one and whole relation (*emphereia*) [of likeness] that exists in both. In the same way, in the case of the symbol of the cross and of the life-giving cross itself, the veneration of the symbol is not lessened by the comparison with the life-giving cross, but rather, it is set on an equal footing by its utter likeness with the prototype.

An objection from the iconoclasts:

8. If the image is in Christ as prototype even before it is artistically reproduced in any other material, then it would be unnecessary to delineate the image, as the latter can be sufficiently seen and venerated in him.

A solution to the above:

It is true that, even before the image of Christ is reproduced by artistic means, it inheres in him as a prototype. What, in fact, is not at all portrayed is not a human being but something monstrous (*amblōthridion*). And, yet, it is not possible to call something a prototype if its image has not been transferred onto some material. Therefore, since it is acknowledged that Christ possesses the characteristic (*logon*) of being prototype—as indeed is the case with everyone else—it is thus absolutely necessary that his image should be transferred from his imprint onto a material of some sort. Otherwise, if he were no longer seen and venerated through the production of an image, he would cease to be a human being.[92]

Further, by way of an example:

9. A seal is one thing, and its imprinted effigy (*apomagma*) is another. Nonetheless, even before the impression of the seal, the imprint is in the seal. A seal would not be a proper seal if it could not be impressed onto a material of some sort. Therefore, Christ also, if he were not impressed on some artificial image, would in this respect be dysfunctional and ineffective; even just to think this, is foolishness.

Further, by way of example:

10. If someone who sees the seal and the imprint sees in both a similar and unchanged form (*eidos*), then the imprint exists in the seal even before the impression. Thus, the seal displays its own propensity to be honored (*philotimia*) whenever it makes itself available to be impressed in many and different materials. In the same way, even if we believe that Christ's own image is in him inasmuch as he is in a human form, whenever we see this image materially depicted in different

manners, we celebrate his magnificence all the more. Indeed, the failure to proceed to a material imprint eliminates his existence in human form.

Further:

11. The image inheres and is seen and is venerated for the sake of the archetype, and the archetype [inheres and is seen and is venerated] for the sake of the image, not in virtue of an identical substance, but in virtue of a unity of likeness, according to which there is a single veneration for both, and the veneration is not distinct for either of the two natures.

Further, by way of example:

12. If the shadow cannot be separated from the body, but its subsistence always exists along with it (*symparyphestōsa*), even if the shadow does not always appear, in the same manner it is impossible that Christ's own image may be separated from him; in the same way as the shadow becomes more visible because of the rays of the sun, so does the image of Christ become more manifest to all, whenever it appears by imprinting itself in diverse materials.

An objection from the iconoclasts:

13. "As our Savior is now in the heavens, it is not seemly to erect an image; indeed, as the holy Apostle says, 'We walk by faith, and not by appearance (*dia eidous*).'"[93]

An answer to the above:

The term *appearance* (*eidos*) is used to make a distinction from what is general (*apo tou genous*), such as humanity in general; alternatively, the same term can be used to indicate the form of each one of us, whereby we differ from one another. But the Apostle does not speak of these here. It is rather to be understood that he uses "appearance" to mean his own vision (*autopsia*) of future realities—a vision that surpasses the figures of the present time. For when Paul says, "We walk by faith, not by appearance," he adds, "We are full of courage, and we would rather be away from the body, and dwell with the Lord."[94] And elsewhere he says, "For now we see as in a mirror and partially; but then we will see face to face. Now I know in part; then I will know fully as I was known. So faith, hope, and love remain."[95] Thus, Paul is saying that we walk by such a faith that we are actually able to see, as in a mirror, the truth of the things that are to come, face to face and without error. And in addition, to make it clear that the goal (*skopos*) of the Apostle was not to ban the portrayal of the physical appearance of Christ (*idea*) after his ascension to heaven, listen to what Paul says elsewhere, "O foolish Galatians, who has led you astray and convinced you no longer to follow the truth, when you could see Christ crucified in front of your very eyes?"[96] If our faith is such that we can behold Christ crucified, it would be all the more foolish not to portray Christ at all times. Indeed, if it were not possible to see perceptibly (*aisthētōs*) through a depiction (*perigraphē*) what is perceived intellectually because of its absence, even this intellectual vision would be lost.[97]

Epigram of Constantine, who copied the book of Theodore the Studite[98]

O noetic foundation of wise teaching,
Overflowing source of rightful dogmas,
As a true Father you were known to all mortals.
Do then protect me, Constantine, with your prayers.

SEVEN CHAPTERS AGAINST THE ICONOCLASTS

[by the same Theodore]

I

Against those who say that Christians make gods out of the images when they venerate (proskynountas) *the image of Christ, the Mother of God, or any of the saints:*

To "make gods" (*theopoiein*), if we consider the very composition of the term, is the action on the part of someone to turn into a god and to worship as such something that is not God, according to what the Apostle said, "And they changed the glory of the incorruptible God into the likeness of the corruptible image of a man, of birds, of four-footed beasts and of serpents";[1] so, for instance, as far as the first type is concerned (it is indeed appropriate to assess those four types), Chronos and Zeus, Hera and Aphrodite, and a variety—as many as there are—who are similar to these in both genders; for the second type, the eagle, the gryphon, or any other one of the same nature of different types; for the third type, the cow or the goat, or any other one of the same nature of different types; finally, for the fourth type, the serpent, the lizard, or any other one of the same nature of different types. And the Greeks, the Barbarians, the Scythes, having turned their images into gods, "worshiped," as scripture says, "the creature instead of the creator,"[2] setting up many gods and goddesses that are dissimilar from each other and fight against each other; and of them none ever was, or is, or will be God.

And it is not the case that all those who portrayed something of what exists should be reproached, given that even Moses, to omit the others, represents the serpent and the Cherubim by way of images;[3] and as he was about to construct the whole of the tabernacle, he was given an image of the latter by God. Indeed, scripture says, "Behold, you will make everything according to the type that was shown to you on the mountain";[4] but given that which was represented, they called it God and worshiped it, creating an endless series of a plurality of gods, because of their ignorance of the one God who truly exists, incorruptible and invisible. To them the blessed apostle says, "As then we are the progeny of God, we should not think that the divine should be similar to gold, or silver, or stone, or to a creation of art or of human skill."[5] This is the act by which those previously mentioned made gods of the icons. For those, instead, whom the Apostle was addressing, "there is one God the Father, who is the maker of all things; and one Lord Jesus Christ, through whom all things were made;"[6] and one Holy Spirit, in whom everything subsists; and it is not "to make gods" to erect the icon of the bodily imprint of Christ—perish the thought (*apage*)!—but rather to confess that he appeared in a form that is similar to us, as it is written, "While being in the form of God, he did not consider it a jealous treasure to be equal with God, but emptied himself, taking the form of a servant, and becoming in the likeness of man, and he was found in the habit of man. And he humiliated himself, becoming obedient until death, and until death on the cross."[7] And his image indeed is not in the similitude of a corruptible man, which has been condemned by the Apostle, but it was in the similitude of man, as the Apostle himself said, though not a corruptible but an incorruptible one. Indeed, "his soul was not abandoned in hell," as the great Peter says, "nor did his flesh see corruption."[8] For this reason Christ, after becoming man, is not a mere human being—he is God. However, because he is like all other men, he is circumscribed according to the form of the body; and because he, alongside the Father and the Spirit, is different from all other creatures, he also remains uncircumscribed according to the essence of the divinity.

And then, how will the Word of the economy be understood, unless he, unlike the Father and the Spirit, apart from the set of properties that he has as Son, could also be represented in his corporeal form? Therefore, to paint and to venerate the image of Christ has nothing to do with turning the icons into gods—perish the thought, O foolish man! Indeed, we do not say that God has been "made," but rather that he has become incarnate; nor do we say that there are two Gods, but rather one in three hypostases. Nor, venerating the image, do we impiously choose to worship the matter (*hylēn*) in which it is imprinted, but rather that very essence that is naturally in Christ, which imprinted itself into the matter like a seal. The artifacts, indeed, do not participate (*ametocha*) in the nature of the archetype within the boundaries of the art; they only display as in a mirror the relation (*emphereia*)[9] to the things of which they are representations. Thus, after a certain material has appeared in a cruciform shape, we should worship any material found in this manner. But enough foolishness! There is only one power in both, one glory, one adoration, as the great Basil claims,[10] as the relationship between image and prototype is not di-hypostatic, but mono-hypostatic.[11] With the exception of the difference (*diaphora*) of substance, the archetype and the image are one and the same, says the divine Denys.[12] And the same goes for the Mother of God. When we depict and venerate her image, we do not hold and worship her in the manner of the Gentiles (*Ellēnikōs*), as divine, but rather as the Mother of God. And the same goes for what concerns the saints; we do not honor and pay respect to many gods and goddesses, but to the one God and his servants. Through him and to him the honor of all flows out and returns.

Or does it not seem to you that the divine unguent was poured as a type of Christ? Is it not clear that the divine altar [lit. "table," *trapeza*] [is a figure] of the life-giving tomb? And that the cloth on the table [represents] the shroud on which and in which Christ was put to be buried? And that the priestly spear [stands for] the one spear on which and in which the side of the divine body was opened? And that the sponge [is a figure] of the one on which and in which he was forced to drink? And that the image of the cross [stands for] the actual tree of the cross that gave us life?[13] Consider all these things, or anything else that may be a divine antitype; whenever one worships one of these things at all, or an image is made to represent and honor Christ, say then that those who fabricate and worship are guilty of making gods (*theopoieisthai*). But this insanity is equal to the Gentiles who blurt out such things. The ones, indeed, at the incarnation confessed that God could be circumscribed even as he is uncircumscribable; the others instead, after the incarnation, continue to insist that he could not be circumscribed, even if he was circumscribable in terms of his body.

II

To those who wonder why in the Gospel nothing is written about the image of Christ:

It seems to me that these sophists ignore that, among the sayings of the Gospels, certain things are said and enunciated directly, and other things indirectly; this is the result of the Spirit's disposition (*oikonomēsantos*), that the [easy] access to edifying teachings would not be truly advantageous to the majority, but rather that through the hard work of research, we would reap more advantageous fruits, so that whatever until now was solid, from now on should not be taken away easily; and this with good reason. And if one were not to look, one would not find. Now we will give an illustration of this issue from a similar matter. Peter says to Christ as follows: "Lord, if it is you, command me to come to you on the water. And Jesus said: 'Come.' And getting off the boat Peter walked on the water, to come toward Jesus. Seeing then the strong wind, he was full of fear; and as he started to drown, he shouted saying, 'Lord, save me!' And immediately Jesus, having extended his hand, took hold of him. And he told him, 'O you of little faith, why did you doubt?' And as they climbed into the boat, the wind ceased."[14]

The text does not say that, after Christ took hold of him, Peter started again to walk on the water, but this is indicated indirectly. And no one would be able to claim with any reasonableness that Peter was taken by Christ through the air, or that Jesus took Peter by force until they ascended into the boat together. Now, let us revert to the topic, and observe with attention what is said. "Those came," scripture says, "who brought the drachma to Peter, and they said to him, 'Your master does not pay the two drachmas?' And Peter said, 'He does.' And as they entered into the house, Jesus came toward them, saying, 'What do you think, Peter? From whom do the kings of the earth receive a tribute or taxes? From their sons, or from outsiders?' And he said, 'From outsiders.' And Jesus then said, 'Thus the children are exempt. However, so as not to scandalize them, go to the sea, throw in a hook; take the first fish that will come up; and having opened its mouth, you will find a *statera*; take that and give it to them for me and for you.'"[15] Now the statement "for me and for you" indicates indirectly "instead of my image and your image." This is not only because the very pronouns of the persons (*prosōpōn*) are indicative (*dēlōtikai*) [of the natures]—indeed, the persons are images (*eikones*)—but also because, apart from his or her own image, each one of those who are subject to a tribute offers in honor of the emperor an imperial image, which is called capital image; the head, indeed, is nothing else but an image; and all of this can be seen from the voice of the Lord, "Why do you tempt me? Bring me a *denarium*, so that I may see it. And they brought it to him. And he said to them: 'Whose image and whose inscription is this?' They told him: 'Of Caesar.' And as he answered Jesus told them: 'Give to Caesar what is of Caesar, and to God what is of God.'"[16] Thus Christ, having submitted himself in his humanity to all things that pertain to obedience, paid—like everybody else—the two drachmas for his own image; and the same happened with Peter and the *statera*, which amounts to two drachmas. The *statera*, no less than the drachma and the *denarium*, carried an image, no less than they carried and were marked by an inscription.

As, then, here we said it could be found in a metaphorical sense (*kata paralēpsin*), there we said that Peter walked over the waters, and it could not be otherwise; thus similarly the expression "for me and for you" should be interpreted to mean implicitly the image of Christ as well as the image of Peter; and this is clear to all who are not fools. I forego to say that of course the image inheres in Christ from the point of view of the nature (*physikōs*). Where the prototype is, it is proper that there should also be an image (*paragōgon*), as the prototype naturally expresses an image.

All these matters are indeed related and conjoint with one another. But apart from what was said above, there is still something else that I must say, which is that Jesus himself, in a hidden manner, shaped the image that he gave to Caesar as a tribute. How is that? Was it not accidental? While the tradition asserts that the fish swallowed the *statera* (indeed, this is the human point of view), it is perhaps more appropriate to suppose that the *statera* was created within the entrails of the fish with a mere word by the Divine Spirit, to which nothing is impossible. This, indeed, is appropriate to God. "Indeed he spoke," says scripture, "and they were made; he ordered, and they were created."[17]

III

To those who say that in heaven there is no human image, but the type of the cross, and therefore one must venerate the latter:

God, who knows all things before they are done, showing the mystery of his dispensation in the flesh before the foundation of the world, represented the cross in heaven by means of stars;[18] and on earth instead he represented himself in the shape of Adam, who, in the words of St. Paul, is a type of the one who has to come.[19] Truly, truly it was fitting that what was in heaven should be represented on earth, and what was on earth should be represented in heaven, so that it should appear to those who contemplate the heaven that, from now on, celestial things will be one with earthly ones.[20] And in any case, it was not appropriate that the image of a man should be seen in heaven, given that men independently of this were misled to worship the stars, much more so if they had seen a human image. For this reason the great Moses says, "Looking into the sky, and seeing the sun, and the moon, and the stars, and all the decoration of the heavens make sure that, being led into error, you will venerate and worship them."[21] Thus, even before the advent of Christ, among the other figures of the stars there was already a type of the cross, and it was not to be adored; as the prototype was despised, it was impossible that the image should not be despised as well.

However, now that Christ suffered on the archetype of this image out of love for humanity (*philanthrōpōs*), the image of the cross should be venerated and it has acquired a salvific power—even the one that can be seen in the heavens; and the same goes for the image of the cross of him who suffered for us, an image that, after its first manifestation, can be seen everywhere on earth, unless perhaps the hand of an iconoclast, anticipating the heresy of these modern enemies of images, has followed the example of the Jews.[22] Thus, the type of the cross should be considered worthy of veneration not because it was in heaven, but because of the life-giving wood when Christ was hung on it; similarly, the image of Christ should be worshiped not because of its prototype in Adam, but because of his incarnation from the Virgin.

IV

To those who say that the priest, when he blesses the children that are taken to him, should not use an image, but the type of the cross:

The priest stands between God and humanity, and whenever the priest invokes God, he is a symbol (*mimēma*) of Christ. The Apostle indeed says, "One is God, one is the mediator (*mesitēs*) between God and humanity, the man Jesus Christ."[23] As the priest is an icon of Christ, it is necessary that he should not use an image—in what way, then, should the image use an image of his own prototype?—but rather he should use the type of the cross, clearly imitating Christ. As, indeed, the latter "defeated the principalities and the powers with great confidence (*en parrhēsia*), triumphing over them" in the cross, as is written; in likewise manner, then, the priest accomplishes the salvation of the child by means of the type of the cross, as he himself is the type of Christ—indeed, the type and the icon are in a relation (*eis emphereian*); thus, for this reason the image of Christ is used, which is clearly the priestly dignity.[24]

V

To those who say that one can dispel disease and demons from oneself using the type of the cross but not the icon:

This problem has the same solution as the previous one. How, and in what way? Because each of the faithful, through the regeneration of baptism and the renewal by the Holy Spirit, is made to conform (*symmorphos*) to the image of Jesus who is God, according to what was said by the Apostle.[25] And in a different place, "Man does not have to cover his head, as he is the image and the glory of God."[26] And to those who are baptized, the prince of the Apostle says, "You are a chosen race; a royal priesthood; a holy people."[27] Thus, everyone can choose what kind of conduct to follow, according to one's understanding of what is conducive to salvation. And even if every faithful is a living icon, it is not useless that there should be icons of Christ [that are painted] on a table. The [image and likeness of Christ][28] that are brought about by the transformation accomplished in baptism concerns the internal person (*ton esō anthrōpon*). In what way, then, can Christ be made similar, in bodily form, to different individuals who differ utterly from each other according to their appearance (*kat'idean*)? The icon of Christ is—and is said to be—the only one among images that are artificially made (*monē technētē*) that carries the features—in other words, the appearance—of the incarnate form as well as all other external characteristics.[29]

It is possible to see the same thing in the type of the life-giving cross. When the Apostle says, "I am crucified together with Christ,"[30] he is not said to have been crucified and suffered in a physical manner (*aisthētōs*) or using a real type of the cross; rather, this is said according to the interior person, and by way of an intellectual (*noētō*) cross, which, I say, is the power to mortify the passions. And this is even clearer from the saying of the Lord, "Take your cross, and follow me."[31] Thus both words, *cross* and *crucifixion,* have a dual meaning; the same goes for the icon of Christ, [which is] either the artificial one or the one taken up by the faithful in their own inner lives.

VI

To those who against the image of Christ oppose the famous saying of the Theologian: "What is venerated is not circumscribed":[32]

Those who say this say so because they do not understand the actual meaning of polyvalent terms, or rather do not want to understand how to act properly. Indeed, the word *venerated* (*septon*) is a polyvalent term that embraces quite a few different meanings. Thus, for instance, the term φῶς ("light") is understood in terms of the sun; but the term can also indicate a human being. Φώς ("a man") is indeed a human being.[33] If, then, I say that the term φῶς does not indicate a human being, it is true, because I refer to the sun. If, then again, I say that the term φώς indicates a human being, it is true, because I refer to the human being; and in itself the term may be confusing, because of its dual meaning. Similarly, then, the term *venerated* is correctly understood to be polyvalent, sometimes referring to uncircumscribability, sometimes to circumscribability. Indeed, about the Father, if one talks about the divine nature, it is possible to say that what is venerated is not circumscribed, in order to oppose those who would want to restrict the divine within circumscription. And it is true. But what was said before did not refer to the economy. One indeed is the rationale of theology, and one is the rationale of the economy, and speaking dogmatically it is not appropriate to affirm the same in both contexts. It so happens, for instance, that even the divine Cyril sometimes refers to the hypostasis by the term *physis* and sometimes by the term *hypostasis*, as the term has a dual meaning.[34] And since Gregory of Nazianzos knows quite well that what is circumscribed can be venerated, he himself says, "Worship (*proskynēson*) the manger, through which you, who lacked reason (*alogos*), were fed by the Word (*hypo tou Logou*)."[35] And what must be worshiped, in the same way it must be venerated. I forego to talk of the Body of the Lord; is it not circumscribed? Who can contradict this? So then? Is it not worthy of veneration? Even the stones will shout it. And what will you say then of the life-giving cross? Of the antitype? Of the altar? Of the holy table? Of the most holy Gospel, or of any other sacred implement? And perhaps the very relics of the saints, are not all of them circumscribed? Of course they are, and in the same way they also are to be venerated, like the icon of Christ; the fathers of the Sixth Holy Council testify together to that in the passages of their writings where they treat of the holy icons.[36]

VII

To those who against the image of Christ oppose that famous saying by St. Gregory: "If anyone venerates the creature, even if he does that in the name of Christ, he commits idolatry":

This saying was directed against the Arians, who claimed that the Son of God was a creature (*ktisma*).[37] But we, when we venerate the image of Christ, do so because we have the intention of venerating Christ himself in an orthodox manner, in virtue of the one veneration that is directed to both natures, and which is not divided in accordance with the distinction (*diaphora*) of the essences,[38] but is on the contrary unified because of the unity of the one hypostasis; we do not venerate a creature—perish the thought!—because Christ is not a creature, even if there is in him an element that is created, because the latter, as they say, takes second rank to what is higher. Do not consider any longer the material from which it is distinguished intellectually; even if in itself—and I say it again—as through a mirror it is seen through an image. And if you claim not to understand this, you have only the eyes of the body, while you are similar to the pig, to which God and the [eternal Word] prohibited that the words of truth, which are similar to pearls, should be thrown.

SOME QUESTIONS POSED BY THE [SAME] THEODORE TO THE ICONOCLASTS,

...who do not want that our Lord Jesus Christ should be depicted according to his corporeal form.[1]

I. If Christ is out of (*ek*) two natures and is in (*en*) two perfect (*teleiais*) natures,[2] please do say according to which nature he cannot be painted: according to the one which assumed, or according to the one which was assumed? And if it was according to the first, could he not be painted according to the other? Or vice versa? If, then, according to both natures, in what way could this be, if one perfect nature and one perfect property were not composed out of two?[3] And let us then assume neither that he could be painted, nor that he could not be painted, but rather simultaneously that he could and that he could not (*graptoagraptos*), being composed of half natures (*ex hēmiseias*) but not being complete according to either. And if this were the case, in what way, then, could Christ not be different in nature (*heteroousios*) from the Father and from us? He would be different from us because we can be painted, as we are made of a body; he would be different from the Father also, as the Father can never be circumscribed because of the simplicity of his nature.

II. As the properties of each nature cannot be changed, circumscription applies to the humanity of Christ; if Christ could not be represented according to his humanity, this would entail surely that this humanity had been moved away; and if it had been moved away, where had it taken residence? Perhaps into the nature of his own divinity? And if this is the case, the Trinity received an addition, assuming a property that it is not connatural (*asymphyes*) to it,[4] which is impossible. If, then, it did not go there, where should it be? And if it disappeared, by necessity the relevant nature should also disappear, despite the fact that in the confession of faith one cannot be separated from the other.

III. What is uncircumscribable is either of the same order (*homostoichon*) as what is circumscribable, or it is of a different order (*heterostoichon*).[5] If what is uncircumscribable is of the same order as what is circumscribable, God the Word is of the same essence as the flesh that has been assumed, even as he is uncircumscribed; and this would be the case because the properties of the same order belong to the same nature in whatever is undivided. If, instead, what is uncircumscribable is of a different order from what is circumscribable, given that the Logos is of an utterly different substance from the flesh, we must conclude that, according to the flesh, the Logos is circumscribed, but, according to the substance of his humanity and to the substance of his divinity—in other words, according to the two orders of their respective properties—he is simultaneously circumscribable and uncircumscribable, in the same way, of course, as he is seen and not seen, or he can be touched and cannot be touched.[6]

IV. If the properties of material and composite things are also material and composite, in which way, then, will Christ be uncircumscribed according to the corporeal form? What is uncircumscribed is immaterial and simple, but the body instead is material and composite. Indeed, it is necessary that every property should be similar to the nature [to which it belongs]; and a diversity (*allotriotēta*) based on a dissimilarity of this kind (*heterotēta*) could in no way be admitted.[7] And then, if the body of Christ were not circumscribed, the properties of his humanity would be different from their underlying nature; and this is impossible, as the immaterial (*aulon*) cannot be identical to the material, and the simple cannot be identical to the composite. Indeed, in terms of the body, Christ is not uncircumscribable; there cannot be any difference between things that are not different, or composition in things that are simple.

V. If Christ is God and man, the human nature is not endowed with the same nature with which God is endowed; indeed, clearly, it is impossible that Christ should be circumscribed by the same property in virtue of which he is uncircumscribed, as each property differs from the other; and neither the natures, nor the properties that inhere in them, can come into the communion that exists in the identity (*koinōnia*) of one substance. If this is the case, in what way, then, will Christ, who consists of two natures, not be the one who can be portrayed and cannot be portrayed?[8]

VI. Is God seen by those who are on this earth by means of the form that can be represented, or by means of the form that cannot be represented? If by means of the form that cannot be represented, the latter is certainly invisible as well; and if one is of the same order as the other, this also applies to what cannot be circumscribed and what cannot be seen. But then, how can the disciples say, "We have seen the Lord?"[9] Thus [Christ was seen in that form] that can be represented, even if he remained invisible in terms of the divine nature. And if indeed he could be seen in that form that can be represented, who then will dare call the circumscribed form uncircumscribable, unless he were to reach the apex of folly?

VII. If we were to say that Christ were only circumscribable, this would amount to stripping him of his divinity, which is characterized by uncircumscribability; it is also clear that if we were to say that he is only uncircumscribable, this would amount to stripping him of his humanity, which is characterized by circumscribability; and both claims are absurd. And [similarly absurd are the claims] of Paul of Samosata, who deliriously said that Christ was a mere man and not God; or of Mane the Persian, who stupidly said that Christ was merely God and not man.[10] Consider, then, how we are going from one abyss to another.[11] Whichever, then, of these two impious opinions you may choose to flee, as if you were made of parts, by necessity, being in the middle, you will embrace the opposite opinion. On the one hand, if you say that you do not wish to follow Paul of Samosata, why do you follow the Manicheans, thereby failing to circumscribe Christ as if he were just the incorporeal Word? This is something that Paul of Samosata rejects. On the other hand, if you say that you do not wish to follow the Manicheans, why do you say with Paul of Samosata that Christ is [merely] an embodied man? This is something that the Manicheans reject. Thus, if you follow the Manicheans, you end up following Paul of Samosata, and vice versa.

VIII. If you confess Christ both in divinity and in humanity, and you are unshakable in your conviction, why, then, do you refuse to say that, in certain respects, Christ can be circumscribed, and, in other respects, he cannot be circumscribed? Indeed, he is known (*gnōrizomenos*) in virtue of the property of each nature; by means of the property in virtue of which he is God, he goes beyond circumscription, as well as sight and comprehension; by means of the property in virtue of which he is man, he falls under the purview of circumscription, as well as sight and quality; unless it is only by voice that you confess that Christ is both in humanity and divinity, while for other reasons of convenience you claim that Christ is without body, and thus uncircumscribable.[12]

IX. Do you not think that what is simple and what is composite are different things, or do you think that they are the same? If the former, you will say with us that Christ is entirely circumscribed, and entirely uncircumscribed, as he is from both. Indeed, in the properties that are opposed to each other, one can see the nature of both the aspects of Christ—I mean, the simple and the composite, the divinity and the humanity. As in the example of the fire and the water, fire does not go downward, nor does water go upward; dryness is not humidity, nor is humidity dryness.[13] Thus, circumscribability is different from the inability to be represented (*agraphia*), and the inability to be represented is different from circumscribability. Indeed, one is opposed to the other as much as possible by a natural opposition, which is much greater in this third case than in the previous two. If, instead, you think that Christ was only uncircumscribable, why then do not you affirm the latter? And even if you do not say that, you will say that the divinity and the humanity will be one nature that will be simple and composite at the same time (*haplosyntheton*), as if, with Severus, you were affirming in a mixed manner (*sygchytikōs*) the existence of aqueous fire (*hydropyron*).[14] The structure of the nature (*ho tēs physeōs logos*)[15] is proved to be unique from the uniqueness of its set of properties.

X. If the negations are opposed to the affirmations, and they are neither conceptually nor terminologically identical, circumscription then is an affirmation; no circumscription is a negation; and Christ is from both natures, in his divinity and in his humanity; and he has the properties of the natures in full; and among these properties, there are some that are in opposition to each other, and they are not mixed into one; rather, they are distinct, and they exist in correspondence to the duality of the natures; and from these, Christ can be known (*nenoētai*) to us, and called circumscribed and not circumscribed. If this is not how matters stand, but he is only uncircumscribable, then things that are distinct (*ta akrata*) are mixed; and things that have different names are called by the same name; and walking and not walking can be understood and called in the same way; and the same, then, for discussing and not discussing; and existing and not existing; and being circumscribed and not being circumscribed; all of which is utter foolishness.

XI. From the union of uncircumscribed and circumscribed, O good ones, it is impossible that something only uncircumscribed should ensue; similarly, it is impossible that from the union of divinity and humanity should emerge someone who is God alone. If indeed the natures are united (*enōtheisai*) according to the hypostasis, they do not undergo change into each other; nor did they change their own appellations; even after the union in one person (*prosōpō*),[16] they preserve the duality in terms of the realities (*tois pragmasi*) and in terms of their appellations; and in the same way, their properties are maintained unchanged, and their natural quality has not undergone any modification; nor did they forego their distinction in terms of the names; rather, [the natures] remain inviolate (*alōbētoi*) in Christ; from which (*aph'ōn*) he is both circumscribed and uncircumscribed, despite the fact that you reject this in an impious manner.

XII. If, as St. Epiphanios says,[17] all the things that are in man are man; and if at his coming, the Only Begotten assumed everything that is human; so that what is fully (*teleiōs*) in man should also, being God, be turned into the fullness of salvation, having let go of nothing human; if he were not circumscribed in terms of the body, he would have let go of something, and not just of something minor, but of the most important and particular characteristic—if truly the most important characteristic of humanity is the fact that its bodily imprint may be represented; is it not the case, O men, as the same saint [Epiphanios] says in the thirty-second chapter of his treatise on the heresies, that whoever denies that Christ can be represented is akin to whoever denies that Christ took flesh? And, of course, even the blessed Sophronios casts anathemas against the latter in his synodical letter.[18]

XIII. To those who are opposed in an even more tenacious manner and claim that, in the act of representing Christ, Christ ends up being divided into two Sons, as Nestorius had said, one must respond that this is not dividing Christ, but rather [one must say] what is most necessary to know.[19] As in the realm of theology, what is proper to the hypostasis does not divide the one nature of the divinity but may be ascribed to each hypostasis accordingly while having everything in common from the point of view of the nature; in the same way, on the contrary, from the point of view of the economy, what is proper to the natures does not divide the one hypostasis of the Word of God but may be ascribed to each nature accordingly while having everything in common from the point of view of the hypostasis. If, indeed, in the act of circumscription what is proper to the human nature were to induce a division, there would also be a division in the one nature that is proper to the One who is *Unbegotten*, the One who is *Begotten*, and the One who is *Spirated*. And yet the nature is not divided; even these three are different from one another. Nor in this sense could the uncircumscribability of the divinity and the circumscribability of the humanity divide the one hypostasis of Christ either, even if they are distinct from each other.

XIV. If, from the incarnation of God, the Word, it is not possible to infer that the Father and the Spirit also took flesh, even if the Trinity is undivided according to the nature, so then, from the circumscription of God the Word according to the humanity, is it possible to infer that the divinity is simultaneously circumscribed as well, even if the latter according to the hypostasis is undivided from the flesh, as the conjunction (*synapheia*) of the natures therein does not confuse the hypostases, nor does the identity of the hypostasis remove the natures from their proper limits?[20]

XV. If Christ because of the divinity cannot be represented like us, so similarly according to the humanity he is not uncircumscribed like the Father; and he has let go of both, or rather has changed the properties one with the other, being circumscribed as God and being uncircumscribed as man. If it is true that having everything that the Father has, he also has uncircumscribability, then clearly, having everything that humanity has, he also has circumscribability if he is perfect from both sides, and not only partially according to one of the parts.

LETTER OF THE SAME THEODORE TO HIS OWN FATHER PLATO ABOUT THE VENERATION OF THE SACRED IMAGES

We ourselves are full of consolation as we address our sacred head. What indeed can be more enticing for a child than to address one's father, and indeed one of such quality and achievement, whose virtue is sung by many cities, regions, and islands; such is my beloved Father, even if the fruit is not similar to the tree, because of the sterility of my unworthiness. But you have been set up for us as the norm of piety; and not for us alone, but also for those who choose to lead a pious life, strive for worthiness, and let themselves be encouraged to run the good course. It is already a long time since your holiness asked me to offer an argument about the way in which one must venerate the blessed icon of Christ, not because you did not know how to go about it, but because in this way you wished to elicit my word, which until then had remained silent (*ton alogon mou logon*). Until now, however, I did not have the opportunity to respond. Having now remembered, it is opportune that I should set out to accomplish, with the help of your sacred prayers, whatever has been ordered to me by one such as you. I will do so even if, probably, I talked enough elsewhere about this topic.

To begin, every artificial image is a likeness (*homoiōsis*) of the one of whom it is the icon, and in itself it mimetically displays the imprint of its archetype, as Denys—expert in divine matters—says: truth in similitude; the archetype in the icon; one in the other, according to the difference in substance.[1] Thus, the one who venerates the icon clearly venerates the one whom the icon displays. Indeed, he did not venerate the substance of the icon, but the one who is depicted in it; nor indeed, as far as the veneration is concerned, did he separate the archetype from the icon. By the way of the likeness, indeed, the image is the same as the archetype. Thus, for example, even the great Basil says that even the image of the king is called king, and there are not two kings.[2] Thus, the power is not split, and the honor is not divided. In the same way as the principle and power to which we are subject is one, so also the honor (*doxologia*) that is given by us is one, and not many. Thus, the honor given to the icon passes over to the archetype.[3] If, then, it passes to the archetype, there are not different venerations, but the honor and the veneration are one and the same, in the same way as what is venerated and the prototype for the icon are one and the same.

The natural image and the artificial image are two different realities. On the one hand, the first one does not have a natural distinction from its cause but a hypostatic one, like the Son from the Father; one, indeed, is the hypostasis of the Son, and one is that of the Father, even if their nature is clearly one. The other one, on the other hand, has a natural distinction but not a hypostatic one, like the icon of Christ in relation to Christ. The nature of the material representation and the nature of Christ are indeed different ones, but the hypostasis is not different—rather, it is one, and the one of Christ and the one that is represented in the icon are the same. Again, the same divine Basil says: What, then, the icon is mimetically, the same, then, the Son is naturally; and in the same way as there is similitude according to the form in artificial matters, so there is a unity in the communion of the divinity in terms of the divine and simple (*asynthetou*) nature.[4] Note then the difference: regarding the natural image and the cause, namely, the Son and the Father, given that there is one nature, there is also one veneration according to the identity of the nature, not of the hypostasis; since, given that there is only one nature, we also recognize one veneration and honor (*doxologian*) to the Holy Trinity in three hypostases, the Father, the Son, and the Holy Spirit.

Regarding the artificial image and the archetype, namely, Christ and the icon of Christ, given that there is only one hypostasis in Christ, one only, then, is the veneration, clearly in virtue of the identity of the one hypostasis, not because of the diversity of the natures of Christ and of the icon. If, indeed, we say that the veneration of the icon in relation to the prototype is one according to the identity of the hypostasis, but is also one according to the identity of the nature, we no longer acknowledge the difference between the image and the one who is represented. In the same way as there is one hypostasis, should we, then, say that the icon and Christ himself share the same nature? We would fall into the polytheism of the Gentiles, turning into a god (*theopoiountes*) the whole matter that has been imprinted with the image of Christ. And, thus, we would excite the tongue of the iconoclasts to claim with reason that we, who venerate one God in three hypostases, actually venerate and honor many gods. If, on the contrary, someone were to say that the veneration of the icon in relation to the archetype [is not the same]—neither according to the identity of the hypostasis, nor according to the identity of the natures—clearly this person would divide the power and separate the glory of the archetype from the image; thus, venerating the image of Christ, he would clearly fall into idolatry, practicing not one but two distinct forms of veneration. This is what the iconoclasts strive to demonstrate, concluding from here, as is clearly manifest (*ōs to eikos*), that Christ cannot be contained in the flesh; the same goes for those who are seen impiously to claim that God manifested himself to those on earth only in appearance and imagination.

But may the impiety of both remain buried in its own darkness; the true faith of the Christians, as was said before, in the same way as it acknowledges one veneration of the Holy Trinity in virtue of the shared character (*koinōnia*) of the divinity, so then, in relation to the icon of Christ, it acknowledges one and the same veneration according to the identity of the hypostasis of Christ. Indeed, [the hypostasis] that is venerated is the same as the one that is represented. If it were not an icon, if it is separated and divided in terms of the honor from the prototype, it would happen to be some item with its own hypostasis (*idioupostaton*). And thus, in the end (*loipon*), in terms of the veneration of the icon of Christ, [it is important to acknowledge] that the veneration and the honor of the much-hymned and blessed Trinity is one, and only one.

But perhaps someone else could say: given that veneration is identical with adoration, it so happens that the icon of Christ is adored together with the Holy Trinity. But it seems that whoever says this would not know the difference in veneration, because we venerate the saints but do not worship them; according to the law of God, we also venerate [our] rulers but do not worship them. Thus, this person should learn that the veneration is not addressed to the substance of the icon; this is alien (*ektopon*) [to us], and [rather] it is typical of those who adore the creation instead of the Creator. On the contrary, as Christ is venerated in the image of Christ, the matter of the icon remains utterly outside the Christ who is venerated in it; and this is so in virtue of the likeness that is proper to the hypostasis of Christ and that is distinct from his physical body, even if seen in it. And it seems to me that this fits with the example of the mirror; indeed, it is possible to say that the face of the viewer appears in the mirror, and yet the likeness remains outside the actual physical mirror. And if anyone can discern his own image in the mirror, one would not include the actual mirror in the conception of one's own image; one does not come close to the mirror because of the object in itself, but because of one's likeness that is represented in the mirror. Indeed, this likeness adheres to the material of the mirror; of course, as soon as the mirror is moved away, the image immediately moves away from it, as it does not inhere in the actual material of the mirror. The same can be said then of the material of the sacred image; if the likeness that is seen in the material of the image and toward which the veneration is directed were to disappear, the material of the image would remain without veneration, because it would not have anything in common with the likeness.

Let us now consider a ring that is imprinted with the image of the emperor, and let the image be imprinted in wax, or in pitch, or in clay. The seal will indeed be one and the same, without any difference in all the materials. The latter, however, are different one from the other; the seal did not remain the same in virtue of the distinct materials but rather in virtue of the fact that it does not have anything in common with the materials. The seal did remain in the ring, but conceptually it is distinct from the materials in which it was imprinted. And the same applies also to the likeness of Christ, whenever the latter is imprinted in any material you can think of, as the likeness of Christ does not have anything in common with the material in which it is imprinted; rather, the likeness remains in the hypostasis of Christ, of which it is also a property (*idion*). And to speak in a straightforward manner, the icon of Christ as such is not the object of adoration (*ou latreuetai*); rather, in the image, Christ is venerated (*proskynoumenos*); and veneration is due to the icon because of the identity of the hypostasis of Christ, despite the difference of the substance of the icon.

Thus, in this way—or at least so it seems to me—the veneration of the image of Christ is confirmed (*epereidomenon*)[5] by the teaching of the holy fathers; if this veneration is eliminated, the economy of

Christ is equally eliminated, and if [the image] is not venerated, the veneration of Christ is similarly eliminated.

And for this reason, divine Father, it is fitting to approach [the image of Christ] and to venerate it with fear and with devotion, as the veneration moves over to Christ; it is also appropriate to believe that the divine grace is present in the image, and that the grace of sanctification is transmitted to those who approach the image with faith. Moreover, concerning the type of the life-giving cross, and the image of the most holy Mother of God and of all the saints, every sacred (*hagiastikē*) veneration of the icons—it is possible to ascend to God by means of the prototypes represented in these images. And for this reason one and undivided is the veneration of adoration (*latreutikē*) of the holy and consubstantial (*homoousiou*) Trinity; it is because of the Trinity that other forms of venerations (*hai diaphoroi proskynēseis*) ultimately exist,[6] and it is to the Trinity that all other venerations ultimately tend. If, then, because of ignorance I said something erroneous, by being either too concise or too verbose, as a good Father, do deign yourself to correct it or to integrate it or to eliminate it—praying and praying again because of my wretchedness that I should be able to understand correctly, and to speak without procuring offense, and to act in an irreprehensible manner.

REFUTATION AND SUBVERSION (BY THE SAME THEODORE) OF THE IMPIOUS POEMS

...by John, Ignatios, Sergios, and Stephen, modern adversaries of Christ, first by way of poems that have the same number of lines as the letter of their own names, and then by way of a separate oration that lays out the blasphemous argument of those who are lacking in piety.[1]

JOHN

Acrostic: The Passion of Christ Is the Hope of John[2]

The divine authors praise Christ with a golden effigy,
Without considering lowly matters, and in accordance with the speech of the prophets.[3]
The speech of both divine authors and prophets rests on nothing but **hope** in God.
Both of them openly despise the ever recurrent (*palindromon*) error
Of the painters of icons (or of the shadows [*skias*] of those who paint) as hateful to God—
And those who agree with these teachings (the emperors), full of enthusiasm,
Raise crosses in a splendid manner and with a pious discernment.[4]

IGNATIOS

Acrostic: The Glory of Ignatios Is to Acknowledge the Cross

O Word, so as to strengthen among the mortals the worship of God,
And in order to grant a clearer understanding of yourself,
You established by law that the **cross** alone would be represented.
You also chose that out of an artificial material,
The cross may also be painted on the walls, and as it was in the past, so it should be now.
So then the great emperors raise the very cross
As a harbinger of victory.

SERGIOS

Acrostic: Sergios Raised the Cross as Salvific

Moses openly defeated the powers of evil raising a type,
And with the aid of a type he crushed the enemy.[5] In the same way now the **cross**,
Glory of the faithful, stops the strong torrent of error.
In a similar way, then, the creation of art, not unlike a hidden arrow
Thrown with an evil intent, penetrates deeply into the souls.
This is how their wound is felt by those who are subject to Christ.[6]

STEPHANOS

Acrostic: The Glory of Stephanos Is to Acknowledge the Cross

As support of the faithful, and as something that is worthy of divine veneration,
You gave us, O Word, the salvific **cross**, the life-giving type of the passion.

Indeed, you chose to suppress as an error
The earlier divine prohibition against representation,
And this is the law that everyone is mandated to follow:
Always worship that cross, to which you were hung, and
  through which you redeemed us.

Into the Bronze Door Under the Cross[7]

As the emperor would not allow that Christ should be painted
Through an image without speech, and devoid of spirit,
Using earthly matter which the scriptures condemn
Leo with his son, the new Constantine,
Impressed the happy type of the cross
Glory of the faithful, on the doors of the palace.[8]

THE ORTHODOX

Where the acrostic is carried right in the middle of each verse, and the pincer (*syllabē*) is not divided.[9]

Acrostic: It Is Praiseworthy to Erect Pictures of Christ

May Christ be praised, he who is simultaneously God and man,
Blossom of the Virgin, and light that illumines the world,
His image, **painted**,[10] dissolves all error,
And defeats the armies of those who claim that
The veneration of images is nothing but worship of created
  things, which is utter impiety.
Let him perish then, whoever refuses
To acknowledge Jesus in the form that is common to all mortals.

Acrostic: It Is Appropriate to Praise the Virgin, as She Is the One Who Was Expected

Having given birth in a divine manner, without the use of seed,
From you, as from a new heaven, the light came forth,
The **praise**[11] of the Cherubim, the cause which precedes
  them,[12]

Decreasing the night of every ancient error.
You embraced him, and now you carry him as he is painted,
Resplendent with a divine beauty in your image,
As Lord, and as your true Son.

Acrostic: It Is Appropriate for Theodore to Praise Christ

God, before the assumption of the flesh, was in a form that could not be depicted.
But now that he is flesh, he can tolerate delineation (*tēn pographēn*).
It is then clear that the blossom, which she who is blessed brought forth as **Christ**,
Can now be depicted in her likeness (*kat'autēn*) by anyone
To whom it is given that he should be able to see the Son of Mary,
Brushing aside him who is endowed with the light of reason,
And yet acts in opposition to the divine plan.[13]

Acrostic: The Cross Is Going to Bring Miracles to Theodore

Do me the favor of pausing to reflect on the wondrous tree, which is joined to God,
And which I acknowledged to be a power that could overcome Hades
(the **cross** talks clearly of the passion of Christ).
I do indeed sprinkle around a dew (*drosos*),[14] which accomplishes truly admirable feats,
So that it may again irrigate the world with its flowing drops;
Showing its powers, and forgetting none of the things that pertain to eternal life;
Whose exact number it is impossible to describe.

Christ must be painted: do not err, O deceivers;[15]
As he appeared not according to the divinity, but according to the human flesh,
Given that he must be known according to both natures,
So that he cannot be painted [in terms of what] he received

from the Father, but he can be painted in terms of what he received from the mother,
Lacking in no property from either nature,
And in either case he is perfect.

In what way, if he were lacking in any property at all,
Could then the Word who became man be perfect at all?
Truly he would be missing in something, if he could not be painted,
And not even in something irrelevant, but in one whole nature;
Especially as we consider that what was most visible in him was the mortal form.
You must realize that if you deny it with an evil counsel, or abolish it as an error,
You are calumniating and denying Christ.[16]

From the same:

Acrostic: Christ Is Peace[17]

The error of the idols disappeared in front of the image of Christ,
A double-edged sword destroyed it: behold,
The image of light that destroys darkness
Is overshadowed by the cross: he carries a sword in the back.[18]
And with the cross, indeed the king of all
Defeated the forces of the ruler of darkness, taking us up from below,
Placing us above, and giving us celestial glory.

From the same:

Acrostic: Praise to the Mother of God

As God has appeared in the flesh, as flesh he should also be portrayed.
Having been seen in the world of matter, he wants to be seen in a material manner.

He must be celebrated by hymns, through which it might be possible to see him.
The fact that he is the Savior should also be clearly visible.
The one who goes beyond the vision of the Cherubim, as God,
Letting go of himself (*katheis eauton*), he takes the form of a servant.[19]
O prodigy! In what way it is made present when he is depicted!

From the same:

Acrostic: An Iambic Eruption[20]

Behold, Christ is here depicted, indeed, even as he is the king of all,
In no way he differs from the mortals. In no way then should
The corrupt mind deviate from this teaching.
So that everyone should know that he is a mortal (*merops*), and that is he is not beyond the flesh,
He is a perfect witness of himself as he is depicted,
And thereby he is shown to be utterly similar to us.

From the same:[21]

Christ is visually depicted as flesh, even if he is the Word,
Anyone who has tasted the divine mysteries should communicate them to the minds that are wise.
He comes indeed carrying the human image (*ton andromorphon eikona*),[22]
By means of that, through the divine power, he defeats
Every shadow, which deceives the mortals.
From now onward, doing what is just, the one who carries the scepter (*skēptrokratōr*)[23]
Swept away in this manner all foolish traps.

From the same:

Christ here depicted shines again,
Not of course in opposition to the symbol of the cross;
Indeed, he carries that forever on his head—

But so as to dissolve the heresy that deceives the people.
And having slaughtered this heresy with the word, as if with a word of judgment,
The Lord most powerful has won.

A Response to John's Poem[24]

The divine authors praise Christ with a golden effigy,
Without considering lowly matters, and in accordance with the speech of the prophets.

I. The divine authors describe Christ with words, O noble man; and you, in your perverse nature, call this speech a "golden effigy." However, they did not do so only on the basis of what the prophets had spoken; rather, they had seen everything with their own eyes (*oikeia autopsia*): "What we have found," says scripture, "with our eyes, that we have seen, and our hands have touched the Word of life."[25] Thus, it is not at all the case that they were avoiding "earthly matters"; rather, raising the eyes of their minds to what they themselves had seen, they contemplated Christ reclining in the manger; others saw him carried by the bent arms of his mother; and some saw him sitting near the well, some walking over the sea, some descending toward Capharnaum, and some ascending toward the mountain.[26] And who could count the innumerable works, which in many ways it is possible to see, and which in no way supplant the mysteries that are above this world? For this reason your claim is false, no matter how you consider it.[27]

Both of them openly despise the ever-recurrent error
*Of the painters of icons (or of the shadows [*skias*] of those who paint) as hateful to God.*[28]

II. As things that are absurd are wont to follow things that are absurd, these second things follow accordingly. Whom do you call the makers of shadows, if not the painters of sacred images (*zōographōn*, lit. "the writers of life")? What then do you call the recurrent error, if not [the injunction] that Christ should be painted? O tongue that is enemy of Christ! And why, then, are we talking of a recurrent error? Surely, you will say, because it is similar to the making of idols. Let us then return to the earlier dispensation, when Christ did not rule over us, nor was there any manifestation of the Trinity, and an image of Christ depicted before his descent into the flesh (*pro sōmatōseōs*) would have been an idol. But if this is the case, the Hebrews won, those who took their name from Christ are in error, and it is necessary to follow the custom of the Jews. The heavens were shaken by this, and they were greatly horrified, says the Lord.[29]

John did two evil things: he called Christ an idol, and he lied, saying that such practice was hateful—indeed, that it was hateful to God. But things do not stand this way, O injurer of Christ! The error is not truth, and the community of the Christian faithful, by whom Christ was seen in human form, and which continues to paint Christ and to worship him until the present, has not turned toward idolatry. Indeed, he was seen so that he could be painted, and so that those who worshiped the idols may worship Christ visually represented in human form.

Now, "The Lord is God, and he illumined us."[30] As long as this is the case, idolatry will cease. However, we are close to the coming of the Antichrist, of which you are the forerunner; and the Antichrist will seek to convince the people to remain mired in error, so that "the man of sin may be revealed, the son of perdition, who is in opposition, and is glorified above everything that is said by God, or is worshiped."[31] It is for this reason that the image has to be made the object of disrespect: so as to deny the prototype himself.[32] So, if you please, take hold of yourself; yours indeed is the false error, born indeed of the false council,[33] then interrupted, and now again spilling forth as of from a fountain of mud.[34]

III. But, John says, [this practice is] hateful to God. Surely, he is not talking from God;[35] he is howling from the mouth of the devil. This practice is not hateful to God, O madman, but it is most pleasing to him! Why, then, should God become what he hates that should be reproduced? There is nothing among the properties of humanity that cannot be portrayed in an image. Man has nothing else first in his properties but what is of the type that can be painted. If someone cannot be represented in an image, that is not a human being, but an abortion (*ektrōma*).

IV. Therefore, which of the things of which you so ineptly speak do you think actually belong to Christ, who because of his great goodness agreed to become man in all things? In what way could he cleanse similar with similar, as the theologian says,[36] if he could not be described in a way that is utterly similar? All that is left to you is to oppose the theologian, and claim that he cleansed the dissimilar with the dissimilar. In what way, then, is it possible to believe that he took flesh from the most holy Virgin, if he could not be represented in it? It is indeed necessary that the one who is given birth should be identical to the one who gives birth; thus, every son is the image of the one who gives birth [the father], and nothing that is present in the nature of the mother should be missing from what is carried by the one who is generated. And one of the first characteristics that are present is the portrayability (*exeikonēsis*) of the bodily character. If, indeed, the body could not be portrayed, the body would not come [from the Virgin] but from some other source, and then of what should it be made? Perhaps it should be celestial, as Valentinos says; or angelic, and so it should have no quantity or quality, it could not be touched or caressed, and it could not eat or sleep.[37] These things and many more should then be ascribed to the body that cannot be represented. In this way, then, the Redeemer did not pay the price (*timēma*) for us, as the divine Basil says, nor did he defeat the kingdom of death by himself.[38] If, indeed, it was other that was defeated by death, then it was something else that was assumed by the Lord (and how could it be otherwise, given that he cannot be depicted in a manner that is equal to us), nor did death cease to rule over the things that belong to it, nor would the sufferings of the divine bearer of the flesh have been of any advantage to us. And so, then, he did not kill sin in the flesh; we, who died in Adam, were not given life back in Christ; what fell was not transformed; what was broken was not restored; what had been distorted by the deceit of the serpent was not returned to God. All these things are eliminated, then, by those who claim that Christ came with a body that cannot be depicted; this is ultimately what their speech entails. Distance yourself from error, O man, if you please, and learn that truly Christ became man and that the divine writers claim that he can be described both by words and by images. Some, indeed, praise him with words, others represent him using paintings, and, in both cases, this leads to the same truth. What, indeed, the word of history represents by hearing, graphic art silently represents by imitation. The same divine inspiration is present. And again, someone is shouting: May Christ—the one who rewards struggles—be depicted in a painting. He indeed is honored, who is the subject of the painting that is honored; and similarly, he indeed is dishonored, who is the subject of the painting that is dishonored. The honor of the icon, indeed, ascends (*anabainei*) to the prototype, and the same also with the dishonor.[39] Behold, then, who is the one whom they despise.

Those who agree with these teachings (the emperors), full of enthusiasm,
Raise crosses in a splendid manner and with a pious discernment.

V. What are you saying? That the cross is honored, as Christ is despised? Is it not the case, then, that the glory of the cross comes from the honor of Christ? In what way is the cross exalted if he is despised in the image? Rather, he will be despised even more, even if you seem to glorify the cross. What do you think you can attain, displaying a scepter that is opposed to the king of the universe? Why do you exalt with divine honors what is inferior and reject what is superior? Foolish and blind, says the Lord, what is greater: the gold, or the temple that sanctifies the gold? And it is certainly no different in the case of those who appear to honor the symbol of the cross and indeed do not honor the image of Christ. Enough.

A Response to Ignatios's Poem

O Word, so as to strengthen among the mortals the worship of God,
And in order to grant a clearer understanding of yourself,
You established by law that the cross *alone would be represented.*

VI. You who endlessly talk in a foolish manner! Why, then, should the Word have given a law that the cross alone should be depicted, in order to establish devotion for the mortals, and to make it easier to understand his mystery? This is indeed not what we have heard today, but rather that "the grace of God has appeared, that grace which will save all men, so that, letting go of impiety, and of earthly desires, we should live in this century, soberly, and justly, and piously, waiting for the blessed hope, and the coming of the glory of our great God and Savior Jesus Christ; who gave himself for us, to redeem us from all iniquity, and to choose for himself an acceptable people, a people that would accomplish good works."[40] The Word, then, gave himself, out of the express good will of the Father, with the cooperation of the Holy Spirit, not in order to judge the world but in order to save it, as he himself said. And he even gave his own body, as he himself said, "And the bread, which I will give, is my flesh, which I will give for the life of the world."

This is according to the first word, what is blessed (*to sebas*); this is the more manifest cognition, the law; this is the participation in the divine mysteries, as long as we obey the divinely given command to do so in memory of him. If it is the cross, this is an excellent thing, but not on an equal level, but inferior.[41] And then the spear and the nails and whatever else has been used in the life-giving passion should be worshiped. And for whatever he suffered, there are corresponding instruments of the passion; the passion is holy and divine, and thus the instruments are sanctified and deified. This is really what matters. How, then, can you put aside the things that are written and speak instead those that are not written? How is it that when you speak, you leave aside what is more important and prefer what is of lesser import? How can you, asserting that this is to be found in scripture, claim that this has been transmitted by way of divine law? O stupor! O licentious madness! Such is falsehood: it has no light, and no probation of truth. Truly, what he says must be denied.

You established by law that the cross *alone would be represented.*
You also chose that out of an artificial material,
The cross may also be painted on the walls, and as it was in the past, so it should be now.

VII. Do you see now how this blessed man[42] is talking in a manner that is removed from common sense (*asyllogistōs*), as if he were to speak to people lacking the ability to hear? For what reason, then, should what the Word allegedly disdained become instead worthy of honor and of being made more widely known in the case of the cross? As if he had not become a human being. But he did become flesh, which can be most certainly circumscribed, as all human flesh, and indeed [it can be circumscribed] with artificial material. Indeed, this is called an artificial (*technētē*) image, whether it is seen on the wall, or on a canvas, or in whatever other material; and the same with the image of the cross. And why, then, is the painting on the walls considered valid, when it is in aid of indecency? Perhaps because the painting is unworthy. In what way then would painting on the cross advance his honor and his popularity? Indeed, whatever is honorable and convenient should be of greater honor to Christ than what is to his detriment.

Any artist prefers to be held in good esteem because of what he has himself accomplished, and not because of the tools of his art. And whoever is eager to see prefers to see the artist engaged in the act of painting rather than the instrument that the artist uses to paint. If, indeed, something is bodiless, it cannot be painted; if it is embodied, the claim that it could not possibly be painted cannot be understood by anyone who is endowed with the faculty of reason. Did you not hear God saying to the prophet, "Take up a book that should be new and great, and write in it with the writing of a human being"?[43] For what cause did God say that? Because the only Son of God became man, and he continues to write with the writing of a human being, even in us, so that we can understand that he, while being uncircumscribed with the Father and the Holy Spirit, chose to be seen for our sake, and he is now circumscribed [in the flesh], as the choir of the saints will confirm with one voice.

In whatever manner you interpret this passage of scripture, you will see that it truly foreshadows circumscription (*perigraphē*), or rather, iconic representation (*exeikonisis*).[44] What does the image of the cross show? Does it not show the life-giving tree? What else does it show but the fact that on the tree of the cross, the life-giving Word was killed in the flesh? Why, then, can what killed be painted, but what was killed cannot be painted? It is not possible to assert this with any coherence, as such belief is incompatible with the nature of things. If we were to follow this train of thought, we would have all sorts of consequences going counter to our reason: what cannot be painted would kill what can be painted; what is not embodied would kill what is embodied. This is absurd, however, because everything that is embodied can be painted; not even those who have invented the deer-goats have conceived such nonsense.[45] Indeed, when Christ was wounded by the spear, did he not let go blood and water from his side? Did he not let go of the spirit having inclined his head? Was he not buried, having been enveloped in a shroud with spices? Are these things not perceptible? And is it not the case that whatever is perceptible can be described (*eggraphesthai*)?[46] And so, he who has suffered these things, which are the same as the things that are also our condition to suffer, should not be circumscribed? And the one who deigned himself to suffer such things (and I include here all that happens in the nativity, and all the things that happened later, the mocking, the insults, the humiliations, the betrayal, the chains, the derisions, the whips, the hittings, the spittings) for the salvation of the world also deigned himself to be painted, so that the image may show to our eyes those things more clearly than speech may be able to declare. Hence, whence is the offense?

Now, imagine that Christ did not suffer of his own will. In this case, someone would consider it an insult if someone were to narrate and depict what he suffered. But Christ suffered of his own will;

hence, he might actually consider it an insult to himself if no one were to narrate or to paint what took place. There is no one, indeed, who does not love that the things that he bore out of charity for one's neighbor should be remembered in speech and in painting, since both speech and painting are going to bring him immortal glory.

VIII. Do you see, then, you who lack in intellect and wisdom, that you procure injury to God? Or do you think perhaps that Christ was displeased with what he had done,[47] or that he did not suffer of his own will? What did you drink, and from what revolting mud of impiety, so that you could vomit such a flood of horrors? Away with such stench! And again I ask: how is it that what can be seen cannot be painted? And in what way, if the Word became man, could he have a [human] nature, but this human nature could not be painted? Such a thing is indeed nothing less than an enigma. It would be the same as if someone were to say that there is a man who is in all things similar to everyone else in his own nature and in the way things are; and yet it is impossible to claim that he has a body, or that he is seen, or that he can be touched, or that he eats, or drinks, or sleeps, or walks, or speaks; nor is it possible to say that he was crucified, or died, or was buried; and yet, despite all this, this man is of such condition and nature that he can be painted in the form of men. What then? Is this not ridiculous and fanciful? And there would be the same laughter and ridicule, if not even more, if someone talking of the incarnate Word—whom everyone confesses in everything to be similar to us—were to affirm all the properties listed above but were simultaneously to assert that it is impossible that the Word should be painted. Hence, circumscription asserts affirmatively (*kataphatikōs*) all the things that are denied; so in Christ the negation of the painting eliminates negatively (*apophatikōs*) all the things that are claimed of him, and [everything] is therefore appearance and imagination, and Marcion again triumphs and so do Manes, and Valentinos, and Ignatios, who belong to the same school.[48]

A Response to Sergios's Poem

Moses openly defeated the powers of evil raising a type,
And with the aid of a type he crushed the enemy. In the same way now the cross,
Glory of the faithful, stops the strong torrent of error.

IX. You seemed to me, O learned man, to have strayed from the right path and to have fallen into the abyss of perdition. Indeed, what does Moses seem to you if not the figure of Christ, when he defeated Amalec in the figure of the cross, which the extended hands displayed?[49] In what way, then, will you accept a typological interpretation in that case, but here instead you fraudulently separate the archetype from the type? You brought forth an example involving the cross, but you rejected the one who was crucified. It was not the cross that destroyed the error, but the Christ who was crucified on it; as it is written, "Having defeated the principalities and powers, he exposed them to public contempt, having triumphed over them in himself."[50]

Should I perhaps go mad and repeat what you said? Which cross do you talk about, if you please, and which error? I understand clearly that you are talking of the symbol of the cross and of the image of Christ; you are calling the symbol "cross" with the name of the prototype, as it is customarily called; you do the same with every image; but in the case of Christ, since even his image is called "Christ," you acted with the violence of a flood and you called Christ "a mistake" that must be taken from the cross![51] O worse than Jewish madness! If these enemies of Christ were said to have a devil and were called Samaritans, they would appear to be less conceited. The sword is taken away from the fighter; Christ is indeed divided upon himself,[52] having been separated from his own weapon. Who will be able to cope with such blasphemy? And really, look, the consequences of this deceit are of such magnitude that the Christian people will leave behind the adoration of the Trinity and will apostatize to Greek polytheism, denying the fact that Christ became man.

Tell us, O men, who were those who were found guilty [of venerating the images], and those instead who stood up against you? Let us know, so that, knowing what constitutes guilt for you, we may be able to resist your teaching if the occasion arises. Let us imagine that someone has never seen Christ depicted in an image. This person could still be induced to believe in Christ in unity with the Father and the Holy Spirit, if he came to know the secrets of theology (*tēs theologias*), as well as the mystery of the divine economy (*tēs oikonomias*). Let us imagine, instead, that the only way to come to know of the incarnation is to see Christ depicted in an image. Now, this at least would confirm that Christ became man.[53]

You should understand, then, that you are really like a violent flow of errors that is never restrained and that constantly comes out again from the sea of the old lack of faith. Because of this lack of faith, there is no certainty as to the incarnation of Christ, and people suffer because of their impiety. Is it not clear then? For you, the sacred temples are places of idolatry; the divine anathemas are profanities; the servants of God have been deceived. Truly, what you said was impious and demonstrated your lack of faith in God; your words were the cause of disaster and spiritual death for many. And let us now turn to what follows.

In a similar way, then, the creation of art, not unlike a hidden arrow
Thrown with an evil intent, penetrates deeply into the souls.
This is how their wound is felt by those who are subject to Christ.

X. What are you saying, O silly man—are you suggesting that the image of Christ, which has saved the cosmos, has actually resulted in the loss of souls? What defeated error is an arrow drawn by an evil intent? Anyone who was bitten by one of these noetic serpents, and who has started to look at it with faith, will immediately run away when he discerns the real poison of evil that carries death.[54] When the Word was not yet incarnate, he worked for our salvation, and he was not a force of destruction. And now that he became incarnate for us in an unchangeable form, you would suggest that his representation is not salvific, but it is actually harmful? "Hark, O heaven, and listen, O earth, because the Lord has spoken. I nourished and exalted the sons, but they despised me. The ox recognized his owner, and the donkey the manger of his Lord," but Sergios "did not recognize me," [55] as scripture says; Ah, if he had run toward me, but instead he caused me much insult. O you, man who truly is lost and impious and an enemy of Christ, you dare to be against Christ? You stand up against the image of Christ—an image that even the angels honor and the demons abhor? And whose name would you rather have? That of Saturn, or Jupiter, or Mars, or Venus, or Diana, or of any of the other false gods, whose naming is deception, and whose accusation is deceit? Without Jesus Christ, no one, then, "can say the Lord Jesus Christ, unless he is in the Holy Spirit,"[56] as scripture says; see what you blasphemed not only in Jesus Christ but also in the Holy Spirit according to the Jewish custom, because you have called the name of Jesus Christ, which is said or painted in the Holy Spirit, dangerous to the life of the souls.[57] O tongue that has talked impiously! O mouth that has spoken iniquity against God the most high! "What is an idol," asks the Apostle, "or anything that is sacrificed to the idols? Whatever is sacrificed by the Gentiles is sacrificed to the demons, and not to God."[58]

For us, instead, there is only one God, who is called holy and who is worshiped in the Father, the Son, and the Holy Spirit. We know also that the Son of man truly became God, and he was called similar to us in everything. And as every human being can be represented by an image, the same goes for Christ; for the sake of our salvation, we can contemplate these painted images, these sacred lights, these memorials of salvation, where we see Christ born, baptized, performing miracles, crucified, buried, risen again, ascended into heaven. In all these mysteries of his life, we readily admit that things did not come to pass as they are represented in the images; we assent to this claim with our senses and with our soul,[59] yet, [in the contemplation of the images] both our senses and our soul are confirmed in their faith in the mystery of the incarnation, which brings about piety and every spiritual fruit.

You, having summed everything up, opposing the figure of the cross, incurred into the highest error. I ask, indeed, for what reason you should want to paint the cross when the one who was crucified should not be painted. You say to everyone: [Christ cannot be represented], because he does not have a nature that can be represented. But if he does not have a nature that can be represented, much less does he have a nature that can suffer; anyone who is endowed with the faculty of reason will agree. Why is this the case? Even an angel, who has no body and therefore cannot suffer, can be depicted the way we are depicted; Moses himself, in obedience to the divine command, represented an angel, and the angel did not have any physical characteristics, nor could he suffer.[60] If we follow what you say, the mystery of the incarnation is a product of the imagination, or a ruse. But it is you, impostor, you, who extracted the evil arrow from the sheath of impiety, who should call yourself an error that is lethal and dangerous to the souls.

This is how their wound is felt by those who are subject to Christ.

XI. So, can the one whose mind is blinded really understand what we have been talking about? Whatever has been said until now—all the aspersions that were cast against the icon of Christ—Sergios sent out to Christ himself. This is the truth, even if he is not aware of it. He said nothing positive about Christ; he launched a harmful invective against his image; and finally he says, "This is how those who are wise understand Christ."[61] What else can be said about such absurdities, apart from what we have been saying until now?

A Response to Stephanos's Poem

As support of the faithful, and as something that is worthy of divine veneration,
You gave us, O Word, the salvific cross, *the life-giving type of the passion.*

XII. That the Word gave us the cross for our salvation, as a support for the faithful and a divine blessing, is clear to everyone, but the cross is certainly not the life-giving type (*typos*) of the suffering of Christ, O you who talk foolishly. How is it possible that in the image of the cross, Christ should be represented as he is captured, he is bound by chains, he is beaten by sticks, he is spat at, crucified, wounded by the lance, or anything else you may wish to add? This is absolutely, utterly impossible. The cross indeed signifies (*sēmainei*) Christ, [it] does not represent (*typoi*) him. For this reason the cross is also called "sign" (*sēmeion*) by the divine scripture.[62] "Moses, then," it says, "put the serpent as a sign,"[63] which refers to the cross.

One thing, indeed, is the sign, and the other is the representation; in the same way, the morning star signifies the day; the sun itself, on the contrary, represents or shows the day. In the same way, Christ is signified by the cross, but he is represented in his own image. The archetype appears in the image; thus speaks the blessed Dionysius,[64] and with him also the other fathers, for whom the terms *image* and *type* are synonymous. This, indeed, is the life-giving type of the passions: the image of Christ! You, who chose to hide the image, have now been shamed in front of everyone.[65] The type of the cross signifies all the mysteries of our salvation. And if the cross, which is only a sign, is the anchor and the blessing of the faithful, how much more beneficial will actual images be? Such, indeed, is the truth, and not as you had claimed with your false speech.

Indeed, you chose to suppress as an error
The earlier divine prohibition against representation,
And this is the law that everyone is mandated to follow

XIII. What is not allowed is evil, and not what is allowed; what is against nature, and not what is in accordance with nature. If then, before the incarnation, someone had made an image of the Word, that would not have been just wrong, but it would also have been an absurd lie, as it would have made the non-incarnate Word resemble the flesh; and he who was not similar to anyone would have been put on display in an effigy that resembles all other members of humanity. This is why God himself said, "To which likeness will you compare me?"[66] This was idolatry, and indeed, it had been banned by God himself.

You who fight God, listen! You who say this after the incarnation are false and deceitful; even if you support the cross, you set out to take away the image that has been given for the salvation of the cosmos. Talking against the image, you tried to show that things that are compatible with each other are actually in opposition to each other, since in the image of Christ, it is also possible to see the cross being expressed. But no, he did not truly exist, no one ever called him a divine man, and he was not seen in our likeness! Nor did he have a body that was sensible to touch and color, from which derive quantity and quality, as well as position in place and extension in time. Anyone who can use reason, even just moderately, will understand that these are properties of circumscription! In what way, then, is it possible to say that he who has such properties is not circumscribed? In what way is it that he who has assumed the likeness of men should not be painted in the likeness of men? In what way can he be found in a form (*schēma*) as a man, if he does not have a form?

What is this ignorance (*anoia*) and this disagreement (*machē*) in such important matters? It is as if someone were to say that as the sun rises, the night is coming! Is it not the case that a line is made up of points? And that lines can form triangular figures as well as others of a different shape? And is it not the case that out of the different geometrical figures one can create a face, and if we paint a face in an image, this will be recognized as that of a human being, as is taught by the scriptures, which are divinely inspired? Or is Christ perhaps without form? The Apostle claims that he took the shape (*morphē*) of a servant;[67] perhaps you would suggest that he lacked shape? Or that as he was found in the form of a man, he nonetheless lacked form? Or that he assumed the likeness of men, and yet he was dissimilar? Indeed, the representation is a similitude (*homoiōma*). "O you, full of every fallacy and every deceit, son of the devil, enemy of every justice, you will never cease to subvert the straight ways of the Lord!"[68] These words are not from me; Paul sings such things to you, the new Elymas.

Moreover, deceitful man, think of this: the characteristics (*idiōmata*) of the same nature are of equal power (*isodynama*) and are complementary (*allēloucha*); as such, if one is present, of necessity even the remaining ones will be there; similarly, if one is taken away, even the other ones will be taken away. To list the properties of the divine nature, for instance, [one can mention] the lack of a body, invisibility, incomprehensibility, uncircumscribability, immutability, impassibility, and all sorts of other ones. If, then, by hypothesis, one of these properties happened to be taken away or to change—such as, for instance, incomprehensibility—and then we were to say that the divinity is circumscribable; if then we were to list all the properties of divinity, as soon as one is eliminated, all the remaining properties are simultaneously eliminated; and it would follow that the divinity could be comprehended, and had a body, and could be seen, and circumscribed, and was liable to mutation, and passible; since it is impossible, as said already, that with the elimination or subtraction of a property all the other ones should not also be eliminated or subtracted.

The same can be said for the humanity of Christ. The properties of humanity are corporeality, visibility, circumscribability, variability, possibility, and all other characteristics that, along with these, inhere in every human being. If, then, you chose to eliminate or subtract one of the properties mentioned above—such as, for instance, circumscribability—Christ, even according to his humanity, would become uncircumscribable, and incorporeal, and invisible, and incomprehensible, and immutable, and impassible. Your words, therefore, should be advertised as they are, without omitting any of them, even if they are full of impiety, and they are only worthy of the arenas.[69]

And this is the law that everyone is mandated to follow:

Always worship that cross, to which you were hung, and through which you redeemed us.

XIV. Yet again this charlatan appears to be speaking unreasonably. It is as if we were to say that the king has saved the city by thrusting the spear into someone, and then the foolish one says that we should forget the king and worship the spear alone. It is thus necessary to say: first, we should worship you, O Christ, and then the cross from which you saved us; first, we shall worship the one who saved us, and after that we shall worship that through which the salvation has come. Oh, what a horrid display of impiety, and what a bitter announcement! Stephanos is truly fighting against Christ.

FURTHER, IN RESPONSE TO STEPHANOS'S SECOND POEM

As the emperor would not allow that Christ should be painted
Through an image without speech, and devoid of spirit,
Using earthly matter which the scriptures condemn
Leo with his son, the new Constantine,
Impressed the happy type of the cross
Glory of the faithful, on the doors of the palace.

XV. "The silly man," says scripture, "will say silly things, and his heart will meditate over error."[70] Is it even proper to ask again for which cause, O you who devise falsity, for what reason the emperor does not wish that Christ should be painted "through an image without speech and devoid of spirit"? It is certainly not proper. What about an image that emits a voice and draws breath? After all, the images of Christ lack these properties. It is only appropriate that all images that are the product of human ability (*technētē*) should be without voice and without breath; otherwise such an image would not be a reproduction, but a prototype, or a natural image, in the same way as everyone has his own father. Why should it be, then, that whatever can be seen in the image of an ordinary human person should not be seen in the image of Christ as well—in the image of the one who is similar in all things to all men, "and in the same way participated with us in flesh and blood,"[71] as scripture says? Perhaps you chose to withhold faith from what is revealed in scripture, and you decided on your own advice (*heautō*) to contemplate a Christ who has no blood and no flesh, in the Manichean manner.[72] However, if you believe what is officially professed by everyone, you will have to accept that Christ can be painted like all other human beings, to whom "he is similar in all things except for sin";[73] if this were not the case, the absence of representation (*hē agraphia*) could be construed as a negation of the incarnation.

It is also important to remember that the image of Christ does not represent the imprint of the invisible soul, or—indeed, even less so—an imprint of the divinity. Rather, the image of Christ is an imprint of his body, as would be the case with every human being. On the cross, however, his holy body lacked in voice and in breath; for this reason it was called a "dead image" (*nekra eikōn*) by St. Gregory the Armenian.[74] As such, it is only right that Christ, in a likeness from a likeness, should be represented as a form that lacks voice and is devoid of breath. You did nothing but expose yourself to ignominy by talking nonsense. Let us have a look again at your fanciful hypothesis (*to theōrēma*).

As the emperor would not allow that Christ should be painted
Through an image without speech, and devoid of spirit,
Using earthly matter which the scriptures condemn.[75]

XVI. I would really like to know from Stephanos in what way, if not "using earthly matter which scripture condemns," the type of the cross could be impressed? In what way does the Lord suffer dishonor from it? But here, the cross is represented instead of Christ; it opposes him, and as it fails to carry Christ, it carries ignominy. Do you see, O wise man, how foolish (*paidia*) such things are in the eyes of Christ? After all, the flesh that carried God is from the same human stock as Adam, and the flesh of human beings is earthly matter. Or perhaps in you there is nothing earthly?

Most foolish man, not all matter is despised by the holy scriptures, but only that which is the explicit target of this censure. Many things that could be included in the list (*graphidōs*) of what God gave to humanity belong to the realm of matter, and they are not condemned by anyone. Instead, all you want to do is to call the image of Christ an idol, acting in an arbitrary manner (*apodeiktikōs*) and thinking that you are obeying those apostolic words, "Remember, then, that when you were pagans, you used to go to the idols that have no voice, according to your inclinations";[76] and thus, you wanted to show that the Christians fall into perdition in the manner of the Gentiles according to the sentence of the Apostle, even now, when there are no more idols in the world, and the blessed name of the Lord is invoked throughout the whole earth; now that we all confess one faith, one Lord, one baptism; now that one pure sacrifice is offered in opposition to the sacrifices to the idols, and that from the rising of the sun to its setting the image of Christ is displayed in all sacred temples; after so many holy councils, which held the image of Christ in front of their eyes;[77] after Christ is now present in the public places (lit. *en prothyrois*, "on the lodges").[78]

You see here an error that is worse than all the heresies that have emerged after the coming of Christ. Indeed, among those, none tried to negate Christ openly (*prophanōs*), but this one heresy tries to do exactly that. He who rejects the type of the cross, does he not deny the cross as well? So, then, he who despises the image of Christ, he also despises Christ in the most extreme manner. If you are ready to admit that the first statement is true, how can you reject the second? Why, then, do you mix things that should not be mixed, and acting in a demonic manner (*daimoniōdōs*), you apply to the icon of Christ whatever is said of the idols? Is it not the case that whatever the law says is said to those under the law? Is it not the case that all those things that the Apostle says are said to those who at his time lived like the pagans? Do you not hear St. Athanasios shouting, "We who are faithful do not venerate the images like gods—perish the thought!—in the manner of the Gentiles, but we show not only the manner, but also the depth of our love (*agapē*) toward the imprint of the countenance (*prosōpon*) of the image"?[79]

Thus, over and over again, having destroyed the imprint, we should throw the image to the fire, as wood that from now on is useless. The Gentiles, however, thought that the wood itself in its own nature, and the gold and the silver, sculpted with human figures, were their own gods. These are the idols that the prophet and the Apostle condemn: idols that do not see, even if they have eyes; idols that have no voice or speech, even if they have a mouth; and idols whose members do not work, if they are represented with any of their members. Stop, then, blaspheming against Christ in a Jewish manner (*Ioudaikōs*).

DECLARATION[80]

XVII. Following the doctrine of the apostles and the fathers, and believing in the power of the church to lay down the law (*thesmothesia*), accepting the six holy and ecumenical councils, as well as that council that was celebrated at the Blachernae and that which met to confirm the latter;[81] following and accepting the orthodox teachings equally affirmed by all the councils, rejecting what they rejected, and receiving what they received; spurning the fabrication and the veneration of images, rejecting the meeting held under Tarasios,[82] and anathematizing those who disagree, I signed this by my own hand (*idiocheirōs*).

XVIII. Every heresy that has emerged in recent times believes that it is rejecting earlier heresies; that it accepts the doctrines of the apostles and the fathers; that it receives the holy councils that were held before its time; and whenever the heresy is assessed against the word of truth, its supporters claim that there is no disagreement between their claims. The same can be said of the heresy that we are considering today, and, with the help of God, we are going to show this in the course of this oration.

First of all, we must ask the following: In what way, O intelligent man, despising all making and worship of images, you claim that you are following the teaching of the apostles and the fathers? The Apostle says the following: "The law indeed possesses the shadow of the future goods, but it does not possess the actual image (*eikona*) of the realities."[83] According to the Apostle, the shadow represents what is old, the image represents what is new, and the realities are nothing but the future goods. Gregory the Theologian, in line with Paul, says that grace and law are examples of one another;[84] and indeed, these words are sometimes used interchangeably. The image is sometimes called type, and the shadow is also called type. "Look," says scripture, "you shall make all things according to the example (*kata ton typon*) that was shown to you on the mountain."[85] In the same way, the same Paul calls those things that belong to the law "antitypes (*antitypa*) of things that exist in reality";[86] therefore, shadow, type, and antitype are the same thing.

Dionysius, the wisest of men, says somewhere, "All the things that were carried out in the sacred rituals in accordance with the law, these things he called the image of the type that was shown to him on Mount Sinai."[87] In the words of David, "We move in this life as if in an image (*en eikoni*)."[88] And again, in the words of Dionysius, "To the extent that it is possible, we rise to divine contemplation by means of sensible images."[89] He calls image the holy altar; and the sacred unguent; and the type of the cross; and he even calls images those who live in such a way as to signify, by way of a similar form (*homoieideis*), the cruciform image of their own sinlessness. All the implements that are seen in the liturgical ceremonies are also called images.

What will you say now? If you consider all these things, are they not tantamount to the making and the veneration of images? Of course they are; and as you despise these things, you clearly hold in contempt not just the teaching of the apostles and the fathers, but also the New Testament; and if you despise the New Testament, you also despise the Old. Indeed, I see that you even despise yourself and the angels. The human being, after all, is an image of God, to the extent that it is possible to imitate what cannot be imitated; to this point, scripture says, "I made man in the image of God."[90] And an angel is also an image of God, says the blessed Denys.[91] You will, then, have to accept, even if you are reluctant, that images can be made and can be venerated, since both angels and men can be the object of veneration. Thus, you made earthly things, as well as celestial things, the object of your contempt. You did not even distinguish between one kind of image and the other—I mean, between the natural image and the one that is painted—but you chose to despise all making and veneration of images, leaving nothing untouched by your contempt apart from the Holy Trinity, as the Trinity alone cannot be associated with the making of an image, because the Trinity is not created, but uncreated.

It is not possible to interpret your claims any differently. But let us now return to the subject matter.

Following the doctrine of the apostles and the fathers, despising all making and veneration of images.

The Voice of Peter, Prince of the Apostles:

XIX. Take the image of our Lord Jesus Christ, and take it to the tower, so that the peoples may see what form the Son of God chose to assume.[92]

The Voice of St. Denys:

XX. The super-essential cause (*teletarchia*), out of love of humanity, described the super-celestial intellects (*noas*) by way of visible images, and inscribed these images in the passages of scripture that describe holy matters.[93]

The Voice of St. Athanasios:

XXI. We who are faithful do not venerate the images as divine—perish the thought—as the Greeks do, but we display the nature (*schesis*) and the intensity (*pothos*) of our love toward the imprint of the form of the image.[94]

The Voice of St. Basil:

XXII. Come to me, O you famous painters of athletic triumphs, and with your art give glory to the mutilated image of the leader. *And after other things*: May also Christ, who was victorious in battle (*agōnothetēs*), be painted on a table.[95]

The Voice of St. Gregory of Nazianzos:

XXIII. Observing the famous Polemon in an image:

Seeing it—and it was awesome indeed—
She left at once, defeated by the sight,
Put to shame by the one depicted, as if he were alive.[96]

The Voice of St. John Chrysostom:

XXIV. And I conceived love for an image molten out of wax, which was overflowing with devotion; in the image an angel was seen, striking the crowds of the infidels. I saw the tribes of the infidels being punished, and David saying with the voice of truth (*alētheuonta*): "Lord, in your city you will reduce their image to nothing."[97]

The Voice of St. Gregory of Nyssa:

XXV. I often saw an image of this pitiable event in painting; and this vision was not unaccompanied by tears; with such mastery (*enargōs*) the art was bringing the story to the sight. Isaac lies down...[98]

Voice of St. Cyril:

XXVI. In a wall painting, I saw a girl who was fighting in the arena; and I did not see this image without shedding tears.[99]

The Voice of the Fathers of the Sixth Holy Council:

XXVII. In a number of paintings of the venerable images, we can see the lamb indicated with a finger by the Forerunner.[100] Among other things, the council fathers also say: So that even what is perfect (*to teleion*) could be represented to the eyes of all using the power of colors, we order that the image of the one who takes away the sin of the world—the Lamb, the anointed of our God—from now on should be represented in the icons according to his human form.

XXVIII. I just selected a few statements out of the many that are available, so as not to cause boredom (*koros*). Here is again the doctrine of the apostles and of our fathers, the sublimity (*hē akrotēs*) of the apostles, the foundation of the tradition, the keys of the dogma, the norm of the correct faith; if anyone were to contradict any of these statement, even if he is an angel,[101] he is condemned and declared to be anathema; he does not come from the apostles or from the fathers, but he is deceitful and carries a false name. In spurning all fabrication and veneration of images, you rejected the norm of the correct faith, even if you did not say that you rejected it, as Moab of old.[102]

And obeying the dispositions of the church.

XXIX. The law, then, is holy; and so are the ancient customs, which the great Basil told us to keep.[103] Our customs are based on the traditions of the church, and these are the customs of the church in all its temples and holy places that are on this earth. Indeed, from its very foundation, and from the beginning of the preaching of God's good news (*tou theiou kerygmatos*), the church venerated the sacred images that you now despise.[104] This is the tradition of church that you tried with all your might to abrogate.

Receiving [the teaching of] the six holy and ecumenical councils.

XXX. If we consider the orthodox councils, both those that are ecumenical and those that are local—no matter how many they were in number, they were, so to speak, all the same—if one considers what truly gave them power and strength, we will see that they were all one in terms of their understanding of the divine wisdom, in the same way as the symbol of faith is one. The councils were convened against the heresies of the time as the need arose (*kata kairon*), and having opposed the heretic viewpoints in all sorts of ways, they remained firmly in the same orthodox dogma. To use an example, the same happens for the grain of wheat, which is one when it is sown but potentially also possesses different types of grains, in virtue of its power to carry fruit at the opportune time.

Let us see, then, in what way, if you accept the first council, you will at the same time accept all the others. Leaving aside the synods that took place at an earlier time, as they are not relevant to the current question, we remember how [the Council of Nicaea] affirmed:

> [I believe] in one Lord Jesus Christ the Son of God the only begotten, born from the Father before all ages; light from light, true God from true God, born, not made, consubstantial with the Father, through whom all things were made. And for us men and for our salvation he came down from heaven, and was incarnate from the Holy Spirit and the Virgin Mary, and was made man.[105]

All the saints confess, then, that [the Son] was born of the Father before all ages, and that he was incarnate and was made man from the Holy Spirit and the Virgin Mary, and that he was one from the point of view of the hypostasis and double, so to speak, from the point of view of the nature, perfect in divinity and perfect in humanity.

Christ is uncircumscribed according to that which he received from the Father, in the same way as the Father is uncircumscribed; he is circumscribed according to that which he received from the mother, as even the mother is circumscribed. As is the Father, the same in all things is also the one who is generated by him (*ho gennētheis*); and as is the mother, the same in all things is also whatever is born (*to gennēthes*) from her;[106] so that, if only one of these properties were to cease, the whole complex system would be eliminated, and everything would perish. The mother is depicted in her nature according to the form of her body, because she is circumscribed; the same applies, then, to Christ, because Christ is a circumscribed issue of the mother. If this were not the case, Christ would not have been generated by the mother in nature and in truth. He is a true son of the mother, in the same way as he is a true Son of the Father. Thus, while he can be represented after the imprint of the body, as far as the divinity is concerned he is uncircumscribable like the Father; as a result, because of the necessary structure of each nature, each has to take testimony from the other.[107] Thus the first holy ecumenical council, as the highest authority in the church, claimed that Christ could be represented, since it confessed that he had taken flesh and had become man. No one, indeed, who has a body is uncircumscribable; no one who can be seen is unable to be represented in an icon.

In the same way [the council of Ephesus] did not call Mary "the Mother of God" in virtue of her own power (*kyriolektōs*), but as the council affirmed that through her the Son of God had taken flesh and had become man, the council declared her to be Mother of God in virtue of the power of Christ. If, then, the one who is generated is God, it follows that the one who generates is the Mother of God; this is how the third council could announce this clearly and explicitly and could refute Nestorios.[108] [The council of Ephesus] did not declare explicitly that in Christ there were two natures and the corresponding two wills, but once it had been recognized that Christ was God as well as a human being, and once his two generations (*gennēseis*) had been openly proclaimed, it did not take long to conclude that there were two natures, and therefore, if there were two natures, there were also two wills. It was left to the fourth and the sixth councils to announce this explicitly and properly, and thus these councils refuted those who preached that in Christ there was only one nature and one will.[109]

It would take long to explain in detail how every heresy came about, somehow anticipating the orthodox dogma that would then be proclaimed by a council at the appropriate time. But once we have established and proved this fact, how is it possible for you to say that you reject the making and the veneration of images, but you do not reject the teaching of the first council? We saw how that council announced implicitly that one could make images of Christ's human form. Similarly, [if you reject the veneration of images], you also fail to receive the remaining councils, because the teaching of all councils is the same.

Receiving also the council that was held at the Blachernae, and that which met to confirm the latter.

XXXI. Clearly, you listen to and agree with those who oppose the truth, and disagree with the teaching of the apostles and the fathers, as we said earlier. After all, [the council fathers at Blachernae] banned the fabrication and veneration of images.

And rejecting what those councils rejected, and receiving what they received.

XXXII. Indeed; but you do so in the manner of the assembly of Caiphas, which accepted Barabbas and denied Christ.[110]

Spurning, however, the assembly that was celebrated under Tarasios.

XXXIII. Listen carefully: if you oppose the first holy council when it announces that Christ can be represented according to his human form, [you will also reject] his image, and the image of the life-giving cross, and that of the Mother of God; you will also deny that there should be any veneration of the images of the saints in honor of their prototypes—those saints, from whom you are now separated, in the same way as Judas was separated from Christ.

And casting anathemas against those who disagree.

XXXIV. Of course, but the truth of the matter is that you are an enemy of all the saints, in the same way as you are an opponent of Christ.

I signed this by my own hand.

Surely, but, like Pilate, you signed with a reed, to condemn Christ.[111]

DECLARATION OF THE ORTHODOX[112]

XXXV. I obey all evangelical and apostolic commands and all the edicts of the church; I am strengthened in the faith by the voice of the prophets and by the decisions of the holy fathers; I receive the teaching of the six holy ecumenical councils and of the other local synods that are in agreement with the former (*homodoxois*), as far as dogmatic and canonical observance are concerned; and together with these, I also accept the Quinisext Council,[113] which addressed the question of the blessed images and issued decrees out of divine fear; I accept the second holy council held in Nicaea,[114] which offered dogmatic opinions in an orthodox manner in accordance to what had been declared before, and also in agreement to the Quinisext Council that had preceded it and that had also discussed the holy icons; and I reject all that had been rejected by all the councils. I accept everything that has been approved by these councils; I submit myself to every sacred deliberation, and I accept every custom that has come down to use from Christ or that we are certain that it was instituted in a holy manner after that; I worship with great devotion every image that ever existed or that was ever produced in the world for the sake of our salvation, whether of Christ our God, of the life-giving cross, of the Mother of God, of the angels, and of every male and female saint. And I firmly reject the assembly held at the Blachernae and the meeting that it confirmed,[115] as both of them are enemies of Christ and of all the saints, and I cast eternal anathemas against all those who disagree; with the help of God, I undersigned with my own hand.

More Iambic Poems by the Iconoclasts[116]

JOHN

Acrostic: The Passion of Christ Is a Hope for John.[117]

With the divine strength of the cross, Christ destroyed
The onslaught of the phalanx of the demons; for those who
are in this mortal life,
Christ has become a refuge and **hope** against all challenges:
His disciples taught so openly, and confided only in him.
Thus, it is not allowed to depict the Lord on the walls.
God indeed is whole, hardly changed by error,
And he gives glory to those who rule the kingdom with justice.

IGNATIOS

Acrostic: To Ignatios, the Cross Is Glory.[118]

The cross, which brought together those things which before were dispersed,
Confirms piety with sincerity.
The cross triumphs over all contemplation of images,
And extolled your glory, O Lord.
Having come to know the value of the true faith.
The emperors worship the cross in an appropriate manner
And expel the enemies that serve the power (*tō kratei*).[119]

I Expel the Enemies, and I Slaughter the Barbarians[120]

Leo and Constantine, the blessed emperors,
Who received their power from God alone,
Remove (*anistorousi*) the type of the Lord;
This is what their hearts led them to do.
And having seen the vain creations of the past,
From then onward they banned the fabrication of images.[121]

APPENDIX

Celebratory Canon

...that is sung for the erection of the sacred images; clearly a work of the holy father Theodore the Studite[1]

ODE 1

Tone 6, according to the hymn: Helper and protector, etc.

Let us sing, O faithful, a song as an action of grace to the God and benefactor of all, because he raised a horn of salvation, and a great power, to protect the true faith.

Truly the divine grace has been shown to the world, and glory and honor are manifest; and for this reason the Church rejoices, having put on the stole of which she had earlier been stripped.[2]

The holy fathers, having woven again the garment of Christ, which had earlier been torn apart by John, the seducer and the maker of poisons, gave it back to the church.[3]

Having taken back the incarnate form of the Lord,[4] the Church exults and rejoices with her children; it has received from him the ensigns of victory, the symbols of orthodoxy.

May the equally insane Lezios and Anthony[5] be accursed in the future, and be considered foolish, together with John and Theodore, both deserters of the faith.

Jannes and Mambres once opposed Moses the legislator,[6] and by him they were confused. In the same way now the evil John and Anthony were unmasked.

You dispersed, O Christ, the host of the enemies of God, and you returned her honor to your church, for which you gave your blood in your goodness.[7]

θ (Tone 2) You, O Trinity, I affirm as God, and I prostrate myself in front of you, and I acknowledge your divine strength; deliver me from all temptations; in you, indeed, I believe, Father, and Son, and most Holy Ghost.[8]

θ' (Tone 3) Taking the royal stole from you, Virgin,[9] God appeared to humanity in the form of men, according to a dual essence, and we hold in veneration the image of his form.

Ode 3

Rejoice, all the throngs of the fathers and the apostles, considering the veneration of the images, which you yourselves have bravely transmitted to us.

I took over my beauty, and I put on my stole—so should the church boast, which John had despoiled.

Be accursed, O you who howl against the Lord; he indeed took up flesh, and appeared in an image, which we welcome and always associate with Christ (*schetikōs*).[10]

Who will recount the impious dogmas and the insane doctrines of the mindless John? Who will expose his tropes, and his sibylline strategies?

Let us issue an anathema against Letius and John, with Anthony, the atheist and blasphemous Theodore, together with the insane Theodotos.[11]

The blood cries, the blood which was spilled by John, and which was spilled because of the flesh-carrying divine likeness of the Lord.

The Lord destroyed the throngs of the enemies (lit. "of the foreign hordes"), and returned to his people what belonged to them; glory then to his goodness. Glory be...

Let us worship, according to the orthodox faith, the eternal will and power and kingdom of the Trinity, always covering Arios with infamy.[12]

Let us honor you, O Lady, in a proper manner, as the one who gave birth to God, relying on the dogmas of the holy fathers, and leaving aside the vain teachings of Nestorios.

Ode 4

Rejoice, Church, and every city and region should throw open its temples in exultation; the dwellings of the virgins and the sacred relics should be venerated; let them decorate with worthy honors the images of the martyrs.

Christ is calling us; come here eagerly, O divine fathers, and celebrate in a divine manner the miracle of his own incarnation, as well as his passion, as the holy Gospel describes.

Come together rejoicing, O you throng of the monks that speak the truth (*en parrhēsia*); if indeed again the enemies of the faith—O wretched ones!—were to prevail, again they would be defeated, and the Lord would disperse the heresy which these men uphold.

The enemies of the fathers, as well as the scars of their wounds have faded away; the frequent exiles have stopped, and peace is given to all; the industry of magic art shall no longer prevail, [for] God indeed is with us.

The vineyard of iniquity extends the trellises of impiety and produces bitter grapes, and the wrath of the dragons is their wine, by which they inebriated the people of God, because of their evil and darkened mind.

The impious ones defiled your temple, through their profane impositions of the hands[13] and their simoniac acts, and for this reason, according to the sacred canons, John and Anthony are cut off from the divine glory, and together with them also Simon Magos.[14]

Let us curse with an anathema those beasts, and the enemies of God, and the profane Anthony and the transgressor John, whose mind is enslaved to Satan, and those that disturb the Church, gathering together the faithful as wolves. Glory be to the Father…

O uncreated monarchy, Father, Son and Holy Spirit, we worship you, whom the Cherubim, adorned with many eyes, and the Seraphim, with six wings, praise shouting: Holy, holy, holy you are, O most high and omnipotent.

Holier than the saints, and higher than all creatures, you alone appeared at the same time as Mother and Virgin, O Bearer of God, as you gave birth to your own Creator, and for that reason we venerate your image.

ODE 5

Christ has won; let the earth rejoice; the tumult quieted down, and so did the tears of the servants of God; the faith then has been promulgated throughout the whole earth.

Looking at the image, let us venerate the crucifixion, honoring Christ and his ensigns, and prostrating ourselves in front of them; yet we shall not honor the images like gods;

The loquacious and blasphemous spirit of Lezios is now silent, which in the past used constantly, day after day, to talk against the form of Christ and his saints.

For what reason, O three times unhappy, did you prosecute the immaculate manifestation of the incarnate Christ, and of all the saints? Perhaps we faithful venerate deaf idols?

Having brought together the symbols of turpitude, they convened a synod of impious priests, against God the most high; as in the past the Jews, Annas and Caiphas.[15]

On the Day of Judgment, O most unhappy among men, the adversaries of your impious soul will rise, and so will the choir of the fathers, whose despoiled bodies you afflicted with innumerable plagues.

All the churches will shout, none of them ceasing, having been despoiled by you of the sacred images of the form of the Lord, and of his saints.

θ Glory to you, glory to you, three-hypostatic unity, Father, Son and Holy Spirit, who contain everything with your power, and who deigned yourself to free those who resort to you.

θ' Similar to a lamp adorned with gold, we worship you, O Lady, who has given birth to the noetic light for the world, and who dissolved the dark cloud.

Ode 6

The vigilant (lit. *agrypnoi*, "sleepless") wardens of the church of Christ shouted asking him to be given peace, and he listened to them and fulfilled their request.

The ruses of the seducer have been uncovered, thanks to the teachings of the Fathers; and so God who has taken the form of the flesh is praised by hymns, he who has remained uncircumscribable.

You who took part in the seduction, shame be on you; and together with Anthony, may it be that Theodotus and Lezios be ruined, and so be Theodore, the nadir of perdition.

O unhappy man, you opened your mouth, not in spiritual canticles, but in blasphemies against the Lord, despising the blessed work of iconography.

You perverted the dogmas of the Father and the teachings of the apostles, writing against them, according to your impious belief, O John, enemy of Christ.

Your smoke filled with tears the eyes of the pious, but this smoke has been dissolved by the wind of the divine teachings, O insane John.

You tore apart the sacred stole, in the same way as Arius of old ripped the garment of Christ; for this reason you have been placed outside the church, having been expelled like a dog.

θ I honor a principle of divinity, in three hypostases, which is indeed one God, Father, Son and Holy Spirit, distinct through the characters (*charaktērsi*) and the persons (*prosōpois*).[16]

θ' O virgin prophetically glorified by God, truly you were announced by the prophets as a city of God, from which was born your true Creator, who preserved you after the birth as you were before.[17]

Ode 7

The furnace of heresy that had been predominant for four weeks of years[18] has now been extinguished by divine grace, which has burnt heretics (lit. "the Chaldeans"), and has refreshed the pious worshippers of the Trinity.

The church is decorated and beautified, and the faithful walk around it (*peribeblētai*), having received the sacred image of the Lord, and of his passion, and of the other mysteries, according to the divine laws.[19]

O Christian people belonging to the Lord, rejoice and celebrate, when you see the church again illumined by the beauty of the divine form, which, being God, he carried, so as to save us as a man.

The Word in the flesh experienced poverty and hunger and thirst; these are the properties of the divine essence, through which the latter is circumscribed. At the same time the Word is simple and uncircumscribed according to the divinity.

The miracles and the prophecies of the enemy of Christ are also dispersed. He was the one, who strutted around with the writings of the Gentiles, which were rightly scattered by the voices of the just.

Which tongue will be able to recount your teachings, which were hidden, and profane, and pernicious to the souls? Or the prediction of your ventriloquist prophetess, O John by the false name, who was truly a forerunner of the Antichrist, Satan?[20]

It was not opportune for you, O falsely named, to be called by such a name,[21] but rather Pythagoras, and Chronos, and Apollos, or any of those other gods, whose life you imitated, and in whose profanities you took delight.

θ We faithful, let us all adore the eternal, omnipotent and incomprehensible Trinity, Father, Son and Holy Spirit, and let us celebrate them with divine praises without confusion (*asynchytōs*), shouting: Holy, holy, holy you are, O God.

θ' Holy Parent of God, Mother and Virgin, you who are celebrated and glorified by hymns, free from all crimes us, who venerate your immaculate birth; indeed, we do not have any other refuge save you, O divine bride.

ODE 8

Let us rejoice in a prophetic manner, and let us exult, all we faithful. This is indeed the day when Christ the Word gave back to the church his own stole.

They were arrayed like an army against the form of Christ, Lezios and John of equal fury, the fellow of Belial, cutting the church into pieces with the axe of iniquity.

Who will not deplore the great audacity, seeing the divine image that is on the bronze door of the palace being hit with stones by evil men, according to the teaching of John?[22]

How did you fail to see, O blind and miserable man whose intellect was darkened, the world (*tēn hyp'ouranon*) beautified with the image of Christ, and instead alone retained the mind (*to phronēma*) of the Jews?

You thought to eliminate entirely from the churches of God Christ's image resplendent with flesh (*sarkolampē*), and that of all the saints; but the divine grace destroyed your tyranny.

The fierce Lezios, together with John—the deserters of piety—lawlessly asserted that the holy relics of the saints and their images should not be worshipped at all.

θ All piously worshipping the divine principal author of all in three persons, we will praise the Father without beginning, and the co-eternal Son, and the resplendent Spirit.

θ' O Lady, you alone are the true bridge of the Christians, glory of the faithful, and their refuge, helping all and freeing them from all dangers.

ODE 9

Clap your hands, O people; choirs of the Fathers, hasten; hermits, and those who are in the mountains, approach; come, you who in the past were deceived by the evil and impious John, to curse his magic arts and his predictions.

Rejoice, deserted and peopled lands, and you all mountains, distill sweetness, and you valleys, be full of gladness, because Christ the Word has given peace to those who are on the earth, and has given the unity of faith to the churches of God.

The God of revenges now acted freely, Christ was near, giving strength to the divine teachers so that they could with courage announce his return (*sygkatabasin*), and truly circumscribe his incarnation in the image.

O magnanimous God, how marvelous are your works! Who will try to measure your love of humanity? In what way did you resist and maintained control, failing to strike the evil-doers, when you saw your priests and monks being killed for your image?

O you, who established your church as indefectible, O Lord, so that the doors of Hades would not prevail upon her, do grant your piece to your people, so that we all with a fervid soul may venerate you and praise you with one expression of praise (*doxologia*).

An anathema may be cast, O Lord, against those who do not venerate the image of your incarnation, first of all John, and then Anthony, and the impious Theodore, Theodotos, and the other deserters of the faith.

O Lord, who gave your peace to your apostles, give us all now tranquility, bringing back with your hand those who are scattered; and like sheep of the Word (*logika probata*), count them with the flock of your holy church.

θ I glorify the Godhead of the Father, and of the Son and of the Holy Spirit, one nature (*physin*) in three hypostases, an undivided essence that is distinct by way of the Persons (*prosōpois*), reigning together, having created everything, omnipotent, having perfect command, containing everything.

θ' You (Virgin) helper of all, refuge and protection, do show that you can intercede for all those who take refuge in you, and that you defeat the impious ones by means of the power of your Son; since indeed, as Mother, you can do all things.

NOTES

Introduction

1. See Leonid Ouspensky, *Theology of the Icon* (Crestwood, NY: St. Vladimir's Seminary Press, 1992), 2:273. Joseph of Volokolamsk (1439/40–1515), also known as Joseph of Volotsk, was an important monastic thinker and reformer from Muscovite Russia; he is well known for disputes with St. Nilus of Soras (1433–1508) on the issue of monastic landownership and for his role in opposing the heresy of the Judaizers. According to tradition, he composed the *Message to an Iconographer* to instruct and encourage the famous painter Dionysius of Moscow (1445–1505), who in 1481 had painted the frescoes of the Dormition Cathedral in the Moscow Kremlin, and between 1484 and 1486 came with his *artel'* (a retinue of co-workers) to decorate the monastery of St. Joseph. In the words of Ouspensky, the author of this text views sacred iconography as a form of art that had to be characterized by "a perfect fusion of dogmatic content, inner prayer, and artistic creation" (see Ouspensky, *Theology of the Icon*). While *The Message to an Iconographer* has not been fully translated into English, the Russian text is available in N. K. Goleizovskii, "The Message to an Iconographer and Echoes of Hesychasm in Russian Painting," *Vizantiiskii Vremennik* 26 (Moscow, 1965).

2. John Damascene's chief works on the question of iconoclasm are his three treatises on the icons; see John of Damascus, *Three Treatises on the Divine Images*, trans. Andrew Louth (Crestwood, NY: St. Vladimir's Seminary Press, 2003).

3. For a more detailed overview of Theodore's life, see Roman Cholij, *Theodore the Stoudite: The Ordering of Holiness*, Oxford Theological Monographs (Oxford: Oxford University Press, 2002).

4. Biographical information about Theodore is much more readily available than in the case of John Damascene, whose land of birth—Syria—had already fallen under the sway of Islam and was removed from the religious and cultural developments of the capital. See Andrew Louth, *St. John Damascene: Tradition and Originality in Byzantine Theology*, Oxford Early Christian Studies (Oxford: Oxford University Press, 2002), 3–15.

5. The versions of the *Vita* can be found in the *Patrologia Graeca* of Migne, 99:113–327. Roman Cholij notes that with "hagiography being designed for edification, not information," the chronology of these lives is "often handled artificially in order to give greater scope for the activities of the hero, with bias and misinformation not infrequently coloring the account." Cholij claims however that "a discerning reading" of these texts can still provide useful insights. See Cholij, *Theodore the Stoudite*, 8.

6. This text is available in Christian van de Vorst, ed., "La Translation de saint Théodore Studite et St. Joseph de Thessalonique," *Analecta Bollandiana* 32 (1913): 50–61. This text rectifies some of the information contained in the *Vita* and corroborates a letter on Theodore's death addressed by Theodore's disciple Naukratios to a number of monastic communities.

7. Plato is the addressee of the *Letter to His Own Father Plato* on the subject of icon veneration.

8. For the two catechetical collections, see J. Cozza-Luzi, ed., *Sancto Theodori Studitae Sermones, Magnae Catecheseos* (Rome: A. Mai. Nova Patrum Biblioteca 9/2, 1888); *Sancto Theodori Studitae Sermones, Parvae Catecheseos* (Rome: A. Mai. Nova Patrum Biblioteca 9/2, 1888); a French translation of the latter was Marie-Hélène Congourdeau, ed., *Théodore Stoudite: Petites Catéchès*, trans. by Anne-Marie Mohr (Paris: Migne, 1993).

9. See Alonso J. A. Fuentes, *El divorcio de Constantino VI y la doctrina matrimonial de San Teodoro Estudita* (Pamplona: Ediciones Universidad de Navarra, 1984).

10. Alas, Irene's involvement in this and other palace coups would not stop Theodore from hailing her as a saint because of her later support for the legitimacy of icon veneration. See "La vie de l'impératrice Sainte Irène," ed. F. Halkin, *Analecta Bollandiana* 106 (1988): 5–27.

11. See his *Epistula 53*, in Georgios Fatouros, *Theodori Studitae Epistulae, Corpus Fontium Historiae Byzantinae* 31/1, 31/2 (Berlin and New York, 1992). This series of events marked a major shift in the application of *oikonomia* to matrimonial questions in the Eastern churches, whose position increasingly diverged from the stricter approach of the West; see Alonso J. A. Fuentes, "'Oikonomia' en la iglesia bizantina ante el divorcio de Constantino VI," in *Hispania Christiana: Estudios en honor del J. Orlandis Rovira* 24 (Pamplona: Ediciones Universidad de Navarra, 1988): 239–55.

12. An account of the Bulgar wars before 813, stopping shortly before Leo V's public profession of iconoclasm, can be found in the chronicles of Theophanes the Confessor; see Cyril Mango, trans., *The Chronicles of Theophanes Confessor: Byzantine and Near Eastern History (AD 284–813)* (Oxford: Clarendon Press, 1997). The reign of Leo V is chronicled by the Scriptor Incertus in his *Historia de Leonae Bardae Armenii Filio*, included in Leo Grammaticus, *Chronographia*, Corpus Scriptorum Historiae Byzantinae

(Bonn, 1842), 335–62. For a short summary, see Cholij, *Theodore the Stoudite*, 53–62.

13. See John Bagnell Bury, *Eastern Roman Empire from the Fall of Irene to the Accession of Basil I (AD 802–867)* (London, 1912; rep. Charleston, SC: Nabu Press, 2010), 56–57.

14. See Joan M. Hussey, *The Orthodox Church in the Byzantine Empire* (Oxford; Oxford University Press, 1988), 55–58; Warren Treadgold, *The Byzantine Revival: 780–842* (Stanford, CA : Stanford University Press, 1988), 207–14.

15. In *Epistula* 71, Theodore accused the new patriarch of acting illegally, as he was unilaterally subverting the decision of the council fathers. See also Thomas Pratsch, *Theodoros Studites (759–826): Zwischen Dogma und Pragma: Der Abt des Studiosklosters in Konstantinopel im Spannungsfeld von Patriarch, Kaiser, und eigenem Anspruch*, Berliner Byzantinistische Studien 4 (Frankfurt am Main, 1998), 204–43.

16. A more detailed chronicle of the last years of Theodore's life can be found in the *Vita Theodori Studitae B* (PG 99, 325d–328a), even if the reliability of this text has been challenged: see van de Vorst, "La Translation de S. Théodore Studite et de S. Joseph de Thessalonique," AnBoll 32 (1913): 439–47.

17. Cholij, *Theodore the Stoudite*, 25.

18. On the "constructive" use of earlier sources by late Patristic authors, see Andrew Louth, *Maximus the Confessor*, The Early Church Fathers (New York: Routledge, 1996), 19–33.

19. See Louth, *St. John Damascene*, 31–38, 84–89.

20. See Antoine Guillaumont, *Les Kephalaia Gnostika d'Évagre Pontique et l'histoire de l'origénisme chez les Grecs et les Syriens* (Paris: Seuil, 1962), 124–70; John Meyendorff, *Christ in Eastern Christian Thought* (Crestwood, NY: St. Vladimir's Seminary Press, 1987), 47–58.

21. See Meyendorff, *Christ in Eastern Christian Thought*, 174–78.

22. See Charly Clard, *Les théories relatives au culte des images chez les auteurs grecs du IIe siècle après Jésus-Christ* (Paris: Fontemoing and Cie, 1915), 24–30, 46–62.

23. Porphyry, *Contra Christianos*, Fragment 77, in *Contra los Cristianos: Recopilación de Fragmentos, Traducción*, trans. E. A. Ramos Jurado et al. (Cádiz: Servicio de Publicaciones de la Universidad de Cádiz, 2006).

24. Celsus, *Sermo Verus*, II, 3, 31–36, in Horacio Lona, *Die "Wahre Lehre" des Kelsos* (Freiburg: Herder, 2005).

25. See, for instance, Clement of Alexandria, *Pedagogos*, 3, 1 (PG 8: 555–60), on the nature of images and "true beauty."

26. Origen, *De Principiis* I, 1, 8 (PG 11: 128–30).

27. The literature on Evagrios is vast and constantly growing. See Evagrios Pontikos, *Ad Monachos*, trans. and ed. Jeremy Driscoll, Ancient

Christian Writers (Mahwah, NJ: Newman Press, 2003); Robert Sinkewicz, *Evagrius of Pontus: The Greek Ascetic Corpus*, Oxford Early Christian Studies (Oxford: Oxford University Press, 2006). For the *Philokalia*, see vol. 1 of *The Philokalia: The Complete Text compiled by St. Nikodimos of the Holy Mountain and St. Makarios of Corinth*, ed. G. E. H. Palmer, Philip Sherrard, and Kallistos Ware (London: Faber and Faber, 1979). Volume 1 contains four texts by Evagrios: *Outline Teaching on Asceticism and Stillness in the Solitary Life*, *Texts on Discrimination in respect of Passions and Thoughts*, some extracts from the *Texts on Watchfulness*, and finally the *153 Texts on Prayer*. Further texts by Evagrios on the theme of spiritual practice were published by Jeremy Driscoll in *Steps to Spiritual Perfection: Studies on Spiritual Progress in Evagrius Ponticus* (Mahwah, NJ: Paulist Press, 2005). An interesting overview of Evagrios's theological system can be found in Julia Konstantinovsky, *Evagrios: The Making of a Gnostic* (London: Ashgate, 2009).

28. Elisabeth Clarke, *The Origenist Controversy: The Cultural Construction of an Early Christian Debate* (Princeton, NJ: Princeton University Press, 1992).

29. In *Philokalia*, 1:38–52; in the *Patrologia Graeca*, see *De Diversis Malignis Cogitationibus*, (PG 79: 1199–1234), though Migne attributes this work to Nilus of Sinai.

30. For instance, angelic thoughts about gold will recall how in Exodus 25:22–39 gold is used to cast the candlestick, the censers, and the vessels for the tabernacle of the Ark of the Covenant, whereas demonic thoughts will "shamelessly suggest the acquisition of physical gold." See Evagrios, *Texts on Discrimination in Respect of Passions and Thoughts*, 7, in *Philokalia*, 1:42–43. Evagrios admits the possibility of merely "human" thoughts, which in this case would bring the image of gold to the mind without any attendant passion or desire, but does not ascribe much importance to them.

31. Evagrios, *Texts on Discrimination*, 2, in *Philokalia*, 1:38–39.

32. According to Evagrios, the first stage in the ascent toward the divine reality is the practice of discernment of spirits, whereby the individual learns how to distinguish the angelic or demonic origin of thoughts. As the Greek term *diakrisis* derives from the verb *krinō* (to judge), another possible translation would be "adjudication": the practitioner would pass a judgment on the origin of the thought.

33. Evagrios, *Texts on Discrimination*, 3, in *Philokalia*, 1:39.

34. Gal 3:28.

35. Col 3:10–11.

36. Mark the Ascetic, *On the Spiritual Law*, 139, in *Philokalia*, 1:119.

37. Matt 5:28.

38. Evagrios, *153 Texts on Prayer*, 56, in *Philokalia* 1:62. This text can be found in the *Patrologia Graeca* as *De Oratione* (PG 79: 1166–98), and it is also attributed to Nilus of Sinai.

39. Evagrios, *On Prayer*, 69, in *Philokalia*, 1:62.

40. Evagrios, *On Prayer*, 67–68, in *Philokalia*, 1:62.

41. In his chronicles composed between 440 and 443, Sozomenos narrates the destruction of the Temple of Serapis in Alexandria (the so-called Serapeum) that took place in 391; see Sozomenos, *Historia Ecclesiastica*, 7, 15 (PG 67, 1451–58). News of these events would have reached Evagrios and the other monastic communities in the desert.

42. What we ordinarily call "souls" are thus the *noes* that dwell in the world of multiplicity and have "descended into the realm of practical activity." Evagrios, *Kephalaia Gnostika*, III, 28 (S2).

43. Ibid., IV, 58 (S2).

44. Ibid., II, 53.

45. Ibid., II, 5.

46. See Khaled Anatolios, *Athanasios: The Coherence of His Thought* (Oxford: Routledge, 1998). A different theology of the atonement that also emphasizes the centrality of Christ's body can also be found in Gregory of Nyssa, *Oratio Catechetica* (PG 45: 77–78).

47. Evagrios, *Kephalaia Gnostika*, II, 53; IV, 8.

48. On the sixth-century condemnation of Origenism and its considerable differences from Origen's own theological vision, see Antoine Guillaumont, *Les Kephalaia Gnostika d'Évagre Pontique et l'histoire de l'origénisme chez les Grecs et les Syriens*, 124–70; also Meyendorff, *Christ in Eastern Christian Thought*, 47–68.

49. See also M. Anastos, "The Argument for Iconoclasm as Presented by the Iconoclastic Council of 754," in *Late Classical and Medieval Studies in Honor of A.M. Friend, Jr.*, ed. Kurt Weitzmann (Princeton, NJ: Princeton University Press, 1955), 177–88.

50. See Leo D. Davis, *The History of the First Seven Ecumenical Councils (325–787): Their Histories and Theologies* (Collegeville, MN: Liturgical Press, 1990), 180–92.

51. Sarah Coakley, "What Does Chalcedon Solve and What Does it Not? Some Reflections on the Status and Meaning of the Chalcedonian Definition," in *An Interdisciplinary Symposium on the Incarnation of the Son of God*, ed. Stephen T. Davis, David Kendall, SJ, and Gerald O'Collins, SJ (Oxford: Oxford University Press, 1999), 143–63.

52. John McGuckin, "Introduction," in Cyril of Alexandria, *On the Unity of Christ* (Crestwood, NY: St. Vladimir's Seminary Press, 1997), 39–74.

53. For an overview of Leontios's Christology, see David B. Evans, *Leontius of Byzantium: An Origenist Christology* (Washington, 1970), 1–7. Other important sources for his thought are J. P. Junglas, *Leontius von Byzans: Studies zu seinen Schriften, Quellen und Anschauungen, Forschungen zur christlichen Literatur—und Dogmengeschichte*, vol. 7, 3 (Paderborn, 1908): 148–62; Silas Rees, "The Literary Activity of Leontius of Byzantium," *J. Theol. Stud.* 19 (1968): 229–42; the *Vita Sabae* by Cyril of Scythopolis (525–58), published in

Eduard Schwartz, *Kyrillos von Skythopolis, Texte und Untersuchungen zur Geschichte der altchristlichen Literatur*, Reihe 4, Band XLIX, Heft 2 (Leipzig: J. C. Hinrichs, 1939), 85–200. Two important articles by Brian Daley, SJ, are "The Origenism of Leontius of Byzantium," *J. Theol. Stud.* 27, no. 2 (1976): 333–69, and "A Richer Union: Leontius of Byzantium and the Relationship of Human and Divine in Christ," SP 24 (1993): 239–65.

54. Leontios of Byzantium, *Contra Nestorianos et Eutychianos Libri Tres* (PG 86: 1276–81A).

55. Ibid. (PG 86: 1281B–85).

56. Ibid. (PG 86: 1285D–1288A).

57. Ibid. (PG 86: 1288D–1289A).

58. Ibid. Instead of being used to capture an infra-trinitarian web of relationality, the term *hypostasis* is used to suggest two opposed "infra-christological" relations.

59. Ibid. (PG 86: 1304A).

60. Evans, *Leontius of Byzantium*, 184–85.

61. Leontios of Byzantium, *Contra Nestorianos et Eutychianos Libri Tres* (PG 86: 1277).

62. Ibid., (PG 86: 1280B). Of course, the two sets of divine properties continue to remain grounded in their respective natures.

63. For a chronology of Maximos's life and works, see Hans Urs von Balthasar, *Cosmic Liturgy: The Universe According to Maximos the Confessor*, trans. Fr. B. Daley, SJ (San Francisco: Ignatius Press, 2003). As with Evagrios, the secondary literature on Maximos is constantly growing. Some fundamental works that focus on Maximos's spiritual theology, as opposed to the monothelite controversy, are Jean-Claude Larchet, *La Divinization de l'Homme Selon Saint Maxime le Confesseur* (Paris: Cerf, 1996); Lars Thunberg, *Man and the Cosmos: The Vision of St. Maximus the Confessor* (Crestwood, NY: St. Vladimir's Seminary Press, 1985), and *Microcosm and Mediator: The Theological Anthropology of Maximus the Confessor*, 2nd ed. (La Salle, IL: Open Court, 1995); Adam Cooper, *The Body in St. Maximus the Confessor: Holy Body, Wholly Deified* (Oxford: Oxford University Press, 2005).

64. Maximos the Confessor, *Ep.* 12 (PG 91: 224A, 469D).

65. On Maximos's theology of Christ's composite subjectivity, see von Balthasar, *Cosmic Liturgy*, 31, 250–51; see also Thunberg, *Microcosm and Mediator*, 21–47.

66. Maximos the Confessor. *Amb.* 7 (PG 91: 1084A).

67. Maximos, *ThPol.* 7 (PG 91: 85A); the text from the Pseudo-Denys is *Ep.* 4 (PG 3: 1072AC). See also Thomas Cattoi, "An Evagrian Hypostasis? Leontios of Byzantium and the "Composite Subjectivity" of the Person of Christ," in *Studia Patristica* 68 (2013): 133–47.

68. Maximos the Confessor, *Ep.* 12 (PG 91: 496C). On the question of the mode of the union late Chalcedonian Christology, see also Brian E. Daley,

"Nature and the 'Mode of Union': Late Patristic Models for the Personal Unity of Christ," in Davis, Kendall, and O'Collins, *The Incarnation: An Interdisciplinary Symposium on the Incarnation of the Son of God*, 164–97.

69. Germanos of Constantinople, *Epistulae Dogmaticae* (PG 98 135–83).

70. Nikephoros, *Antirrheticus I* (PG 100: 280–332); Nikephoros would later formally condemn the theological positions of Constantine V. See also Theodore's *Antirrheticus* 1, 3.

71. Theodore will discuss this issue in *Some Questions Posed to the Iconoclasts*, IX, 132.

72. See the same argument in *Antirrheticus* 2, 7–8; 2, 38; 3A, 42.

73. On the Council of Hieria, see Meyendorff, *Christ in Eastern Christian Thought*, 181; Jaroslav Pelikan, *The Christian Tradition: A History of the Development of Doctrine*, vol. 3, *The Spirit of Eastern Christendom* (600–1700) (Chicago, 1974), 113; Milton V. Anastos, "The Ethical Theory of Images Formulated by the Iconoclasts in 754 and 815," DOP 8 (1954): 153–60.

74. Evagrios, *Kephalaia Gnostika*, II, 53.

75. See also Milton V. Anastos, "The Argument for Iconoclasm as Presented by the Iconoclastic Council of 754," in *Late Classical and Medieval Studies in Honor of A.M. Friend, Jr.*, ed. Kurt Weitzmann (Princeton, NJ: Princeton University Press, 1955).

76. See Nikephoros, *Antirrheticus I* (PG 100, 272).

77. Ibid. (PG 100, 628); Theodore, for his part, will note in his *Antirrheticus* 3A, 17, that Christ is circumscribable because he comes from a "circumscribable" mother.

78. Evagrios, *153 Texts on Prayer*, 67–68, in *Philokalia*, 1:63.

79. *Antirrheticus* 1, 7; 1, 10.

80. Ibid., 1, 4; 3A 15; 3A 17; 3A, 34.

81. Ibid., 3A, 3; 3A, 58.

82. Ibid., 1, 2; 1, 3; 1, 12.

83. Ibid., 1, 12; *Some Questions Posed to the Iconoclasts*, XIV.

84. See Evagrios, *Kephalaia Gnostika*, 3, 6–8; 4, 9; 5, 69; 6, 20; Maximos the Confessor, *Amb.* 7 (PG 91: 1089B; 1097B).

85. Maximos the Confessor, *Amb.* 31 (PG 91: 1276B); *Q.Th* 63 (CCSG 22: 173).

86. Maximos the Confessor, *Amb.* 38 (PG 91: 1330BC); *Ep.* 33 (PG 91: 627); also Walter Völker, *Maximos the Confessor als Meister des geistlichen Lebens* (Wiesbaden: F. Steiner, 1965), 410–32.

87. See, for instance, Jean-Michel Garrigues, *La Charité: Avenir Divine de l'Homme* (Paris: Beauchesne, 1976).

88. See Maximos the Confessor, *Liber Asceticus*, 34 (PG 90: 340b).

89. In a passage of the *Capita Theologiae et Oeconomiae*, Maximos notes that in virtue of the shared divinity of Father, Son, and Holy Spirit, the person who follows the divine commandments becomes the dwelling place of the

three persons of the Trinity (PG 90: 1156d). This trinitarian dimension of holiness, however, is always subordinate to the christological aspect. See *Antirrheticus* 1, 6.

90. Maximos the Confessor, *Amb.* 31 (PG 91: 1276c); also *Amb.* 48 (PG 91: 1364c).

91. Maximos the Confessor, *Ep.* 2 (PG 91: 408a). An English translation of this epistle is included in Louth, *Maximus the Confessor*, 84–94.

92. Maximos the Confessor, *Capita Theologiae et Oeconomiae* 2, 30, in *Philokalia*, 2:145 (PG 90: 1137d).

93. See Maximos the Confessor, *Amb.* 41 (PG 91: 1304–12A); also Louth, *Maximus the Confessor*, 155–61.

94. On Paul of Samosata, see McGuckin, "Introduction," 18–39.

95. Maximos connects the church's liturgical actions with Christ's cosmic healing and preservation of ontological difference through the mystery of the hypostatic union. See Maximos the Confessor, *Mystagogia* (658–718); also Thomas Cattoi, "The Symphonic Church: Chalcedonian Themes in Maximos the Confessor's Liturgical Theology," *Studia Patristica* 48 (2010): 123–29.

96. *Antirrheticus* 1, 17–18.

97. The Greek text of Theodore's *Antirrhetici* can be found in Migne's *Patrologia Graeca*, alongside the usual Latin translation. *Antirrheticus* 1 is in PG 99, 327–52; *Antirrheticus* 2 is in PG 99, 351–88; *Antirrheticus* 3 is in PG 99, 387–436.

98. Catherine Roth, *On the Holy Icon: St Theodore the Studite* (Crestwood, NY: St. Vladimir's Seminary Press, 1981), 15.

99. See, for instance, *Letter to His Own Father Plato*, par. 2; *Antirrheticus* 1, 16.

100. *Antirrheticus* 1, 1; 2, 4.

101. Ibid., 1, 1. If the three persons of the Trinity are known to us distinctly in virtue of their specific properties, Theodore also stresses that one can distinguish between the humanity and the divinity of the incarnate Christ in virtue of their distinct set of *idiōmata*; see *Antirrheticus*, 1, 3; 3, 22–23; *Seven Chapters against the Iconoclasts*, 1.

102. On the Council, see Meyendorff, *Christ in Eastern Christian Thought*, 181; also Pelikan, *The Christian Tradition*, 113.

103. Throughout the whole *Antirrhetici*, as well as in his other writings, Theodore plays on the double meaning of the verb *graphō* ("to write," but also "to paint an icon"), as well as of its cognates, such as *perigraphē* ("circumscription," but also "representation"), *perigraptos* ("circumscribed," but also "capable of representation"), *aperigraptos* ("uncircumscribable," but also "not capable of representation"). To admit Christ's circumscribability is thus to admit that Christ can be represented (and worshiped) in an image, and vice versa. See, for instance, *Antirrheticus* 2, 8; 2, 48; 3A, 4–5; 3A, 46–48; 3A, 50.

104. *Antirrheticus* 1, 2; 3, 53.

105. See, for instance, Maximos the Confessor, *Disputatio cum Phyrro* (PG 91: 287–360); *Capita Theologiae et Oeconomiae* (PG 90: 1083–1177).

106. See also *Refutations and Subversions*, IX–X (in response to the poem by "Sergios"); *Seven Chapters against the Iconoclasts*, III.

107. See Davis, *The History of the First Seven Ecumenical Councils*, 180–92; Coakley, "What Does Chalcedon Solve and What Does It Not?" 147.

108. See *Antirrheticus* 3A, 22–23, where the iconoclast accuses those who venerate images of falling back into Nestorianism. In the second part of *Refutations and Subversions*, Theodore debunks the claim of the iconoclasts to be in continuity with the earlier councils: see *Refutations and Subversions*, XXX.

109. *Antirrheticus* 1, 3; see also *Antirrheticus* 3A, 12–13.

110. Similarly, in the spiritual theology of Maximos the Confessor, deification does not deprive men of their human individuality, although their assimilation of the divine properties ensures that their human nature starts functioning "in a divine manner." See Maximos the Confessor, *Amb.* 7 (PG 91: 1088C).

111. In *Antirrheticus* 1, 12, Theodore observes that, in the hypostatic union, the divine nature does not assume those properties that are "unsuited" to it (*ta anoikeia*). This is an important qualification; if it were not so, the teaching on the communication of the two properties would have untenable consequences, such as the mortality of the divine nature (or conversely, the omnipresence or omniscience of Christ's humanity).

112. It is interesting to note that, in more recent times, theologian John Hick (1922–2012) rejects the *communicatio idiomatum* precisely on the grounds put forth by the iconoclasts, as he argues that the exchange of properties between humanity and divinity would result in the ascription of contradictory attributes to the same nature. See John Hick, *The Metaphor of God Incarnate: Christology in a Pluralistic Age* (Louisville, KY: Westminster Press, 2006), 47–61.

113. See Lars Koen, "Partitive Exegesis in Cyril of Alexandria's Gospel according to St. John," in *Studia Patristica* 25 (1991): 115–22.

114. *Antirrheticus* 1, 4.

115. Ibid.

116. See also ibid., 2, 7–8.

117. See also ibid., 2, 38; 3A, 42; *Some Questions Posed to the Iconoclasts*, XIII.

118. See *Antirrheticus*, 1, 7.

119. Hab 2:18.

120. Porphyry, *Contra Christianos*, Fragment 77.

121. Theodore goes back to this point in his discussion of the iconoclastic poems: see *Refutation and Subversions*, XV, as Theodore responds to "Stephanos"' second poem.

122. See also *Antirrheticus* 3A: 15. It is important to remember how Neo-Platonic thought also distinguished between the human nature and the human *genos*: while the former is the ontological matrix of our substance, which unfolds in time in different manners according to the choices made by the individual subject, the latter is the set of all those subjects that are endowed with the same human nature. It is important to remember that Christ assumed our common human nature, but he did not assume the human species; if he had, he would have become incarnate as many times as there have been or will be members of the human race. See Sara L. Rappe, "Explanation in 'Enneads' VI. 7.1–15," in *Neoplatonism and Nature: Studies in Plotinus' Enneads,'* ed. Michael Wagner (Albany, NY: State University of New York Press, 2001), 71–99.

123. *Antirrheticus* 1, 7.

124. See Theodore's critical commentary to the poem by "John" in *Refutations and Subversions*, I–V; *Seven Chapters against the Iconoclasts*, III.

125. See *Antirrheticus* 1, 36. Theodore presents Old Testament practices as a *skiagraphia* (foreshadowing) of the new covenant, choosing the term that was used for Greek vase painting whereby figures and scenes emerged from a black background; see Plato, *Phaedrus*, 69.

126. See *Antirrheticus* 1, 7; also 2, 24–5.

127. The deliberations of the Quinisext Council are also mentioned when Theodore critiques the iconoclastic profession of faith in his *Refutations and Subversions*: see *Refutations and Subversions*, XXIX.

128. *Antirrheticus* 1, 10; on this issue, see also Nikephoros, *Antirrhetici* (PG 100, 272). The contention on the part of the iconoclasts was that the Eucharist alone could be considered an image of Christ, as it was not distinct from Christ in terms of essence. See also *Antirrheticus* 2, 25, and the discussion of natural and artificial image in the *Letter to His Father Plato.*

129. Basil of Caesarea, *Homily* 19 (PG 31: 509).

130. Interestingly, *Antirrheticus* 1, 17 insists that "hearing" is equal to "sight."

131. *Antirrheticus* 1, 12.

132. This language is reminiscent of Leontios's discussion of Christ's subjectivity; see Leontios of Byzantium, *Contra Nestorianos et Eutychianos Libri Tres* (PG 86, 1285d–88a). Leontios, however, thought that the hypostasis of the incarnate Word emerged out of some sort of relational dialectic, whereas in this case Theodore is talking of the ontological relationship between the image and its prototype.

133. See, for instance, *Antirrheticus* 2, 7.

134. See Ibid. In *Refutations and Subversions* XXX–XXXVIII, Theodore notes that the church only defines dogmas when the need arises to counter some heretical teaching.

135. *Antirrheticus* 2, 7–8.

136. Ibid., 2, 16; see also *Seven Chapters against the Iconoclasts,* I. The point is that the properties are present in the prototype "in an eminent manner" and are therefore transmitted to the image.

137. *Antirrheticus* 2, 15; also 1, 15.

138. Pseudo-Denys, *De Eccl. Hier.* 4, 3, 1 (PG 3, 473); Basil of Caesarea, *Homily* 42, 4 (PG 31, 608); Athanasios, *Contra Arios* 3, 5 (PG 26, 332).

139. *Antirrheticus* 3A, 5; 3A, 8; 3A, 43: 3A, 51.

140. Ibid., 3A, 15–17.

141. At the very beginning of the first *Antirrheticus,* Theodore mentions a work by the name of *Steleutikos,* which is seemingly lost. The theme of iconoclasm is also treated in some of Theodore's letters; see G. Fatouros, *Theodori Studitae Epistulae,* Corpus Fontium Historiae Byzantinae, 31/1, 31/2, Series Berolinensis (Berlin: 1992).

142. Louth, *St. John Damascene,* 219–23; John A. McGuckin, "The Theology of Images and the Legitimation of Power in Eighth Century Byzantium," SVTQ 37 (1993): 39–58.

143. The *Seven Chapters* can be found in PG 99: 485–98.

144. The *Questions Posed by Theodore to the Iconoclasts* can be found in PG 99: 72–486.

145. See *Antirrheticus* 3A, 4–7; 3A, 12.

146. The *Letter to Plato* can be found in PG 99: 499–506.

147. See Pseudo-Denys, *De Eccl. Hier.* 4, 3, 1 (PG 3: 473).

148. The *Refutations and Subversions* can be found in PG 99: 436–78.

149. The poem is at the very beginning of *Refutations and Subversions*; for Theodore's critical commentary, see *Refutations and Subversions,* I–V.

150. The poem is the third poetic composition in *Refutations and Subversions*; for Theodore's critical commentary, see *Refutations and Subversions,* IX–XI.

151. Num 21:6–9.

152. Exod 17:8–16.

153. On the Council of Hieria, see again Meyendorff, *Christ in Eastern Christian Thought,* 181; also Pelikan, *The Christian Tradition,* 3:112–14 for the context of these assemblies.

154. See *Refutations and Subversions,* XIX–XXVII.

155. See ibid., XXX.

156. Evagrios, *153 Texts on Prayer,* 67–68, in *Philokalia,* 1:63.

157. 1 John 1:1–3.

158. On the Triumph of Orthodoxy, see Henry R. Percival, ed., *Nicene and Post-Nicene Fathers, 2nd Series. 14: The Seven Ecumenical Councils* (Peabody, MA: Hendrickson Publishers, 1994), 576; Metropolitan Kallistos (Timothy) Ware, *The Orthodox Church* (London: Penguin Books, 1964), 38.

159. This *Celebratory Canon* is included in an appendix to this volume; the Greek text can be found in PG 99: 1767–80. For another version, see the

texts for the First Sunday of Great Lent in Mother Maria and Kallistos Ware, trans., *The Lenten Triodion* (Waymart, PA: St. Tikhon's Seminary Press, 2002). John is most likely John the Grammarian (837–43), who as patriarch had authored some iconoclastic works.

160. Maximos's teaching of dythelitism was accepted as official church doctrine at the Third Council of Constantinople (682); see Davis, *The First Seven Ecumenical Councils*, 279–84.

First Refutation of the Iconoclasts

1. *Kenophōnia* is a Pauline term indicating vain speech, or heresy: see 1 Tim 6:20: "O Timothy, preserve the deposit of faith, rejecting the defiled heresies (*kenophōnias*)"; 2 Tim 2:16: "flee the accursed heresies (*kenophōnias*)."

2. An echo of Eccl 3:7: "There is a time to talk, and one to be silent." All citations from the Old Testament are from the Septuagint.

3. Theodore is resorting to the customary humility *topos.*

4. The reference to Gregory of Nazianzos, like later references to the same or to works by Basil of Caesarea that are scattered throughout the *Antirrhetici*, cannot be traced with any certainty. While it is possible that Theodore may have had access to works by the Cappadocian fathers that are no longer extant, it is also clear that Theodore is often quoting other authors from memory. As a result, his citations are often approximate; at times, the original text is slightly modified to fit the flow of his argument.

5. This work is not included in Migne's *Patrologia Graeca.* The title *Stēliteutikos* comes from *stēliteuo* ("to write on a stele, so as to expose to public infamy"), clearly indicating the apologetic intent of the work.

6. Ps 67(68):11.

7. Faith, adoration, and honor are used synonymously to indicate the one adoration that is due to the Three Persons of the Trinity in virtue of their shared divine nature.

8. Theodore tends to use *physis* to indicate nature, and he alternates between *hypostasis* and *prosōpon* to indicate the person. On occasion, he will also use the term *oikeōsis* (likeness) as synonymous with hypostasis.

9. The term can also mean "a flow of words," or "context," but in this passage it indicates the "rule of faith" that found a dogmatic articulation at the councils of Nicaea and Chalcedon.

10. The notion that the different hypostases of the Trinity, as well as the two natures of Christ, are known to us by their specific set of properties (*idiotēs*) is a recurrent theme throughout Theodore's writings.

11. This citation is from the decrees of the iconoclastic Council of Hieria, 754. See John Meyendorff, *Christ in Eastern Christian Thought* (Crestwood, NY: St. Vladimir's Seminary Press, 1987), 180–83.

12. Throughout all his writings on the subject of iconoclasm, Theodore will play with the fact that the verb *graphō* ("to write") is also customarily used to indicate the painting of sacred images. As a result, the adjectives *perigraptos* and *aperigraptos* ("circumscribable" and "uncircumscribable") will also be used to mean "passible of representation" (which could be rendered as "portrayable") and "not passible of representation" (or "non-portrayable").

13. 2 Cor 6:14–15.

14. 2 Kgs 23:13. In other words, if the veneration of the idols (= the effects) were legitimate, one might as well venerate the pagan deities themselves (= their causes).

15. Rom 1:25.

16. Theodore wishes to emphasize that, no matter which of the various pagan gods one may worship, the sin of idolatry remains the same.

17. The first of numerous references to the traditional distinction between *theologia* and *oikonomia*; the first concerns the divine realm in itself, the latter refers to God's plan for the world and, more specifically, to the mystery of the incarnation.

18. In the Origenist worldview, the *epinoiai* are the characteristics of the eternal Logos; see Origen's reflection on the "titles" of Christ in his *Comm. in Joannem* (PG 14: 21–828). In this case, however, the term is used more broadly to indicate philosophical reasoning.

19. The blurring of the boundaries between the two natures that would be the consequence of this monophysitism would make the divine and the human natures cognitively inaccessible to humanity, as their distinct properties.

20. The allegation of the iconoclasts is that Theodore's position is akin to Nestorianism, as it would drive a wedge between the humanity, which can be represented, and the divinity, which transcends representation. In Chalcedonian theology, the term *diairesis* indicates a difference that is a source of conflict, whereas the term *diaphora* indicates a difference that is a source of mutual integration. Maximos the Confessor, mindful of the Chalcedonian claim that in the hypostatic union the two natures exist without division (*adiairetōs*), claims that the event of the incarnation inaugurates a process of cosmic healing, whereby all instances of *diairesis* can turn into instances of *diaphora*; see *Amb.* 42 (PG 91: 1341–56).

21. The term has a sarcastic overtone, indicating a sophistical wish to dissent; see Plato, *Thaetetus*, 146.

22. The passage goes back to the theology of Cyril of Alexandria, especially his discussion of the communication of the idioms (*koinōnia idiomatōn*); see Cyril of Alexandria, *De Unitate Christi* (PG 75: 1254–1363); see also, Cyril of Alexandria, *On the Unity of Christ*, trans. John McGuckin (Crestwood, NY: St. Vladimir's Seminary Press, 1995), esp. 49–55. Theodore is invoking the tradition of partitive exegesis of scripture, whereby certain statements are ascribed

to Christ's humanity and others to Christ's divinity, all the while affirming the unity of Christ's subjectivity.

23. The cognate *asynchytōs* is one of the four Chalcedonian adverbs characterizing the union of humanity and divinity in the hypostatic union; the other three are *adiairetōs, atreptōs,* and *achōristōs.* Theodore deliberately uses Chalcedonian language to stress that his emphasis on the difference (*diaphora*) between the natures is not a form of Nestorianism but is fully faithful to the orthodox tradition.

24. Theodore proves the invalidity of this syllogism by showing the falsity of both premises. Migne translates the expression *psilos anthrōpos* as "*nudus homo.*"

25. One could also read, "when you counter what is demonstrable with a lack of demonstration, and what is proved by logic with your lack of logic." According to the first reading, the iconoclasts bring forth flawed arguments; according to the second, the iconoclasts do not bring forth any arguments at all.

26. To deny the presence of a center of human subjectivity in Christ, Theodore is here deploying the argument developed by Leontios of Byzantium, who had emphasized the absence of an individual human hypostasis in Christ but, at the same time, had affirmed the necessary indwelling of all natures in a hypostasis, as natures were neither accidental realities nor entities "that could be contemplated in themselves"; see Leontios of Byzantium, *Contra Nestorianos et Eutychianos* (PG 86A: 1277CD). As noted in the introduction, Theodore inherited Leontios's discourse on anhypostasis via its Chalcedonian appropriation by Maximos the Confessor. Even more than Maximos, however, Theodore exploited Leontios's insight to affirm the paradoxical conclusion that Christ's universal human nature is actually concretely embodied in a particular individual with specific individuating characteristics that can be portrayed in an image.

27. The *agraptodocetae* emphasized anhypostasy to the point of denying that Christ's nature could be described at all; their position is exposed by St. Nikephoros of Constantinople (758–828) in his treatise, which is also known as *Antirrhetici.* See Nikephoros, *Antirrhetici* (PG 100: 628A); Meyendorff, *Christ in Eastern Christian Thought,* 187; also Thomas Cattoi, "Salvific Asymmetry: Anhypostasy and Icon Veneration in Theodore the Studite's *Antirrhetici,*" in *Studia Patristica* 51 (2009): 181–94.

28. Theodore turns the accusation of Nestorianism upside down; it is actually his opponents who introduce an unnecessary wedge between the divinity and the humanity.

29. Exod 20:4–5.

30. Gal 3:23.

31. In other words, to those people (the Hebrews) who were entering into a covenant with the Godhead, who had not yet revealed his triune

nature. *Monarchia* is a term that the Cappadocians associate with the Father inasmuch as the Father was the cause (*aitia*) of the Trinity; see Gregory of Nazianzos, *Or.* 28 (PG 36: 25–74). In this case, however, the term refers to the fact that God ruled over Israel as a monarch.

32. In the *Philokalia*, Evagrios opposes the *dianoia* (deductive reasoning) to the more intuitive character of the *nous*. *Dianoia*, which explores created reality, has to fade away before one may discern the Divine Mystery by means of the *nous*. See Evagrios, *Texts on Discrimination*, in *Philokalia*, ed. G. E. H. Palmer, P. Sherrard, and K. Ware (London: Faber and Faber, 1979), 1:38–52; also, *Antirrheticus* 3, 16. The claim that there were philosophical concepts that could express the reality of God fully can be traced back to the Eunomianism attacked by Gregory of Nyssa; see Gregory of Nyssa, *Contra Eunomium* (PG 45: 239–1122).

33. Isa 40:18. The Septuagint uses *homōiosis*, which is the term also used in Gen 1.

34. Exod 25:18–22.

35. The quotation is actually not from Leviticus but from Num 21:8–9—another indication that Theodore is most likely quoting from memory.

36. John 3:14.

37. The passage echoes the allegorizing interpretation of Old Testament sacrifices in chapter 9 of the Letter to the Hebrews.

38. Hab 2:18. The passage in Habakkuk lambasts idolaters because they worship what they themselves have created. Again, the argument of the heretic appears to echo the Evagrian mistrust for images ascribing form and shape to the deity; see again Evagrios, *153 Texts on Prayer*, 56–57, 66–58, in *Philokalia*, 1:62–63. Clearly, for Theodore, the "noetic contemplation" posited by Evagrios as the highest stage of inner spiritual progress fails to take into account the irreversible change in the divine economy brought about by the event of the incarnation.

39. Jer 10:3–4.

40. Luke 14:11.

41. This tantalizing passage leaves us wondering how Theodore would connect the sacrament of baptism with the intellectual contemplation of Christ, as well as with the notion that Christ is shaped in us by the Holy Spirit. Alas, this topic is not addressed in any of his extant works. For the notion of repeated "incarnations" of Christ in us, see Maximos the Confessor, *Capita Theologiae et Oeconomiae* (PG 90: 1156d).

42. Heb 4:15.

43. As usual, the term *diaphora* is used to indicate a positive difference. See *Antirrheticus* 1, 3.

44. 1 Cor 1:18.

45. Gal 6:14.

46. This is a standard Aristotelian claim that we find, for instance,

throughout Athanasios, *Contra Arios* (PG 26: 9–525); the study of creation (= the effect) leads us to a greater understanding of God (= the cause).

47. Basil of Caesarea, *De Spiritu Sancto* 18, 45 (PG 32: 149).

48. Maximos the Confessor uses the term *diabainein* to indicate a motion that goes through something but does not let go of it; in other words, the spiritual interpretation of a scriptural passage goes beyond the literal meaning, but the literal meaning retains its value. Similarly, for Theodore, the honor that is ascribed to the image goes over to the prototype, even as the image itself continues to be worthy of veneration. See Maximos the Confessor, *Amb.* 20 (PG 91: 1236–42).

49. Once again, Theodore uses the term *diaphoroi* to indicate that the ontological distinction between different individuals is part of the divine plan; this remains the case even if in Christ there is only one hypostasis and as a result no such distinction is present.

50. *Eidos* indicates the set of all the hypostases that share the same nature; Migne translates here *species*, which can indicate appearance, but in this particular sense *eidos* could also be rendered as *genus*.

51. Luke 22:19.

52. This is the position developed by Constantine V Copronymous (718–75); see Nikephoros, *Antirrheticus* 1 (PG 100: 301C).

53. *Anepitimēton* is a *vox media* and could also mean "wondrous, irreproachable." According to this reading, Theodore would be using sarcasm against his opponents, saying, "Since it would not be appropriate to ignore any of your wondrous claims..."

54. Theodore uses the term "mystery" to indicate the sacrament of the Eucharist, but he also deploys it in a broader sense, including acts such as the carrying of branches on Palm Sunday, which the Western tradition would call "sacramentals." The Slavic tradition would use the term *maĭha* ("secret").

55. While Theodore uses *synkephalaiōsis*, Irenaeus of Lyon uses *anakephalaiōsis* to signify the same concept; Theodore emphasizes the sense of a plurality brought into a unity, while Irenaeus underscores how everything is brought together at a higher level. See Irenaeus, *Contra Haereses* 3.21.9–10; 3.22.3 (PG 7A 953–55; 957–58).

56. The sense seems to be that the celebration of the Eucharist is a sort of synecdoche, commemorating the whole of Christ's life through one specific action.

57. Theophany is the Eastern name for the Feast of the Epiphany, which however, differs from its Western counterpart as it commemorates the baptism of Christ in the Jordan.

58. *Theōria* usually indicates contemplation, but in this case the term is used to indicate some hidden or questionable insight.

59. Isa 10:23 (from the Septuagint version); Rom 9:28.

60. Basil of Caesarea, *Homily* 19, "On the Forty Martyrs" (PG 31: 509).

61. This is in fact the position developed by some iconoclasts, who thought that only the Eucharist could be a real image of Christ. See Jaroslav Pelikan, *A History of the Development of Doctrine II: The Spirit of Eastern Christendom (600–1700)* (Chicago: Chicago University Press, 1974), 108–9.

62. In this passage, Theodore uses *ousia* and *physis* as synonyms.

63. 2 Kgs 16:18.

64. This is the term used in the Nicene Creed to indicate that the Holy Spirit is worshiped with the Father and the Son (*simul adoratur*).

65. While the term *sarx* is used, and no mention is made of the soul of Christ, it would appear that *sarx* here indicates the whole of the humanity of Christ, as had arguably been the case in the writings of Athanasios; see David M. Gwynn, *Athanasius of Alexandria: Bishop, Theologian, Ascetic, Father* (Oxford: Oxford University Press, 2012), 116–71, 185. In any case, in responding to this particular argument, Theodore does not accuse his opponents of Apollinarism.

66. *Synapheia* had been Nestorius's favorite term to indicate the association of the humanity and divinity in Christ. While the term as such had also been used by other authors whose orthodoxy was not in question (such as Basil of Caesarea in *Ep.* 210.5 or John Chrysostom in *Hom 11.2 in Johannem*), *synapheia* was eventually replaced by *hēnosis* to indicate the commingling of the natures in the hypostatic union; see Norman Russell, *Cyril of Alexandria* (London: Routledge, 2000), 130–75. See *Antirrheticus* 2, 38; *Some Questions Posed by the [Same] Theodore to the Iconoclasts*, 14.

67. In this passage, Theodore seems to restrict the scope of the *communicatio idiomatum* to preserve the concreteness of the humanity of Christ.

68. The hypostasis of the eternal Logos, as the locus of the *communicatio idiomatum*, is also the locus of Christ's suffering, which cannot possibly touch his divine nature.

69. In the sense that you will be even less justified to claim that the uncircumscribable divinity is actually present in the image. Migne points out that some manuscripts read "circumscribable" (*perigrapton*), but the thrust of the passage suggests "uncircumscribable" (*aperigrapton*).

70. In this context, the term indicates liturgical implements, or votive offerings.

71. If "natural union" entails a blurring of the two *physeis* and the emergence of a *tertium quid*, this conceptualization of the incarnation would be rejected as incompatible with Chalcedon, which preserves the two natures intact. In this case, however, Theodore seems to use "natural union" in an orthodox sense, suggesting that in the case of the image we do not have a natural union of any kind.

72. The term would associate "material depiction" with something that slithers on the ground or with a serpent, which of course symbolizes the devil.

73. John 4:24.

74. In this case, the "letter" indicates the inscription.

75. See Ezek 9:4: "Pass through the city, through Jerusalem, and put a cross [in the Septuagint, *to sēmeion*, which is often understood as a cross] on the foreheads of the men who sigh and groan over all the abominations that are committed in it."

76. Lev 26:1.

77. Theodore probably has in mind the decisions of the Quinisext Council of 692, where icons of the Father were forbidden, because they would presume to represent the invisible nature of God. He is saying here that in fact the iconoclast argument is correct if it is applied to the invisible nature of God. See Meyendorff, *Christ in Eastern Christian Thought*, 177–79.

78. Gen 1:26. Of course the distinction between the two terms is at the basis of the teaching of deification, but Theodore does not develop this line of argument; in fact, he insists here that the two terms mean the same thing.

79. Matt 22:20. Christ refers here to the image of the emperor on the coin, leading to the famous statement: "To God what is of God, and to Caesar, what is of Caesar."

80. Theodore does not seem to distinguish conceptually between the image of God that is given and that likeness of God that has to be achieved; as such, he also uses "icon" to indicate the divine likeness.

81. The Emperor Constantine V Copronymous supported iconoclasm, but he also opposed the veneration of saints altogether. See Pelikan, *A History of the Development of Doctrine II*, 110–12.

82. Some iconoclasts viewed themselves as following the example of the Maccabees, who had cleansed the temple of Jerusalem and thrown out idols that had found their way even into the Holy of Holies; see 1 Macc 4:36–59.

83. Exod 19:13; Heb 12:20. In Exodus, we are told that any beast that will touch the mountain of God shall be put to death; for Theodore, this indicates that iconoclasts are unworthy to enter the churches of God. See the penultimate anathema in the next paragraph; clearly, some supporters of sacred images claimed that it was possible to share the sacraments with the iconoclasts, but Theodore takes a harsher line.

84. This last paragraph contains a series of anathemas.

85. Lit. "it is not divided in the image"; yet another reference to Basil of Caesarea, *De Spiritu Sancto* 18, 45 (PG 32: 149).

86. See Basil of Caesarea, *Homily* 19 (PG 31: 509).

SECOND REFUTATION OF THE ICONOCLASTS

1. Again, the term *diairesis* indicates that, in doctrinal matters, "differences" can only lead to conflict and strife.

2. In this passage, *historia* seems to indicate images portraying specific episodes in the earthly life of Jesus, serving a propaedeutic purpose rather than mere representations of Christ.

3. Theodore seems to suggest that some iconoclasts did not oppose images openly but merely argued that icons had to be relegated to higher positions, thinking that in this way they could conceal the extent of their actual opposition to them. Theodore argues that this pretense of moderation does not fool anyone.

4. See 2 Kgs 18:3–4; 2 Kgs 23:4–20; 2 Chr 23:4–20. Theodore would have followed the usage that labeled the two books of Samuel, the two books of the Kings, and the two books of Chronicles as the six books of the Kings.

5. Lit. "which have their being out of the histories" (*onta ex historiōn*).

6. The structure is here the opposite of the one deployed in the *First Refutation*: there, the heretic makes a claim and the orthodox refutes it, here the orthodox poses questions to the heretic, who tries to answer, leading to further questions. The orthodox, of course, has the last word.

7. Gregory of Nazianzos, *Ep.* 101 (PG 37: 177).

8. The fact the *anthrōpos* and not *anēr* is used was also problematic, since one could see it as an assertion that Christ possessed human nature in general but not a specific gendered body; apparently, this was the position of the so-called *agraptodocetae.* See Thomas Cattoi, "Salvific Asymmetry: Anhypostasy and Icon Veneration in Theodore the Studite's *Antirrhetici,*" in *Studia Patristica* 51 (2009): 181–94.

9. Athanasios of Alexandria, *Contra Apoll.* 2, 2 (PG 26: 1133).

10. Deut 6:13.

11. Theodore is thus conceding that the argument of the iconoclasts is correct, but only as far as the realm of *theologia,* and not in the realm of the divine dispensation.

12. The sense of the question appears to be that the passage distinguishes an object of *proskynēsis* and an object of *latreia,* so that the former would be given to the Son, and the latter to the Father. Interestingly, this would seem to suggest an element of Arianism in the iconoclastic view (*proskynēsis* being lower than *latreia*), and in the answer Theodore insists that Father and Son ought to be given the same level of worship.

13. John 1:18.

14. Heb 1:6. Migne's Latin version uses *adorare* rather loosely for both *latreuein* and *proskynein.*

15. Migne translates freely: "*una Deus permanens,*" "simultaneously remaining God."

16. The term *homologia* refers here to the Nicene Creed, as "the same words" would be accepted by all the faithful.

17. See the same argument developed later in *Seven Chapters against the Iconoclasts,* II.

18. Theodore has his opponent resort to the teaching of anhypostasy ("he is not a mere man") as supporting the claim that Christ cannot be represented; this is the agraptodocetic position.

19. Alternatively, he has the characteristic (*logos,* in the sense of *logos spermatikos*) of being a prototype. There might be an echo of the claim of Maximos the Confessor that there are different sorts of *logoi* that preside over being, division, and judgment. See Maximos the Confessor, *Amb. 10* (PG 91: 1133A–37C).

20. Lit. "written" (*gegrammenou*); technically, one writes icons rather than drawing them. The use of the term *paragōgon* as "model" is unusual; the manuscript might have placed it here instead of *prōtotypos.*

21. Basil of Caesarea, *Homily* 17. 3 (PG 31: 489).

22. The rare adjective *theēgoros* ("who speaks of divine matters") comes from the verb *theēgoreō*, from *theos* + *agoreuo.*

23. See Pseudo-Denys, *De Eccl. Hier.* 4, 3, 1 (PG 3: 473).

24. Namely, of the fact that this is the emperor's portrait.

25. Basil of Caesarea, *Homily* 42, 4 (PG 31: 608); see also *Homily* 24 *Contra Sabellianos* (PG 31: 599–612).

26. Basil of Caesarea, *Contra Eunomium* 5 (PG 29: 724).

27. See Basil of Caesarea, *De Spiritu Sancto* (PG 32: 149). Lit. "It is from you, and not from the Father (= Basil) that comes the metonymy (*hē metonymia*)."

28. Athanasios, *Contra Arios* 3, 5 (PG 26: 332).

29. Lit. "through the extension on it," *tē en autō ektasei.*

30. 1 Cor 2:8.

31. 1 Cor 1:24.

32. John 8:12; 9:5.

33. Phil 2:10; the original text refers to Christ in the third person.

34. John 11:25.

35. Athanasios, *Contra Arios* 3, 5 (PG 26: 332), as cited above.

36. Unusually, Cyril of Alexandria refers to *hē Graphē* to mean "the image," when the expression normally indicates Holy Scripture. Migne translates *hē Graphē* as *pictura.*

37. See Cyril of Alexandria, *Thesauros* (PG 75: 184–85).

38. Migne notes how a different codex says, "of the nature" (*tēs physeōs*).

39. The description that follows appears to be that of an iconostasis, with three major figures on top (Christ, the Mother of God, and John the Baptist), and a lower row of small icons representing the prophets and the apostles. The three figures might be a variation of the more common Deesis

theme (from *deēsis*, supplication), which includes John the Evangelist, rather than the Baptist. See Maria Cheremeteff, "The Transformation of the Russian Sanctuary Barrier and the Role of Theophanes the Greek," in *The Millennium: Christianity and Russia, A.D. 988–1988*, ed. Albert Leong (Crestwood, NY: St. Vladimir's Seminary Press, 1990), 110–18.

40. The use of this term, instead of the more usual *Kyrios*, might suggest an image of Christ as *Pantokratoros*, or "ruler of the world."

41. See Matt 9:36, where Christ "was taken by pity (*splagchisthē*)" for the crowds.

42. See Sophronios of Jerusalem, *Ss Cyri et Joanni Miracula* (PG 87C: 3557–60). Sophronios was the spiritual teacher of Maximos the Confessor, and he is most likely the model for the elder in Maximos's *Liber Asceticus* (PG 91: 911–58). The story finds its way into the acts of the Second Council of Nicaea; see Erich Lambertz, *Concilium Universale Nicaenum Secundum. Concilium actiones I–III*, Acta Conciliorum Oecumenicorum 2, 3, 1 (Berlin, 2008).

43. Why Theodore should refer to angels at this point is not quite clear.

44. See Pseudo-Athanasios, *De Pass. Imaginis D. N. Jesu Christi* (PG 28: 814). The text is listed under "Spuria" by Migne and has only survived in the Latin version. The image in question is said to be in Berytum, in Syria, and the events are supposed to have taken place "during the reign of Constantine the Elder (Constantine V Copronymous) and Irene his spouse."

45. This time the term is not used to indicate the creed of Nicaea, as in par. VI above, but merely "a shared opinion."

46. A deliberate misapplication of a word for rhetorical purposes.

47. It is of course the intellect (*nous*), and not the senses, that ultimately has to discern the presence of the divine nature in the incarnate Christ.

48. They have an equal *dynamis*, or energy.

49. Again, Basil of Caesarea, *De Spiritu Sancto* 18, 45 (PG 32: 149): this is the most frequently cited passage in the whole of the *Antirrhetici*. Basil seems to suggest that since the divine nature is undivided, there is only one type of deification, since we all participate in the same divine nature. At the same time, the saints do not lose their own individuality.

50. The objection of the iconoclast is not entirely unfounded, given that, in the passage in question, Basil does speak of Christ as the image of God the Father. In what follows, Theodore partially concedes this and notes that Basil's simile is used by him in a different way than Basil originally intended.

51. Lit. "...the honor of all under the hand" (*tōn hypo cheira pantōn*).

52. Wis 6:5–6.

53. The term is used by Neo-Platonic thinkers who address questions of linguistic or logic; see Plutarch, *Moralia*, 969.

54. See Basil of Caesarea, *De Spiritu Sancto* 18, 45 (PG 32: 149). *Mymēsis* is here seen in opposition to *physis.*

55. Here, the term *prototype* is applied to a relationship, as will be the case again in the third *Antirrheticus,* Part B.

56. Apparently some iconoclasts would honor images of Christ and the saints as long as they were hung in high places—a stratagem that was supposed to diminish the risk of idolatry.

57. Rev 4:11.

58. Rev 5:12.

59. Rev 5:13.

60. John 5:23.

61. Isa 28:16.

62. Exod 20:12.

63. Eccl 3:3–4.

64. 1 Pet 2:17.

65. *Homostoichos* can also be translated as "belonging to the same order," "the same category"; both *homostoichos* and *homodynamos* are clearly calques of the Nicene term *homoousios.* See *Some Questions Posed by the [Same] Theodore to the Iconoclasts,* III.

66. The acclamation at the end of the Eucharistic Prayer in the Liturgy of Saint John Chrysostom.

67. Basil of Caesarea, *De Spiritu Sancto* 18, 45 (PG 32: 149); Athanasios, *Contra Arios* 3, 5 (PG 26: 332).

68. See John Chrysostom, *Homilia enkōmiastikē eis ton en hagiois patera ēmōn Meletion archiepiskopon Antiocheias tēs megalēs kai eis tēn spoudēn tōn synelthontōn* ("Funeral Eulogy for Our Father in the Saints Meletios Archbishop of Antioch the Great, and for the Edification of Those Present") in PG 50: 516. The text is not accompanied by a Latin translation.

69. Meletios of Antioch (ca. 327–81) was a bishop of Antioch and a great opponent of the Arian heresy.

70. Heb 9:1–5.

71. Thereby referring to a part for the whole.

72. An exclamation from the Liturgy of Saint John Chrysostom, proclaimed by the celebrant shortly before distributing communion to the congregation.

73. Theodore uses here the term *skiagraphia,* which is the type of classical vase painting whereby figures and scenes emerge out of a black background. The Old Testament injunctions are thereby likened to the darkness that surrounds the novelty of the New Testament and makes us see it for what it is.

74. The reference is to Heb 10:1, even if Paul seems to say that the law *is* a shadow, and therefore it is the law that is said to differ from the realities that followed it.

75. Theodore moves back and forth from using *nomos* as a synonym of the first five books of the Old Testament (hence the tent and the implements for sacrificial worship are said to be "in the law") to using it in its strict sense of law, in opposition to grace. Clearly, the conflation of the two legitimizes Theodore's allegorical reading.

76. The term *technologia* (which can be translated as "sophistry") is used by the Cappadocians to indicate a type of theological discourse that presumes to control the divine reality by means of its art (*technē*), as opposed to *theologia*. In the late fourth century, Gregory of Nyssa famously accused Eunomios of *technologia* and wrote an apologetic treatise to expose what he thought were the faulty viewpoints of his adversary; see Gregory of Nyssa, *Contra Eunomium* (PG 45: 239–1122).

77. *Koryphaiotatoi*: lit. "Those who are most *koryphai* of all." The *koryphai* is the term used in Classical Antiquity for those individuals who would open a procession; see Plato, *Theaetetus*, 173.

78. Gregory of Nazianzos, *Or.* 2, 93 (PG 35: 496). For the story of Eli, see 1 Sam 2:12–7; for Uzzah, 2 Sam 6:6–7; 1 Chr 13:9–10.

79. Gregory of Nazianzos, *Or.* 2, 94 (PG 35: 497).

80. The reference is unidentified.

81. Acts 17:23.

82. Lit. "He who inspires to piety."

83. Acts 25:21.

84. Acts 25:25.

85. By a sleight of hand, Theodore references scripture to argue that the Christian emperors of his time were worthy of veneration, even if, of course, the New Testament does not refer to Christian monarchs.

86. Again the Nestorian term *synapheia*, which Theodore had already used in *Antirrheticus* 1, 12. See below *Some Questions Posed by the [Same] Theodore to the Iconoclasts*, 14.

87. The text seems to refer to truth as the fulfillment of the law, but the general sense of the passage seems to view law in opposition to truth and grace together.

88. The Greek text says, "*ton tou airontos...*," without ever specifying the noun to which the article *ton* refers. A possible implicit referent might be *charaktēr* ("shape," or "imprint").

89. Lit. "led by the hand."

90. This appears to be the only instance when we find the term *apolytrōsis* ("redemption") in Theodore's writings, and in fact we find it within a citation.

91. Canon 82, Quinisext Council. The same council also condemned the practice of representing God the Father as an old man, according to the Book of Daniel. Both canons were only haphazardly applied. See

Giandomenico Mansi, *Sacrorum Conciliorum Nova et Amplissima Collectio*, 11:977–80.

92. The text would then endorse the condemnation of the veneration of sculptures, which was always a rather rare phenomenon in Eastern Christianity. The reference is actually to Theodore of Jerusalem (745–67), whose synodical letter was read publicly during the Second Council of Nicaea. See Mansi, *Sacrorum Conciliorum Nova et Amplissima Collectio*, 12:1135–46.

93. See 2 Kgs 18:34. A medieval legend, however, continues to see Moses's original serpent in a bronze sculpture at the Basilica of Saint Ambrose in Milan, Italy.

94. See Gregory of Nazianzos, *Or.* 45, 22 (PG 36: 653), which is a collage of 1 Cor 15:55 and Hos 13:14. In the *Patrologia Graeca*, the citation is made to end one sentence earlier, but this is already rectified in the Latin version.

95. The prototype of the bronze serpent is not Christ but the biting serpent, which is not worthy of veneration; hence, it is only fitting that the bronze serpent should be destroyed once it is no longer of use.

96. Cyril of Alexandria, in his treatise *De Adoratione et Cultu* (PG 68: 133–1126), develops an extensive allegorical interpretation of the Mosaic sacrificial laws. See also Cyril's *Glaphyrorum in Leviticum liber* (PG 69: 580A–89B).

97. Maximos the Confessor, *Acta* 18 (PG 90: 156). The passage refers to the end of the dispute that saw Maximos oppose Theodosios, bishop of Caesarea in Bithynia, on matters of christological doctrine. Eventually, Theodosios and his followers came to embrace Maximos's dythelite position.

98. The term *historia* appears to indicate a verbal description (see Plato, *Phaedrus*, 96), either written or oral, but in this context the term indicates a painted image.

99. 2 Cor 5:16.

100. Since in the Eucharist it becomes the channel of deification.

101. Gregory of Nazianzos, *Or.* 45 (PG 36: 640–41).

102. Luke 24:39.

103. As is made clear by the following citation from Basil, the iconoclasts are tempted to read all references to Christ's corporeality after the resurrection as mere metaphors for his ongoing activity in the created order, much as references to God's members in the Old Testament were not to be taken as literal descriptions of God's nature. The Greek text adds, rather redundantly, "Reality, which is asserted in theology, or in other words, in the explanation of the divine nature." The sense seems to be that, in the mystery of the incarnation, the divine nature inhabits a human body, and therefore any description of the divine nature must also include references to Christ's bodily members.

104. Basil of Caesarea, *Contra Eunomium* 1, 5 (PG 29: 757). The point, of course, is that references to God's members in the old dispensation are to

be understood differently from references to Christ's members after the incarnation.

105. *Pachytēs,* which the Latin version in Migne translates as *crassitudo,* is a term that connects us to the era of the Origenist controversy. In Evagrios's *Kephalaia Gnostika,* the noetic realities, which came into being at the beginning of time, acquired "thickness" when they turned away from God and descended into the realm of plurality; the goal of spiritual practice, of course, is to return to a pure noetic state. See, for instance, Antoine Guillaumont, trans., *Les Six Centuries des 'Kephalaia Gnostika' d'Évagre le Pontique* (Paris: Firmin Didot, 1958), Book I, 1–45, where Evagrios compares different kinds of "spiritual" and "carnal" bodies and modes of perception.

106. The use of the perfect indicates that the effect of the action lasts in time ("*et effectus durat*"). In his reflections on the transfiguration, Maximos the Confessor similarly noted that the disciples who accompanied Jesus on Mount Tabor had to "purify their spiritual and bodily senses," so that they could "apprehend the spiritual *logoi* of the mysteries that are disclosed to them"; see *Amb.* 10 (PG 91: 1125D–26D). Arguably, the other disciples had not gone through this process of purification, and as a result they would not have been able to "see" the transfiguration, even if they had been physically present at the event.

107. John 20:29.

108. Toward the end of the tenth and the beginning of the eleventh centuries, Symeon the New Theologian opposed the claim that it was no longer possible to have the kind of spiritual experiences that were available to the disciples of Christ and the early Christian communities. See Basil Krivocheine, *In the Light of Christ: Saint Symeon, the New Theologian (949–1022), Life, Spirituality, Doctrine* (Crestwood, NY: St. Vladimir's Seminary Press, 1986).

109. Pseudo-Denys, *De Dov. Nom.* 2, 9 (PG 3: 648).

110. This passage seems to suggest an ontological change in the humanity of Christ after the resurrection, which seems to contradict the Chalcedonian assertion that Christ's natures are united "in an unchangeable manner (*atreptōs*)" even in the presence of the *communicatio idiomatum.* See Meyendorff, *Christ in Eastern Christian Thought,* 170–71.

111. 2 Cor 5:16.

112. 1 Cor 10:16.

113. In line with Maximos the Confessor's critique of Origenism, Theodore is adamant that the goal of spiritual practice is not dissolution in an undifferentiated noetic unity with the Divine; rather, the experience of deification preserves and ratifies our individual subjectivity, which continues to grow in a relationship with God. See, for instance, Maximos the Confessor, *Amb.* 7 (PG 91: 1088C); *Mystagogia* 2, 4 (PG 91: 667–71, 684). Theodore argues that if Christ were uncircumscribed after the resurrection, we would lose our own individual identity.

114. 1 Tim 2:5.

115. Gregory of Nazianzos, *Or.* 30, 14 (PG 36: 121).

116. Ibid., *Ep.* 101 (PG 37: 177).

117. Ibid. (PG 37: 181).

118. Theodore is referencing a number of texts that attacked the veneration of the images and that were attributed to Epiphanios of Salamis (310–403), the author of the *Ancoratus* and the *Panarion.* As we can see, the authorship of these texts—which were a collection of occasional writings rather than a single, coherent treatise—was already controversial at the time of Theodore; see Pelikan, *The Christian Tradition,* 2:102–3. More recently, in his *Epiphanios of Salamis, Doctor of Iconoclasm? Deconstruction of a Myth* (Rollinsford, NH: Orthodox Research Institute, 2008), Orthodox scholar Stephen Bigham argues convincingly against the traditional attribution of these texts to Epiphanios.

119. As with other citations that Theodore attributes to Basil of Caesarea, the text referenced here is unknown.

120. Theodore may be referring to a passage in John Chrysostom, *Hom in Cor.* 2 (PG 61: 18–22), but the exact reference is uncertain.

121. Gal 1:8–9.

122. Valentinos (ca. 100–160) apparently taught that Christ's body was of the same material as the stars and the planets; see Ismo O. Dunderberg, *Beyond Gnosticism: Myth, Lifestyle, and Society in the School of Valentinus* (New York: Columbia University Press, 2008), 119–34. While most accounts of the life of Mani (ca. 216–76) are largely legendary, the founder of Manicheism appears to have taught that the incarnate Christ was a manifestation of the eternal preexistent divine Light; see Marella Franzmann, *Jesus in the Manichean Writings* (London: T & T Clark, 2003), 15–51.

Third Refutation of the Iconoclasts

1. 1 Sam 17, Ps 23. Theodore was most likely familiar with Psalm 151 in the Septuagint, where David speaks in the first person and describes his struggle with Goliath.

2. This might indicate that the third *Antirrheticus* was composed sometime after the first two were already in circulation.

3. Accusations of *technologia* ("sophistry") were traditionally leveled to holders of unorthodox positions, echoing the Cappadocians' critique of Eunomios (335–ca. 339) in the late fourth century: see Gregory of Nyssa, *Contra Eunomium* (PG 45: 239–1122); see also Jaroslav Pelikan, *Christianity and Classical Culture: The Metamorphosis of Natural Theology in the Christian Encounter*

with Hellenism (New Haven, CT: Yale University Press, 1993), chap. 4 ("God and the Ways of Knowing"), 57–74.

4. Lit. "into what is clearly arranged," from *eu* ("well") and *krinō* ("to judge," "to apportion").

5. *Emphereia* indicates that the image "takes (*pherei*)" the viewer "into (*en*)" the reality to which it refers.

6. Theodore is here retrieving the classical discussion on the "common intellect" (*koinos nous*) or "natural reason" (*physikē ennoia*) that are shared by all members of the human race; see, for instance, Clement of Alexandria, *Strom.* I, 19 (PG 8: 805–14) or Gregory of Nyssa, *De Anima et Res* (PG 46: 11–160).

7. Isa 6:1.

8. Ezek 1:18.

9. Individuals come to know the human nature of Christ through the properties of his humanity and his divine nature through the properties of his divinity. In this passage, Theodore uses *physis* to indicate Christ's humanity and divinity, while *ousia* is reserved for the essence of the nature, which is then accompanied by a specific set of properties (*idiōmata*). Other authors use *ousia* to indicate the nature in its totality; see, for instance, Basil of Caesarea, *Ep.* 214, in *Nicene and Post-Nicene Fathers*, vol. 8, ed. Philip Schaff and Henry Wace (Grand Rapids, MI: Wm. B. Eerdmans, 1991).

10. As noted earlier, *diaphora* indicates a positive kind of difference.

11. Prov 8:22.

12. Prov 8:25.

13. To suggest that Christ is created (*ktistos*) would of course be a return to the Arian heresy; see Athanasios, *Contra Arios* 3, 5 (PG 26: 332).

14. *Deductio ad absurdum,* rather than *reductio ad absurdum,* seems to suggest that the absurd conclusion is reached by way of association rather than by way of direct inference.

15. Phil 2:7.

16. A possible reference to Isa 53:3 in the Septuagint translation.

17. 1 Cor 11:24.

18. John 1:18.

19. John 9:37.

20. In other words, while Christ does not have a human hypostasis, he is still in need of a center of subjectivity, as no nature can exist unless it is individuated in a particular hypostasis. Conversely, the fact that Christ's humanity has specific individuating characteristics does not indicate that Christ has a human hypostasis, since his divine hypostasis plays the role of center of subjectivity that would be ordinarily served by the human hypostasis.

21. See again Leontios of Byzantium, *Contra Nestorianos et Eutychianos* (PG 86A: 1277CD); the same argument had been deployed in *Antirrheticus* 1,

4. Theodore rhetorically connects the position of the iconoclasts with the Manicheans' portrayal of Christ as a celestial light; see also *Antirrheticus* 2, 48.

22. According to Evagrios, *nous* is the intuition beyond the realm of concepts, whereas *dianoia* is deductive reasoning that is tied to the world of form. See *Antirrheticus* 1, 5.

23. In *153 Texts on Prayer*, 57, 66, 68, Evagrios had enjoined his followers to flee from contemplation of earthly matters and to approach the immaterial in a purely immaterial manner, as the Deity did not possess either quantity or form; see Evagrios, *153 Texts on Prayer*, in *Philokalia*, 1:62–63. That kind of disembodied spirituality would have been comfortable with the notion that Christ's general humanity could only be contemplated by the mind. While Theodore does not address Evagrios directly, he would have classified Evagrios among those for whom Christ could at most have been incarnate in the imagination (*phantasma*) since the Logos could not possibly have been tainted by matter. Since Christ instead became incarnate in a particular individual, Christ can be not only contemplated by the mind, but he can also be seen and touched in the flesh.

24. John 20:29.

25. John 20:27.

26. Luke 1:31.

27. This passage may have been influenced by the discussion of "proper names" and "common names" in Gregory of Nyssa, *Ad Ablabium: Cur Non Sint Tres Dei* (GNO III: 1, 42; NPNF 2.5, 331). Gregory's discussion, however, hinges on the distinction among the three Persons of the Trinity.

28. Matt 16:13.

29. John 18:4–5.

30. Matt 17:26–7.

31. While Nestorios stopped short of positing two full-fledged persons in Christ, he and Cyril emphasized the duality of natures and subjectivities in the incarnate Christ; hence Cyril's apologetic treatise in defense of Christ's unity. For a comprehensive account of the dispute between Cyril and Nestorios, see John McGuckin, *St. Cyril of Alexandria and the Christological Controversy* (Crestwood, NY: St. Vladimir's Seminary Press, 2004).

32. See Leontios of Byzantium, *Contra Nestorianos et Eutychianos* (PG 86A: 1297B; 1300AB).

33. The term *Akephaloi* was initially associated with certain fifth-century Monophysite groups; St. Nicodemos the Hagiorite writes in the preface to the Canons of the Fourth Council (held at Ephesus in 431) that "all Monophysites were called *akephaloi*, an allusion to the fact that they were cut off from the Patriarchate of Alexandria...and showed allegiance to no single head, but some to one, and some to yet another." See Pelikan, *The Christian Tradition*, 2:27. Named after Apollinaris of Laodicea, Apollinarism taught instead that Christ had a human body and a lower soul—the seat of the emo-

tions—but the role of the intellect was played by the eternal Word of God; hence, Christ lacked a real human soul, or in other words, he had a composite nature. See Ekkehard Mühlenberg, *Apollinaris von Laodicea* (Göttingen: Vandenhoeck and Ruprecht, 1969), 18–32. While the two belief systems were quite different, they agreed in their rejection of Christ's consubstantiality with the Father and with humanity as taught by the Council of Chalcedon.

34. While Montanism was far from having a coherent set of beliefs, most members of this movement appeared to espouse some form of incarnational Docetism; see the study of David I. Rankin, *Tertullian and the Church* (Cambridge: Cambridge University Press, 1995).

35. John 6:52.

36. Deut 4:12.

37. Again, Isa 53:3 from the Septuagint.

38. Isa 53:3.

39. This term could also mean "exact image," but this does not seem to be the case here.

40. Isa 50:6.

41. Ps 22:16–17.

42. The Latin version translates *epigraphē* as "circumscription," but this should rather be *perigraphē*.

43. Phil 2:7; Matt 2:23; John 1:14.

44. John 1:29.

45. A typical strategy of the objections is to misinterpret the *communicatio idiomatum*, and to unwittingly—or perhaps deliberately, as part of a broader rhetorical strategy—ascribe the properties of one nature to the other, rather than to ascribe both sets of properties to the hypostasis that indwells both natures. The resulting logical inconsistencies are then used to excoriate the alleged absurdity of the orthodox position.

46. The Theopaschites (or Patripassians) argued that as the Father and the Son share the same divine nature, God the Father shared in the sufferings of Christ on the cross. From a Chalcedonian perspective, they failed to understand that the divine Person of the Logos suffered on the cross in virtue of the *communicatio idiomatum* with his humanity. For an excellent overview of the Theopaschite arguments, see David R. Maxwell, "Christology and Grace in the Sixth-Century Latin West: The Theopaschite Controversy," PhD diss. (Notre Dame, IN: University of Notre Dame, 2003).

47. Some iconoclasts suggested that images of Christ could only portray his humanity and not his divinity; in this perspective, since an icon effectively "divided" Christ into two, the veneration of the images amounted to a surreptitious form of Nestorianism. See Pelikan, *The Christian Tradition*, 116–20.

48. The last few words are puzzling, as they might appear to suggest that Christ is uncircumscribed even with respect to the humanity, which

would contradict what Theodore has repeatedly claimed up to this point. The meaning is probably that it is not the human nature as such that determines circumscribability, but rather the properties of the human nature that are individuated in the hypostasis.

49. John 14:9.

50. This would suggest that Christ has a human hypostasis, which Theodore, of course, cannot accept. See above, *Antirrheticus* 3, 16–17.

51. Again, this stresses that in the *communicatio idiomatum*, the properties of either nature are not ascribed to the other nature, but to the hypostasis of the Word.

52. Maximos the Confessor would note that the hypostasis of Christ is composite (*synthetos*), as it comes from two natures (*ek dyo physesin*). See Maximos the Confessor, *Ep.* 12 (PG 91: 224A; 469D; 484A).

53. Isa 8:3; the prophetess is a type of the Virgin Mary, who prophesied as she recited the Magnificat (Luke 1:46–55).

54. Luke 2:21.

55. Theodore's understanding of angels as corporeal and therefore circumscribable differs radically from the later Western tradition, which came to envisage angels as pure spirits endowed with the gift of ubiquity. For Theodore, God alone can be regarded as pure spirit, as anything lower than the Divine is already entangled in the world of matter. In addition, if Theodore had espoused the angelology developed by Thomas Aquinas in the *Summa*'s "Treaty on Angels" (ST I, 50–64), he would not have been able to talk of "the nature of the angels," as according to Aquinas, each angel is endowed with its own nature and exhausts its own genus; see ST I, Q 54, Art. 1–2.

56. 1 Cor 15:40. Origen, for instance, would have read this passage as an indication that stars and planets were the "bodies" of particularly advanced spirits; see Alan Scott, *Origen and the Life of the Stars: A History of an Idea* (Oxford: Oxford University Press, 2004), esp. 14–56.

57. See, however, Matt 18:10, where Jesus warns his disciples not to despise little children, as "their angels in heaven always see the face of my Father." The passage could imply that guardian angels are simultaneously in heaven and on earth with their wards, but Theodore was clearly of a different opinion.

58. Phil 2:6–7.

59. John 8:58.

60. The note "as it were" (*ōsper*) is added before *eis enotēta physikēn*, since the notion of a natural union, as opposed to a hypostatic union, might be taken to suggest a blurring of the boundaries of the two natures. Any such blurring, and the resulting creation of a *tertium quid*, would be incompatible with the teaching of Chalcedon.

61. Deut 4:12.

62. See Evagrios, *153 Texts on Prayer*, 67, in *Philokalia*, 1:63. Theodore's

point is that this claim is true when applied to the divine nature as such, but in the new dispensation, it is no longer accurate when we talk of the incarnate Christ.

63. Luke 9:29.

64. Rom 1:23–25.

65. Rom 1:21–22.

66. 1 Tim 1:7.

67. In Migne's Greek text, the latter part of the sentence is included in the citation, which appears to be a mistake.

68. Phil 2:6–8.

69. Rom 1:23.

70. Rom 1:25.

71. This echoes 1 Cor 12:27.

72. The distinction between *logos* and *tropos* is a crucial theme in the theology of Maximos the Confessor, who distinguishes between a blueprint that grounds the nature of different aspects of realities (so that different aspects of realities have different *logoi*) and a dynamic principle, or energy, that determines how this nature plays out in time. See Maximos the Confessor, *Q.Th.* 22 (CCSG 7: 139).

73. Christ's divinity is consubstantial to the divinity of the Father, and Christ's humanity is consubstantial to our humanity, but the two natures are not consubstantial with each other.

74. Theodore claims that every created, circumscribable reality has, at least potentially, an artificial image, in the sense that such an image could be produced. If the Virgin Mary is circumscribable, she has the potentiality of being reproduced in an artificial image. Since Christ is consubstantial with (i.e., is a natural image of) his mother according to his humanity, he must also share with her the property of potentially having an artificial image, otherwise he would not be consubstantial with her.

75. This can also indicate a seal that is imprinted in wax.

76. Matt 22:20.

77. Matt 22:21.

78. The use of the past perfect entails that Christ assumed a human nature and he still has it.

79. Compare this discussion with the more convoluted—and somewhat unconvincing—argument in *Seven Chapters against the Iconoclasts,* 2.

80. Origen, for his part, had called Christ *autobasileia,* the very manifestation of the kingdom of God; see, for instance, Origen, *Hom. in Lucam* 32 (PG 13: 1882–84).

81. Gen 1:26.

82. Heb 5:7.

83. The verb *diorizō* also indicates separation and distinction.

84. It appears that Theodore is here using the term *homoiōsis* ("likeness") to indicate the hypostasis.

85. An approximate citation from Basil of Caesarea, *De Spiritu Sancto* 18, 45 (PG 32: 149).

86. The implication is that the decision to venerate an image "by position" (*thesei*) is arbitrary, so that in theory one could make the same decision about all sorts of other material objects, and the result would be idolatry.

87. This is actually a citation from Isa 42:8, which continues, "I will not share my praise with carved idols." Theodore extrapolates the passage from its original context and makes Christ the subject of the speech.

88. John 14:6.

89. See *Antirrheticus* 3C, 11.

90. Presumably, when he observes that no interval of time intervenes between the prototype and the image, Theodore also means that the risen Christ whom we worship exists at the same time as the images that we venerate.

91. *Charaktēr* is used, rather unusually, to indicate the trinitarian hypostasis.

92. This argument, which is repeated in slightly different form in the following two paragraphs, appears to be rather weak. One could object that many members of the human race throughout history were never represented iconographically and, yet, did not cease to be human beings. Theodore seems to suggest that the production of an image is a prerequisite for Christ's continuing to be human, which is clearly not the case. What Theodore may want to say is that, without the production of sacred images, the humanity of Christ would cease to be soteriologically effective, as no one who is on earth today can see Christ's human form.

93. 2 Cor 5:7.

94. 2 Cor 5:7–8.

95. 1 Cor 13:12–13.

96. Gal 3:1. Paul was not referring to an actual image but to the fact that the mystery of Christ crucified had been preached to the Galatians in a vivid manner.

97. Or "circumscription": *perigraphē* may be both, and the ambiguity is probably deliberate.

98. A brief prayer by a copyist, which Migne has preserved as a conclusion to the *Antirrhetici.*

Seven Chapters against the Iconoclasts

1. Rom 1:23.
2. Ibid.

3. Num 21:7–10; Exod 25:18.
4. Exod 25:40.
5. Acts 17:29.
6. 1 Cor 8:6.
7. Phil 2:6.
8. Acts 2:31–35.
9. The term *emphereia* seems to indicate that the image "takes" (*pherei*) the viewer "into" (*en*) the prototype.
10. A possible reference could be the usual passage in Basil of Caesarea, *De Spiritu Sancto* 18, 44–45 (PG 32: 147–51), although similar passages can be found throughout the writings of this Cappadocian father.
11. In the sense that the hypostasis of the eternal Word is also the hypostasis of the icon, which, like the humanity of Christ, does not have a hypostasis of its own.
12. Pseudo-Denys, *De Eccl. Hier.* 4, 3, 1 (PG 3: 473).
13. This refers to the rite of prosthesis/proskomedia (the preparation of the gifts) before the Byzantine liturgy, when a small liturgical knife is used to cut from a larger loaf the bread that will be used for the Eucharist; this passage indicates that by the early tenth century, this ritual had already taken the form that it still has today. A reflection on the prosthesis image can be found in Klaus Gamber, *Zeige Uns, O Herr, deine Barmherzigkeit: vom byzantinischen Prothesis-Bild zum spätmittelalterlichen Erbärmde-Christus* (Regensburg: F. Pustet, 1986).
14. Matt 14:28–32.
15. Matt 17:23.
16. Matt 22:18.
17. Ps 148:5. The logic of this section, however, is far from invulnerable. To the objection that the Gospels never mention the image of Christ, Theodore refers us to the episode of Christ paying the tribute to the emperor; as every Roman coin bore the image of the emperor, and Christ and Peter paid their tribute with these coins, the images on the coins become "the images" of Christ and Peter. Finally, as if Theodore sensed that his argument does not really follow, he adds that most likely Christ himself "shaped" the image on the coin by creating the *statera* in the entrails of the fish. The fundamental problem with this example is that the image on the coin is an image of the emperor, not an image of Christ. As such, it is unlikely that the iconoclasts would find this passage convincing.
18. This mention of a cross in the skies, which a few lines below we are told is worthy of veneration, may be a reference to the cross in the constellation of Cygnus, which Ptolemy had already described around the year AD 130 in his treatise *Almagest.*
19. Rom 5:12–21.
20. The notion that the cross unifies "the things of heaven" and "the

things of earth" is a *tropos* in the writings by Maximos the Confessor; see *Amb.* 41 (PG 91: 1304D–16A).

21. Deut 4:19.

22. Theodore is saying that the image of the cross in the stars only became worthy of veneration after the passion of Christ, though after this event, images of the cross on which Christ suffered started to appear everywhere on earth. The iconoclasts' rejection of the cross is linked with the Jewish rejection of the incarnation of Christ.

23. 1 Tim 2:5.

24. Theodore does not seem to consider the possibility that in a paraliturgical context, a priest might bless the faithful with an icon of Christ.

25. Rom 8:29.

26. 2 Cor 11:7.

27. 1 Pet 2:9.

28. In Migne, these words are missing in the Greek text and added in the Latin text. The Greek text is probably corrupt.

29. The implication seems to be that images of Christ, alone of all images made by human hands, carry a special ontological link with their prototype that makes them channels of salvific grace.

30. Gal 2:19.

31. Matt 6:24.

32. See, for instance, Gregory of Nazianzos, *Or.* 38, 7 (PG 36: 317–18), though the same claim can be found elsewhere in Gregory's work. In his sermon on the nativity of Christ, Gregory juxtaposes the mystery of God's transcendence and God's extraordinary condescension in the event of the incarnation.

33. Φώς is a poetic term occasionally used as a synonym of *anēr* (a male individual). A classical precedent is Sophocles, *Electra,* 1224, 1354.

34. Cyril of Alexandria, *On the Unity of Christ,* 7, 79. Cyril's use of *physis* to indicate Christ's principle of subjectivity, as well as his two natures, led to a series of misunderstandings whose consequences are still with us today. See Hans van Loon, *The Diophysite Christology of Cyril of Alexandria* (Leiden: Brill, 2009); for an analysis from a traditional Eastern Orthodox perspective, see John S. Romanides, "St. Cyril's 'one *physis* (or hypostasi)s of God, the Logos Incarnate' and Chalcedon," in *Does Chalcedon Divide or Unite?* ed. P. Gregorios, W. H. Lazereth, and N. Nissiotis (Geneva: World of Council of Churches, 1981), 50–75.

35. Gregory of Nazianzos, *Or.* 38, 17 (PG 36: 327–30).

36. This is actually a reference to the Quinisext Council of 692, which banned the representation of Christ in the shape of the lamb, but simultaneously asserted the legitimacy of icon veneration. See John Meyendorff, *Christ in Eastern Christian Thought* (Crestwood, NY: St. Vladimir's Press, 1987), 177–78.

37. See Athanasios, *Or. Contra Arios* 2, 9 (PG 26: 163–66).

38. *Diaphora* is a positive kind of difference, as opposed to *diairesis*, which presupposes conflict; for this reason we are told that in the hypostatic union, the humanity and the divinity of Christ exist in an *adiairetōs* manner. See Thomas Cattoi, "The Symphonic Church: Chalcedonian Themes in Maximos the Confessor's Liturgical Theology," in *Studia Patristica* 48 (2007): 123–29.

Some Questions Posed to the Iconoclasts

1. Throughout this brief work, Theodore resorts to the strategy of *reductio ad absurdum*. With biting irony, he outlines the objection raised by the iconoclasts and exposes the absurdity of the consequences of their assertions.

2. This is a reference, or at least an echo, of the teaching of the composite nature of Christ's hypostasis that was discussed in the introduction. See Maximos the Confessor, *Ep*.12 (PG 91: 224A; also 469D, 484A; 489BC).

3. Given that Chalcedonian Christology cannot countenance the emergence of a third "Christic" nature that is only proper to the incarnate Word.

4. In other words, it would be incompatible with the divine *physis*.

5. Another possible translation is "of the same element" and "of a different element." The term *stoicheion* is commonly used in Neo-Platonic thought and ultimately comes from the discussion of the four elements in the R. G. Bury translation of *Timeus* 32 bd (Loeb Classical Library, 1929).

6. In other words, it is possible to say that the eternal Logos is circumscribed according to the flesh but certainly not according to the divine nature that is omnipresent throughout the cosmos. If what is uncircumscribable were of the same order as what is circumscribable, one would have to say that the human nature of Christ is omnipresent and ungraspable and that his divine nature is fully contained and circumscribed in his incarnate body—both of which are logically untenable positions. To express the same concept using the Cyrillian notion of the *communicatio idiomatum*, the hypostasis of the incarnate Logos is both circumscribable and uncircumscribable because it exists in two natures (or out of two natures!); the humanity of the incarnate Logos is circumscribable in the flesh in the incarnate Christ; and the divinity of the incarnate Logos is uncircumscribable and omnipresent throughout the cosmos.

7. *Heterotēs* refers to the distinction between the humanity and the divinity, which is acceptable; *allotriotēs* refers to the difference that would ensue between a nature and its properties if the humanity of Christ were uncircumscribable, which is not acceptable.

8. He can be portrayed according to the humanity, and cannot be portrayed according to the divinity.

9. John 20:25. It is interesting that the chosen citation should refer to a post-resurrection appearance.

10. Paul of Samosata (200–275) famously taught a form of trinitarian monarchianism where Christ "received" the Logos at his baptism; See Patricio de Navascués, *Pablo de Samosata y sus adversarios: estudio histórico-teológico del cristianismo antioqueno en el siglo terzo* (Rome: Institutum patristicum Agostinianum, 2004), 422–58. For Mani, see *Antirrheticus* 2, 48.

11. Lit. "consider this dual abyss" (*amphykrēmnon*).

12. The implication for the veneration of the icons is that Christ is known to us by way of his humanity, which places him within the purview of our senses, and as such he can be portrayed in an image.

13. This is a classic example that one can trace to Heraclitus's discussion of the unity of opposites; see Philip E. Wheelwright, *Heraclitus* (Princeton, NJ: Princeton University Press, 1959), 12–49.

14. Severus of Antioch (465–ca. 540) was a non-Chalcedonian patriarch of Antioch whose name would eventually become a byword for opposition to the Christology of Chalcedon; a strict follower of Cyril of Alexandria, he thought it was more appropriate to talk of only one "nature" (*physis*) of the incarnate Christ, which would then be manifest through the properties of the eternal Logos and of the incarnate humanity of Christ. For Theodore, this form of monophysitism is logically untenable, as it erases the ontological incompatibility of the properties of the two natures (hence the claim that Severus asserted the existence of "aqueous fire"). See Roberta C. Bondi, *Three Monophysite Christologies: Severus of Antioch, Philoxenus of Mabbug and Jacob of Sarug* (Oxford: Oxford University Press, 1976), 18–66.

15. This expression is typical of Maximos the Confessor, who distinguishes the structure of the nature (*ho tēs physeōs logos*) from the manner of its usage (*ho tropos tēs hyparxeōs*). See Maximos the Confessor, *Q.Th* 22 (CCSG 7: 139).

16. Again, the term *prōsopon* is used as opposed to *hypostasis.*

17. Epiphanios of Salamis, *Ancoratus* 32 (PG 43: 73). The *Ancoratus*—the earliest work by Epiphanius, Bishop of Salamis (320–403)—addresses a series of heresies that threatened the Christian faith as it had been formulated at the Council of Nicaea.

18. The *Synodical Letter* by Sophronios of Jerusalem (560–638) chastises the heresy of monoergetism, which Sophronios regarded as dangerously veering toward monophysitism, and therefore as intrinsically incompatible with the Chalcedonian paradigm. See Pauline Allen, ed., *Sophronius of Jerusalem and Seventh-Century Heresy: The Synodical Letter and Other Documents* (Oxford: Oxford University Press, 2008), 85–119.

19. For the classical discussion of Nestorius's understanding of the

incarnation, see Cyril of Alexandria, *De Unitate Christi* (PG 75: 1254–1363); see also, in the translation by John McGuckin, Cyril of Alexandria, *On the Unity of Christ* (Crestwood, NY: St. Vladimir's Seminary Press, 1995), esp. 49–55.

20. It is interesting that Theodore should use *synapheia* in an "orthodox" sense just a few lines after critiquing Nestorios's "two-Sons" Christology. See *Antirrheticus* 1, 12; 2, 38.

Letter to His Own Father Plato

1. Pseudo-Denys, *De Eccl. Hier.* 4, 3, 1 (PG 3: 473).
2. Basil of Ceasarea, *Homily* 42, 4 (PG 31: 608); see also Cyril of Alexandria, *Thesaurus* (PG 75: 184–85).
3. Basil of Caesarea, *De Spiritu Sancto* 18, 45 (PG 32: 149).
4. Basil of Caesarea, *Contra Eunomium* 5 (PG 29: 724), though the argument is repeated in various places wherever Basil addresses the question of the veneration of images; see also his *Homily* 42, 3–4 (PG 31: 604–8).
5. The Greek participle *epereidomenon* is neuter; one would expect *epereidomenē* to fit the noun *proskynēsis* ("veneration"), and the Latin version in Migne translates accordingly. The Greek text is probably corrupt.
6. The veneration (*proskynēsis*) of the images of the Virgin Mary and of the saints should be seen as instrumental and subordinate to the adoration (*latreia*) that is due to the Trinity alone.

Refutation and Subversion of the Impious Poems

1. This work is divided into two parts: paragraphs 1–16 include a number of poems by iconoclastic authors, followed by some poems by Theodore in support of sacred images and by a more detailed refutation of some of the iconoclastic compositions; paragraphs 17–35 contain a detailed discussion of an iconoclastic profession of faith, which Theodore concludes with an alternative, "orthodox" profession. The authors of the iconoclastic poems—John, Ignatios, Sergios, and Stephanos—cannot be identified with any certainty, although John might be John the Grammarian (780–867), who was patriarch of Constantinople between 837 and 843.
2. For each of these poems, the first letter of each line, the middle letter of each line, the middle word of the middle line (highlighted in the translation), and the last letter of each line constitute a sentence that Theodore poses as an acrostic at the top of the poem.
3. The stanza appears to refer to the New Testament authors who narrate the life of Christ in line with the teaching of Old Testament prophets and

never refer to "lowly matters" such as Christ's physical aspect. The aspect of any actual description of Christ is, then, interpreted as an echo of the Old Testament injunction against images. The error of the painters of images is said to be "recurrent" (*palindromon*), as it had already been condemned in the Old Testament, and it continues to resurface.

4. *Krisis* may refer to a specific edict or legal pronouncement, or more broadly to a general good judgment on the part of the emperors. The implication is that, while the veneration of icons is idolatrous, the veneration of the cross, which is sponsored by the emperors, is praiseworthy and acceptable to God.

5. A possible interpretation that would be in line with the overall preoccupation of the text with the dialectic of prototype and image would point to the story in Num 21:6–9, when Moses raised a bronze serpent (a type of the cross) to save the Israelites from the bite of poisonous snakes. However, as the bronze serpent was itself an image, an iconoclast would not want to draw attention to an episode that could be regarded as setting a precedent for the veneration of images. In paragraph VII, Theodore interprets this stanza as a reference to the story in Exod 17:8–16, when Moses prays with his hands extended in the shape of a cross so that the Hebrews can defeat the Amalekites in battle. In the iconoclastic perspective of the author of this stanza, the cross is the weapon that will defend the faithful from the threat posed by the images.

6. From an iconoclastic perspective, images are like poisoned arrows.

7. This verse does not follow the acrostic system, which resumes in the response by "the Orthodox." The bronze door refers to the doors of the imperial palace in Constantinople.

8. Given the possible date of this poem, this passage could refer to Leo VI (866–912) and to his son from his fourth controversial marriage, Constantine VII Porphyrogennetos (905–59). It is more likely, however, that the iconoclast author should refer to Leo III the Isaurian (685–741) and to his son Constantine V Copronymous (718–75). Constantine V was the convener of the Council of Hiera that in 754 condemned the veneration of the images and inaugurated the first iconoclastic crisis; see John Julius Norwich, *Byzantium: The Early Centuries* (New York: Random House, 1988), chap. 17, 345–66. The iconoclastic author presents these two emperors as supporting the veneration of the cross in opposition to the veneration of sacred images.

9. *Syllabē* (from *syn* + *lambanō*, "to hold together") seems to indicate the acrostic that uses the first as well as the last letter of each line, so that it contains the verse like a pincer. This explicatory superscript is contained in the Greek text by Migne.

10. Lit. *grapton*, "written" or "described."

11. Migne renders the Greek term *ainos* as "gloria."

12. Christ is the creator of the angelic hosts, hence, he can be characterized as their cause (*aitia*).

13. The passage may refer to a specific iconoclastic author, or to anyone who uses reason to condemn the veneration of sacred images, and therefore engages in a futile attempt to oppose God's plan for the world.

14. Theodore is comparing his own writings to "a dew" that irrigates the minds and the souls of the faithful so as to bring them closer to Christ.

15. The next thirteen lines of the refutation by "the Orthodox" do not follow the rigid pattern of the previous acrostics, but they continue the same argument in free verse until a simplified acrostic structure resumes below.

16. "It" clearly refers to the doctrine of dual consubstantiality.

17. The remaining acrostics in this section use only the first letter and the last letter of each line; hence, no word is highlighted in the body of the poem.

18. The passage is obscure. As noted by a footnote in Migne, "*romphaĩa,*" meaning a double-edged sword, appears to be a reference to the fact that some primitive icons carried the image of Christ on one side and the symbol of the cross on the other. Theodore would then suggest that on the back of the image of Christ there is a cross, which Christ uses like a sword to defeat death and the devil.

19. This is a usual reference to *kenōsis* in Phil 2:5–8, even if the actual term is not used, most likely for metric reasons.

20. A less literal translation could be "a poetic outburst."

21. The acrostic structure ceases again.

22. Four stanzas above, it was the cross that Christ used as a weapon to defeat evil, whereas here it is the human image, or shape, which receives the divine power by way of the communication of the idioms.

23. This might be a term indicating Christ's sovereignty over the universe, albeit *skēptros* might actually refer to the cross, which is an instrument of victory.

24. What follows is a refutation-commentary to the poems of the iconoclasts, which are analyzed verse by verse.

25. 1 John 1:1.

26. John 4:6; John 6:19; John 2:12; Matt 5:1.

27. Theodore notes that the evangelists wrote what they themselves had seen; as such, they did not merely follow the teaching of the Old Testament prophets, who had not been direct witnesses of Christ's earthly ministry. At the same time, the fact that in the Gospels the evangelists describe scenes from the life of Christ does not mean that they consider them "lowly matters" that detract from the divine majesty. As such, the claim by the iconoclasts is doubly false.

28. The text in Migne omits one line from the original poem ("the speech of both divine authors and prophets rests on nothing but hope in God") and continues to include the line "And those who agree with these teachings, the emperors who carry crowns..." which is repeated below.

29. Jer 2:12.

30. Ps 117:2.

31. 2 Thess 2:3–4.

32. The suggestion is that iconoclasts, by preaching contempt for the images of Christ, are paving the way to the Antichrist, who will preach contempt for Christ himself.

33. Most likely the iconoclast Council of Hieria (754); see Meyendorff, *Christ in Eastern Christian Thought*, 180–83.

34. The Second Council of Nicaea had reestablished the veneration of icons in 787, but iconoclasm had broken out again in Theodore's time.

35. Lit. "he is talking from the earth" (*ek tēs gēs*), he is not following a divine inspiration.

36. This is a reference to Gregory of Nazianzos's famous saying that "whatever is not assumed is not healed." See Gregory of Nazianzos, *Ep. Ad Cledonium*, in *On God and Christ: The Five Theological Orations and Two Letters to Cledonius*, ed. F. J. Williams and L. R. Wickham (Crestwood, NY: St. Vladimir's Seminary Press, 2002), 155–66.

37. See note to *Antirrheticus* 2, 48.

38. It is not clear to which of Basil's texts Theodore may be referring.

39. Basil of Caesarea, *De Spiritu Sancto*, 18, 45 (PG 32: 149).

40. John 12:47. "Today" should be read as a rhetorical reference to the never-ending day of the new dispensation.

41. Christ is substantially present in the Eucharist but is not substantially present in the cross.

42. An expression of irony.

43. Isa 8:1.

44. Theodore is playing with the double meaning of *graphō*, which indicates writing as well as painting.

45. Aristotle, in his *Posterior Analytics*, 7–10, discusses the role of different kinds of definitions and mentions the deer-stag as an example of an untenable concept.

46. We could also translate as "whatever is perceptible can be painted." Throughout the whole passage, the verb *graphō* and its cognates are used with the dual meaning of circumscribing and painting.

47. If Christ was displeased with what he has done, he would not want his life and his passion to be told and to be the subject of sacred images, but this is clearly not the case.

48. Ignatios, the author of the iconoclastic poem that is the subject of Theodore's comments, is lumped together with heretics such as Marcion, Manes, and Valentinos. Marcion of Sinope (85–160), under the influence of Gnosticism, understood the incarnation in a docetic manner, and thought that Christ's body was a mere appearance; see Adolf von Harnack, *Marcion: The Gospel of the Alien God*, trans. John E. Steely and Lyle D. Bierma (Eugene.

Or.: Wipf and Stock, 2007), 24–49. For Valentinos and Manes, see note to *Antirrheticus* 2, 48.

49. Exod 17:8–16.

50. Col 2:15.

51. In this rather convoluted passage, Theodore acknowledges that Sergios interpreted the actions of Moses in Exod 17:8–16 as a prefiguration of the cross of Christ, but goes on to accuse him of being inconsistent, since he will honor the cross but not Christ, who was crucified on it. Indeed, Theodore claims, since the word *Christ* is used for both the image and the prototype, Sergios would go as far as wanting to take the real Christ down from the cross.

52. Matt 12:26: "If Satan drives out Satan, he is divided against himself. How then can his kingdom stand?" The implication is that the iconoclasts do to Christ what in the Gospels is said of Satan, which is utter blasphemy.

53. The implication is that iconoclasts would deprive the people even of this means to come to know of the incarnation; they would rather leave humanity in the darkness of error.

54. Theodore implies that anyone who has seen an image of Christ and has started to consider it with faith will not only not come to harm, but will actually learn to discern the true poison of heresy.

55. Isa 1:2–3.

56. 1 Cor 12:3.

57. Matt 12:31–32. The rhetorical purpose behind this citation is to associate iconoclasm with the only sin Christ himself calls "unforgivable."

58. 1 Cor 10:19.

59. Lit. "sight (*opsis*) comes together with the contemplation (*theōria*) of the intellect (*nous*)." Theodore knows fully well that icons do not portray the events of Christ's life as they really happened, but this discrepancy does not jeopardize the propaedeutic and salvific impact of contemplating the sacred images.

60. Exod 25:17–22.

61. A paraphrase, rather than an exact repetition, of the last line of the stanza.

62. In other words, the image of the cross is a type of the life-giving cross where Christ was crucified, but it cannot be regarded as a type of the actual sufferings that Christ endured on the cross, or of any of the other events in the economy of salvation.

63. Num 21:9.

64. Pseudo-Denys, *De Eccl. Hier.* 4, 3, 1 (PG 3: 473).

65. You tried to conceal what cannot be hidden, much as your foolishness has now been revealed to everyone.

66. Isa 11:18.

67. Phil 2:7.

68. Acts 13:10. In this passage, Paul is addressing Elymas the sorcerer, so that Stephanos can become "a new Elymas."

69. The conclusion is rather abrupt. Theodore seems to imply that the words of his opponents are utterly absurd and indecent, but one should report them as they are, without passing anything under silence, as only in this way, people will become fully aware of the absurdity of these arguments.

70. Isa 32:6.

71. Heb 2:14.

72. See *Antirrheticus* 2, 48.

73. Heb 3:15.

74. Saint Gregory the Illuminator (257–331) is the founder and patron saint of the Armenian Apostolic Church. On the Armenian *topos* of Christ as a "dead image," see Agathangelos, *History of the Armenians*, trans. Robert Thomson (New Haven, CT: Yale University Press, 1974), 91–95. Theodore draws the rather curious conclusion that it is only appropriate that images of Christ should lack breath and voice, as the dead Christ on the cross similarly lacked breath and voice.

75. These lines from Stephanos's second poem were already reproduced before paragraph XV.

76. 1 Cor 12:2.

77. The idea is that the council fathers could see an image of Christ in front of their eyes as they were deliberating—something that was probably not the case in the fourth and early fifth centuries.

78. The last passage most likely refers to images of Christ that are on display on public buildings.

79. Pseudo-Athanasios, *Quaestio* 39 *ad Antiochum* (PG 28, 621–22). Theodore still attributed this work to Athanasios of Alexandria, but Migne already considered this work spurious.

80. This "declaration" (*hypographē*) is an iconoclastic profession of faith. Theodore comments on in it for the next seventeen paragraphs and then adds an orthodox "declaration" in paragraph XXXV to conclude the discussion.

81. The Council of Hieria, held in 754, condemned the veneration of the images; the author of this iconoclastic "declaration" clearly regards this assembly as an orthodox council in line with the teaching of the first six ecumenical councils. The synod that "met to confirm the latter" is most likely the iconoclastic synod held at Hagia Sophia in 815, which condemned the Second Council of Nicaea and attempted to reconfirm the validity of the assembly of 754. See Milton V. Anastos, "The Ethical Theory of Images Formulated by the Iconoclasts in 754 and 815," *DOP* 8 (1954): 153–60; Paul Julius Alexander, "The Iconoclastic Council of St. Sophia (815) and Its Definition," *DOP* 7 (1953): 37–66.

82. St. Tarasios (730–806) was patriarch of Constantinople during the latter phase of the iconoclastic crisis; in 787, he chaired the Second Council of

Nicaea, which reaffirmed the legitimacy of the veneration of the images and rejected the decisions of the Council of Hieria. See George Ostrogorsky, *History of the Byzantine State* (New Brunswick, NJ: Rutgers University Press, 1969), 178–80.

83. Heb 10:1. The New International Version translates, "The law is only a shadow of the good things that are coming—not the realities themselves." The term *eikōn*, which usually indicates an image, here indicates the reality of what is promised. Theodore accepts the traditional attribution of this letter to Paul.

84. The reference from Gregory of Nazianzos is unidentified; perhaps *Or.* 29 (PG 31: 89–91).

85. Heb 8:5. The reference is to Moses, who saw "a type" of the tabernacle on Mount Sinai.

86. Heb 9:24.

87. See Pseudo-Denys, *De Coel. Hier.* 1, 2 (PG 3: 121–22).

88. Ps. 33:7 in the Septuagint.

89. Pseudo-Denys, *De Coel. Hier.* 1, 2–3 (PG 3: 121–40).

90. Gen 9:6.

91. See Pseudo-Denys, *De Coel. Hier.* 1, 4 (PG 3: 141–44).

92. See *Vita Sancti Pancratii*, in the *Acta Sanctorum*, 10: 241–42.

93. Pseudo-Denys, *De Coel. Hier.* 1, 3 (PG 3: 121–24).

94. See Pseudo-Athanasios, *Quaestio* 39 *ad Antiochum* (PG 28: 621–22).

95. See Basil of Caesarea, *Homily* 17, "In Barlaam Martyrem" (PG 31: 489–90). At the end of this sermon, Basil calls the faithful to depict the martyrdom of the glorious Barlaam as well as the image of Christ.

96. This is a fragment from Gregory of Nazianzos's poem "On Virtue" (*Peri aretēs*); see Gregory of Nazianzos, *Carm.* 1, 2, 10 (PG 37: 738). To get the sense of the citation, it is necessary to reproduce a longer passage of this unusual poem (indeed, the only one where Gregory of Nazianzos talks of an actual image), in the translation by Jønstein Bortnes:

Neither will I pass over Polemon,
For it was a marvel much spoken of;
Formerly he was not counted among the wise,
But rather he was a servant of exceedingly shameful pleasures;
Later he was possessed by longing for the good,
Having found a counselor—I need not say who,
Whether a wise man, or even himself;
Suddenly he was seen getting the better of the passions,
So that I shall relate one of the marvels concerning him.
A dissolute youth invited in a whore,
But when—they say—she came up to the gateway,
There, gazing at her, was Polemon in a painting.
Seeing it—and it was awesome indeed—
She left at once, defeated by the sight,

Put to shame by the one depicted, as if he were alive.

The Athenian Polemon was the head of the Academy from 314 to 276 BC and was known to have turned to philosophy after being a licentious youth. See Jonstein Børtnes, "Rhetoric and Mental Images in Gregory," in *Gregory of Nazianzos: Images and Reflections,* ed. Jonstein Børtnes and Thomas Hägg (Copenhagen: Museum Tusculanum Press, 2006), chap. 3, 37–58.

97. The reference to John Chrysostom is unidentified. The scriptural quotation is from Ps 72:22–23 in the Septuagint.

98. This is a reference to a brief *Oratio in Abraham et Isaac* that was attributed to Gregory of Nyssa but is now believed to be spurious. The Greek text of this sermon is contained in an Appendix to Silvio Mercati, *S. Ephraem Syri Opera,* Monumenta Biblica et Ecclesiastica. (Rome: Pontifical Biblical Institute, 1915), 107–11. In the passage quoted by Theodore, the author is talking of an iconic representation of the sacrifice of Isaac.

99. The reference is unidentified. Cyril (or the author of the passage) is talking of an icon representing the martyrdom of a young woman.

100. This is actually a reference to the Quinisext Council of 692; see Meyendorff, *Christ in Eastern Christian Thought,* 177–78.

101. Gal 1:8.

102. Num 25:1–15. It is curious that iconoclasts should be associated with Moab, who actually induced the Israelites to worship idols.

103. The reference is unidentified.

104. A rhetorical exaggeration, of course.

105. The version quoted by Theodore is actually the creed from the First Council of Constantinople held in 381, which revised the original creed of 325. See Philip Schaff, *Creeds of Christendom* (Ada, MI: Baker, 1969), 1:24–29; also Leo Donald Davis, *The First Seven Ecumenical Councils (325–787): Their Histories and Theologies* (Collegeville, MN.: Liturgical Press, 1990), 56–65, 115–19.

106. It is interesting that Theodore should use the masculine *ho gennētheis* for the divine nature, and the neuter *to gennēthes* for the human nature. A possible explanation might be that while the Father generates the eternal Son, who is the subject of all the actions of Christ, Mary generates the human nature—a substance, but not an individual hypostasis; see *Antirrheticus,* 1, 4. Mary, however, is professed to be the Theotokos at Ephesus, so this explanation would be problematic for different reasons.

107. The humanity of Christ only exists because it rests in the divinity of the eternal Word, and the divinity of the eternal Word is manifest in this world only because it indwells the humanity that Christ took from his Mother. In this sense, within the hypostatic union, each nature is in need of the other.

108. On the christological reasons behind Ephesus, see McGuckin, *The Christological Controversy,* 193–222; see also Davis, *The First Seven Ecumenical Councils,* 140–64.

109. The Council of Chalcedon (451) affirmed the dual consubstantiality of Christ with the Father and with humanity but did not address the question of Christ's wills. This issue, which resulted in the greatest church crisis of the seventh century, was finally resolved with the official acceptance of dythelitism by the Sixth Ecumenical Council (Constantinople III) held in 681. Interestingly enough, Theodore does not mention the Fifth Ecumenical Council (Constantinople II), held in 553, which asserted the identity between the pre-existent Word of God and the principle of subjectivity of the incarnate Christ. See Leo Donald Davis, *The First Seven Ecumenical Councils*, 180–92, 240–47, 279–84.

110. Matt 27:15–21; John 18:39–40. In fact, it is the crowds rather than the "assembly of Caiphas" that demand the release of Barabbas. Theodore may want to associate the iconoclastic councils with the assembly of the Jewish priests who rejected Christ.

111. A rhetorical statement, as the Gospel accounts (Luke 23; John 18: 28–38) do not tell us that Pilate actually "signed" a death warrant. The reed is one of the traditional instruments of the passion (*Arma Christi*), following Matt 27:29.

112. This is Theodore's own "declaration," in response to the iconoclastic text before paragraph XVII.

113. The Quinisext Council, held in 692 and also known as the Council in Trullo, banned the representation of Christ as lamb as well as the icon of God the Father. See Meyendorff, *Christ in Eastern Christian Thought*, 177–78.

114. The Second Council of Nicaea, held in 787 under Tarasios of Constantinople, was eventually accepted as the Seventh Ecumenical Council. See notes 81–82 above.

115. The Council of Hieria; see John Meyendorff, *Christ in Eastern Christian Thought*, 180–83.

116. Migne places these two iconoclastic poems at the end of this section, without any commentary by Theodore.

117. This acrostic uses the first, the middle, and the last letter of each line, as well as the middle word of the middle line, which is here highlighted.

118. This acrostic only uses the first, the middle, and the last letter of each line.

119. Presumably, this indicates the powers of evil.

120. In Migne, these words form a cruciform pattern.

121. This stanza refers to the destruction of the famous image of Christ above the door of the imperial palace, which was carried out in 726 after the publication of the iconoclastic edict of Emperor Leo III. See Stephen Gero, *Byzantine Iconoclasm during the Reign of Leo III, with Particular Attention to the Oriental Sources* (Louvain: Secrétariat du Corpus SCO, 1973), 3–19. Leo III (685–741) and his son Constantine V Copronymous (718–75) were the great imperial sponsors of the first wave of iconoclasm. See also *Ode* 8.

Appendix

1. This canon, which is sung on the Sunday of the Triumph of Orthodoxy, was traditionally ascribed to Theodore the Studite, but the attribution is unlikely, as Theodore passed away sixteen years before the final restoration of the images in the year 842. This text was more likely composed after the synod held in Constantinople that year, either by St. Methodios of Constantinople (788–847), who was instrumental in reaching the final settlement with the iconoclastic party, or by someone close to Methodios. The rubrics in the Lenten Triodion say, "After the Dismissal of Matins and before the Liturgy, we go out in procession, together with the wood of the Cross and the sacred images, to the place where the Synodikon is to be read. As we go and as we return, we sing the following Canon." Given the crucial role of Theodore during the second wave of the iconoclastic crisis, it is only fitting that the tradition should view him as the author of this most important para-liturgical text.

Migne prefaces the text of this canon with an explanatory note from Baronius, *Ecclesiastical Annals*, t. 9, p. 1059:

> Another confessor, even if it could not have been Theodore the Studite (as the latter had already left this life before this time), at a different time, under the inspiration of God, wrote a hymn, which with its harmony delights the Church, and with a spur torments the perfidious iconoclasts; and at the time the church of Constantinople accepted that this hymn would be sung in procession, while the sacred images were carried in triumph; and so that nothing may be lacking from your joy for the defeat of impiety, and for the exaltation of the Catholic faith, we put this hymn here, so that it could be sung, decorated with the following inscription: *Celebratory, or victorious, canon, authored by Theodore the Studite, confessor, and separated from his Odes, received into use so that it may be sung, while the wood of the sacred cross of the Lord and the venerable images are carried in procession in Constantinople on the first Sunday of Lent.*

2. The stole refers to the sacred images, whose veneration was forbidden and is now again allowed.

3. John is probably John the Grammarian, who was patriarch of Constantinople between 837 and 843; see note 1 to *Refutations and Subversions.*

4. The church is no longer ashamed in rejoicing in the incarnate "form" of Christ.

5. These appear to be the names of two of Theodore's opponents. For Migne, Lezius is the same Leontios that is mentioned in some of Theodore's letters.

6. See 2 Tim 3:8, which was traditionally understood as a reference to the magicians defeated by Moses in Exod 7:9–12.

7. The Latin version reads "as a good shepherd."

8. As noted by Migne, the sign "θ" marks the trinitarian and the Marian doxologies that close Greek hymns; the first is followed by "Glory be..." and the second by "as it was in the beginning..."

9. In this case, the stole appears to refer to the human nature of Christ, which he took from the Virgin.

10. Lit. "which we consider in relationship."

11. Another list of leading iconoclasts, most of whom cannot be identified with certainty. Theodotos was the patriarch of Constantinople who reintroduced iconoclasm in 815; see Roman Cholij, *Theodore the Stoudite: The Ordering of Holiness*, Oxford Theological Monographs (Oxford: Oxford University Press, 2002), 56, 61.

12. The customary condemnation of Arios—and of Nestorios in the following line—serve to position the ode in continuity with the teaching of Nicaea and Chalcedon. See *Refutations and Subversions*, XXVII–XXXVIII.

13. Probably a reference to uncanonical ordinations.

14. The leaders of the iconoclastic party are associated with practitioners of the magic arts, such as Simon Magos; see Acts 8:9–24.

15. Matt 26:3; Acts 4:6. The Council of Hieria is associated with the Jewish priests who condemned Christ; see *Refutations and Subversions*, XXXII, 167.

16. It is interesting that the author did not use the term *hypostasis*, which would have been the more common Cappadocian language.

17. This might be a reference to Mary's virginity *in partu* and *post partum.*

18. The twenty-eight years mentioned in this verse would go from the first year of the reign of Leo V the Armenian (813/14) until the death in 842 of Emperor Theophilos; see Patricia Karlin-Hayter, "Iconoclasm," in Cyril Mango, *The Oxford History of Byzantium* (Oxford: Oxford University Press, 2002), 153–69.

19. This is clearly a reference to the practice of walking around the church in procession with the sacred images.

20. The passage is obscure; it is unlikely that John the Grammarian was accompanied by a female prophetess who opposed icon veneration, although this may be a veiled polemical reference to Empress Eudokia (840–81), wife of Basil I and mother of Leo VI, who came from a famous iconoclastic family; see Karlin-Hayter, "Iconoclasm," 153–69. John is also said to be "of the false name" as he is unworthy of having the same name as John the Baptist (the forerunner of Christ), when in fact he should rather be the forerunner of Satan.

21. Presumably the baptismal name, John.

22. This passage may refer to the destruction of the famous image of Christ above the door of the imperial palace, which was carried out in 726 after the publication of the iconoclastic edict of Emperor Leo III. However, in 814, Leo V had again ordered the destruction of a prominent image. See also the very last iconoclastic poem at the end of *Refutations and Subversions.*

BIBLIOGRAPHY

The material is divided into four sections: (1) works by Theodore, (2) Christian works in the original language, (3) Christian and classical works in translation, and (4) secondary literature and reference works.

ABBREVIATIONS

CCSG: *Corpus Christianorum Series Graeca.* Edited by R. Demeulenaere. Leuven: Brepols: 1977– .

PG: *Patrologia Graeca.* Edited by J.-P. Migne. 162 vols. Paris, 1857–86.

WORKS BY THEODORE

Bios kai Politeia (Vita et Conversatio). PG 99: 113–327.

Antirrhētikos Prōtōs Kata Eikonomacōn (Antirrheticus Primus Adversus Iconomachos). PG 99: 327–52.

Antirrhētikos B' Kata Eikonomacōn (Antirrheticus II). PG 99: 351–88.

Antirrhētikos Γ' (Antirrheticus III). PG 99: 389–436.

Elegchos kai Anatropē tōn asebōn poiēmatōn (Refutatio and Subversio Impiorum Poematon). PG 99: 435–78.

Problēmata Tina Pros Eikonomachous (Quaestiones Aliquae Propositae Iconomachis). PG 99: 477–86.

Kata Eikonomachōn Kephalaia Epta (Adversus Iconomachos Capita Septem). PG 99: 485–98.

Epistolē pros Platōna Ton Eautou Patera Peri Tēs Proskynēseōs Tōn Eikonōn (Epistula ad Platonem Ipsius Patrem De Cultu sacrarum Imaginum). PG 99: 499–506.

Canon Epinicius seu Victorialis. PG 99: 1767–80.

Sancto Theodori Studitae Sermones, Magnae Catecheseos. Rome: A. Mai. Nova Patrum Biblioteca 9/1, 1888.

Sancto Theodori Studitae Sermones, Parvae Catecheseos. Rome: A. Mai. Nova Patrum Biblioteca 9/2, 1888.

Fatouros, Georgios. *Theodori Studitae Epistulae, Corpus Fontium Historiae Byzantinae,* 31/1, 31/2, Series Berolinensis. Berlin, 1992.

Christian Writers in the Original Language

Acta Sanctorum. Vita Sancti Pancratii. Vol. 10, 241–42.

Athanasios, *Contra Arios.* PG 26: 9–525.

———. *De Incarnatione Domini Nostri Jesu Christi Contra Apollinarium.* PG 26: 1093–1169.

Basil of Caesarea. *Adversus Eunomium.* PG 29B: 497–772.

———. *De Spiritu Sancto.* PG 32: 67–218.

———. *Epistulae.* PG 32: 219–1115.

———. *Homiliae.* PG 31: 163–619.

Clement of Alexandria. *Pedagogus.* PG 8: 247–684.

———. *Stromateis.* PG 9: 9–602.

Cyril of Alexandria. *De Adoratione et Cultu.* PG 68: 133–1126.

———. *Glaphyrorum in Leviticum liber.* PG 69: 539–90.

———. *Quod Unus Sit Christus.* PG 75: 1254–1363.

———. *Thesaurus de Sancta et consubstantiali Trinitate.* PG 75: 9–1075.

Cyril of Scythopolis. *Vita Sabae.* Edited by Eduard Schwartz. In *Kyrillos von Skythopolis,* 85–200. Leipzig: Texte und Untersuchungen zur Geschichte der altchristlichen Literatur 4 (XLIX, 2), 1939.

Epiphanios of Salamis. *Ancoratus.* PG 43: 11–237.

Evagrios Pontikos. (In Migne: Nilus of Sinai) *De Diversis Malignis Cogitationibus.* PG 79: 1199–1234.

———. (In Migne: Nilus of Sinai) *De Oratione.* PG 79: 1166–98.

———. *Praktikos.* PG 40: 1219–51.

Germanos of Constantinople. *Epistulae Dogmaticae.* PG 98: 135–83.

Gregory of Nazianzos. *Poemata* (*Lib. I: Poemata Theologica*). PG 37: 397–969.

———. *Ep. 101 "Ad Cledonium."* PG 37: 175–90.

———. *Orationes.* PG 35: 387–1252; PG 36: 9–662.

Gregory of Nyssa. *Ad Ablabium* (*Cur Non Sint Tres Dei*). PG 45:115–35.

———. *Contra Eunomium.* PG 45: 239–1122.

———. *De Anima et Resurrectione.* PG 46: 11–160.

———. *Oratio Catechetica.* PG 45: 11–107.

Ireneus. *Contra Haereses.* PG 7A: 433–1225.

John Chrysostom. *Homiliae in Corinthos.* PG 61: 381–611.

———. *Homilia enkōmiastikē*. PG 50: 516–20 (spurious).

John Damascene. *De Fide Orthodoxa*. PG 94: 790–1226.

Leontios of Byzantium. *Contra Nestorianos et Eutychianos Libri Tres*. PG 86A: 1267–1394.

Mark the Ascetic. (In Migne, Mark the Monk) *Opuscula 1: De Lege Spirituali*. PG 65: 906–29.

Maximos the Confessor. *Ambigua*. PG 91: 1031–1417.

———. *Disputatio cum Phyrro*. PG 91: 287–360.

———. *Epistulae*. PG 91: 363–649.

———. *Liber Asceticus*. PG 91: 911–58.

———. *Mystagogia*. PG 91: 658–718.

———. *Opuscula Theologica et Polemica*. PG 91: 9–214.

———. *Quaestiones ad Thalassium*. PG 90: 244–785; also CCSG. Vol. 7, Vol. 22.

Nikephoros. *Antirrhetici*. PG 100: 206–534.

Origen, *Comm. in Evangelium Joannis*. PG 14: 21–828.

———. *De Principiis* (*Peri Archōn*). PG 11: 111–413.

———. *Hom. in Lucam*. PG 13: 1801–1901.

Pseudo-Athanasios, *Quaestiones ad Antiochum*. PG 28: 597–699.

———. *De Pass. Imaginis Domini Nostri Jesu Christi*. PG 28: 805–12.

Pseudo-Denys. *De Coelesti Hierarchia*. PG 3: 115–368.

———. *De Divinis Nominibus*. PG 3: 586–996.

———. *De Ecclesiastica Hierarchia*. PG 3: 369–585.

Scriptor Incertus. *Historia de Leonae Bardae Armenii Filio*. In Leo Grammaticus, *Chronographia*, 335–62. Corpus Scriptorum Historiae Byzantinae. Bonn, 1842.

Sophronios of Jerusalem, *Ss Cyri et Joanni Miracula*. PG 87C: 3363–3697.

Sozomenos, *Historia Ecclesiastica*. PG 67: 843–1131.

Christian and Classical Works in Translation

Aristotle. *Posterior Analytics*. Translated by Hugh Tredennick and E. S. Forster. Cambridge, MA: Loeb Classical Library, 1960.

Basil of Caesarea. *Epistles*. In *Nicene and Post-Nicene Fathers*, 2nd series, edited by Alexander Roberts, James Donaldson, Philip Schaff, and Henry Wace, vol. 8: *Basil: Letters and Select Works*. Peabody, MA: Hendrickson Publishers, 1994.

Celsus. *Sermo Verus* (*True Discourse*) (fragments). Translated and edited by Horacio Lona in *Die "Wahre Lehre" des Kelsos*. Freiburg: Herder, 2005.

Cyril of Alexandria. *On the Unity of Christ*. Translated by John McGuckin. Crestwood, NY: St. Vladimir's Seminary Press, 1997.

Evagrios Pontikos. *Kephalaia Gnostika.* Translated and edited by Antoine Guillaumont in *Les Kephalaia Gnostika d'Évagre Pontique et l'histoire de l'origénisme chez les Grecs et les Syriens.* Paris: Seuil, 1962.

———. *153 Texts on Prayer.* In *The Philokalia,* vol. 1, edited by Geoffrey E. H. Palmer, Philip Sherrard, and Kallistos Ware, 55–71. London: Faber and Faber, 1979.

———. *Outline Teaching on Asceticism and Stillness in the Solitary Life.* In *The Philokalia,* vol. 1, edited by Geoffrey E. H. Palmer, Philip Sherrard, and Kallistos Ware, 31–37. London: Faber and Faber, 1979.

———. *Texts on Discrimination in Respect of Passions and Thoughts.* In *The Philokalia,* vol. 1, edited by Geoffrey E. H. Palmer, Philip Sherrard, and Kallistos Ware, 38–52. London: Faber and Faber, 1979.

———. *Praktikos.* In *The Praktikos and Chapters on Prayer,* translated by J. E. Bamberger, OCS, 15–42. Kalamazoo, MI: Cistercian Publications, 1981.

———. *Ad Monachos.* Translated and edited by Jeremy Driscoll. Ancient Christian Writers. Mahwah, NJ: Newman Press, 2003.

———. *The Greek Ascetic Corpus.* Translated by Robert Sinkewicz. In *Evagrius of Pontus: The Greek Ascetic Corpus.* Oxford Early Christian Studies. Oxford: Oxford University Press, 2006.

John Chrysostom. *Homilies on the Gospel of John.* In *Nicene and Post-Nicene Fathers,* 1st series, edited by Alexander Roberts, James Donaldson, Philip Schaff, and Henry Wace, vol. 14: *Chrysostom: Homilies on the Gospel of John, Hebrews.* Peabody, MA: Hendrickson Publishers, 1994.

John Damascene. *Three Treatises on the Divine Images.* Translated by Andrew Louth. Crestwood, NY: St. Vladimir's Seminary Press, 2003.

Gregory of Nazianzos. *On God and Christ: The Five Theological Orations and Two Letters to Cledonius.* Translated by Frederic Williams and Lionel Wickham. St. Vladimir's Popular Patristic Series. Crestwood, NY: St. Vladimir's Seminary Press, 2002.

Mark the Ascetic. *On the Spiritual Law.* In *The Philokalia,* vol. 1, edited by Geoffrey E. H. Palmer, Philip Sherrard, and Kallistos Ware, 109–24. London: Faber and Faber, 1979.

Plato. *Thaetetus.* Translated by Harold N. Fowler. Loeb Classical Library, 1921.

———. *Timeus.* Translated by R. G. Bury. Loeb Classical Library, 1929.

———. *Phaedrus.* Translated by Harold N. Fowler. Loeb Classical Library, 1999.

Plutarch. *Moralia* (vol. 5). Translated by Frank. C. Babbitt. Loeb Classical Library: 1936.

Porphyry. *Contra Christianos* [*Against the Christians*] (Fragment 77). In *Contra los Cristianos: Recopilación de Fragmentos, Traducción,* edited by E. A. Ramos Jurado, J. Ritoré Ponce, A. Carmona Vázquez, I. Rodríguez Moreno, J. Ortolá Salas, and J. M. Zamora Calvo. Cádiz: Servicio de Publicaciones de la Universidad de Cádiz, 2006.

Pseudo-Gregory of Nyssa. *Oratio in Abraham.* In *S. Ephraem Syri Opera,* edited by Silvio Mercati, 107–11, Monumenta Biblica et Ecclesiastica. Rome: Pontifical Biblical Institute, 1915.

Sophocles. *Electra.* Translated by Hugh Lloyd-Jones. Loeb Classical Library, 1994.

Theophanes the Confessor. *Chronographia.* Translated and edited by Cyril Mango. *The Chronicles of Theophanes Confessor: Byzantine and Near Eastern History (AD 284–813).* Oxford: Clarendon Press, 1997.

SECONDARY LITERATURE AND REFERENCE WORKS

Agathangelos. *History of the Armenians.* Translated by Robert Thomson. New Haven, CT: Yale University Press, 1974.

Alexander, Paul Julius. "The Iconoclastic Council of St. Sophia (815) and Its Definition." *DOP* 7 (1953): 37–66.

———. *The Patriarch Nicephorus of Constantinople: Ecclesiastical Policy and Image Worship in the Byzantine Empire.* Oxford: Clarendon Press, 1958.

Allen, Pauline, ed. *Sophronius of Jerusalem and Seventh-Century Heresy: The Synodical Letter and Other Documents.* Oxford: Oxford University Press, 2008.

Anastos Milton V. "The Ethical Theory of Images Formulated by the Iconoclasts in 754 and 815." *DOP* 8 (1954): 153–60.

———. "The Argument for Iconoclasm as Presented by the Iconoclastic Council of 754." In *Late Classical and Medieval Studies in Honor of A. M. Friend, Jr.,* edited by Kurt Weitzmann. Princeton, NJ: Princeton University Press, 1955.

Anatolios, Khaled. *Athanasios: The Coherence of His Thought.* Oxford: Routledge, 1998.

Bagnell Bury, John. *Eastern Roman Empire from the Fall of Irene to the Accession of Basil I (A.D. 802–867).* London, 1912; rep. Charleston, SC: Nabu Press, 2010.

von Balthasar, Hans Urs. *Cosmic Liturgy: The Universe According to Maximos the Confessor.* Translated by Fr. B. Daley, SJ. San Francisco: Ignatius Press, 2003.

Bigham, Stephen. *Epiphanios of Salamis, Doctor of Iconoclasm? Deconstruction of a Myth.* Rollinsford, NH: Orthodox Research Institute, 2008.

Bondi, Roberta C. *Three Monophysite Christologies: Severus of Antioch, Philoxenus of Mabbug and Jacob of Sarug.* Oxford: Oxford University Press, 1976.

Børtnes, Jonstein. "Rhetoric and Mental Images in Gregory." In *Gregory of Nazianzos: Images and Reflections,* edited by Jonstein Børtnes and Thomas Hägg, 37–58. Copenhagen: Museum Tusculanum Press, 2006.

Cattoi, Thomas. "The Symphonic Church: Chalcedonian Themes in Maximos the Confessor's Liturgical Theology." *Studia Patristica* 4 (2007): 123–29.

———. "Salvific Asymmetry: Anhypostasy and Icon Veneration in Theodore the Studite's *Antirrhetici*." *Studia Patristica* 51 (2009): 181–94.

———. "An Evagrian *Hypostasis*? Leontios of Byzantium and the "Composite Subjectivity" of the Person of Christ." *Studia Patristica* 68 (2013): 133–47.

Cheremeteff, Maria. "The Transformation of the Russian Sanctuary Barrier and the Role of Theophanes the Greek." In *The Millennium: Christianity and Russia, A.D. 988–1988*, edited by Albert Leong, 110–18. Crestwood, NY: St Vladimir's Seminary Press, 1990.

Cholij, Theodore. *Theodore the Stoudite: The Ordering of Holiness*. Oxford Theological Monographs. Oxford: Oxford University Press, 2002.

Clarke, Elisabeth. *The Origenist Controversy: The Cultural Construction of an Early Christian Debate*. Princeton, NJ: Princeton University Press, 1992.

Clerc, Charly. *Les théories relatives au culte des images chez les auteurs grecs du IIe siècle après Jésus-Christ*. Paris: Fontemoing & Cie, 1915.

Coakley, Sarah "What Does Chalcedon Solve and What Does It Not? Some Reflections on the Status and Meaning of the Chalcedonian Definition." In *An Interdisciplinary Symposium on the Incarnation of the Son of God*, edited by Stephen T. Davis, David Kendall, SJ, and Gerald O'Collins SJ, 143–63. Oxford: Oxford University Press, 2002.

Cooper, Adam. *The Body in St. Maximus the Confessor: Holy Body, Wholly Deified*. Oxford: Oxford University Press, 2005.

Daley, Brian E., SJ. "The Origenism of Leontius of Byzantium." *J. Theol. Stud.* 27, no. 2 (1976): 333–69.

———. "A Richer Union: Leontius of Byzantium and the Relationship of Human and Divine in Christ." *Studia Patristica* 24 (1993): 239–65.

———. "Nature and the 'Mode of Union': Late Patristic Models for the Personal Unity of Christ." In *The Incarnation: An Interdisciplinary Symposium on the Incarnation of the Son of God*, edited by Stephen Davis, David Kendall, SJ, and Gerald O'Collins, SJ, 164–97. Oxford: Oxford University Press, 2002.

Davis, Leo D. *The History of the First Seven Ecumenical Councils (325–787): Their Histories and Theologies*. Collegeville, MN: Liturgical Press, 1990.

Driscoll, Jeremy. *Steps to Spiritual Perfection: Studies on Spiritual Progress in Evagrius Ponticus*. Mahwah, NJ: Paulist Press, 2005.

Dunderberg, Ismo O. *Beyond Gnosticism: Myth, Lifestyle, and Society in the School of Valentinus*. New York: Columbia University Press, 2008.

Evans, David B. *Leontius of Byzantium: An Origenist Christology*. Dumbarton Oaks, Center for Byzantine Studies. Washington, DC, 1970.

Franzmann, Marella. *Jesus in the Manichean Writings*. London: T&T Clark, 2003.

Fuentes, Alonso J. A. *El divorcio de Constantino VI y la doctrina matrimonial de San Teodoro Estudita.* Pamplona: Ediciones Universidad de Navarra, 1984.

———. "'Oikonomia' en la iglesia bizantina ante el divorcio de Constantino VI." In *Hispania Christiana: Estudios en honor del J. Orlandis Rovira* 24, 239–55. Pamplona, Ediciones Universidad de Navarra, 1988.

Gamber, Klaus. *Zeige Uns, O Herr, deine Barmherzigkeit: vom byzantinischen Prothesis-Bild zum spätmittelalterlichen Erbärmde-Christus.* Regensburg : F. Pustet ed., 1986.

Garrigues, Jean-Michel. *La Charité: Avenir Divine de l'Homme.* Paris: Beauchesne, 1976.

Gero, Stephen. *Byzantine Iconoclasm During the Reign of Leo III, with Particular Attention to the Oriental Sources.* Louvain: Secrētariat du Corpus CSCO, 1973, 346, 41.

———. "The Eucharistic Doctrine of the Byzantine Iconoclasts and Its Sources." *Byzantinische Zeitschrift* 68 (1975): 4–22.

———. "The Resurgence of Byzantine Iconoclasm in the Ninth Century According to a Syriac Source." *Speculum* 51 (1976): 1–5.

Goleizovskii, Nikita K. "The Message to an Iconographer and Echoes of Hesychasm in Russian Painting." *Vizantiiskii Vremennik* 26 (Moscow, 1965).

Grumel, V. "L'iconologie de Théodore Studite." *Échos d'Orient* 20 (1921): 264–71.

Gwynn, David M. *Athanasius of Alexandria: Bishop, Theologian, Ascetic, Father.* Oxford: Oxford University Press, 2012.

Halkin, François, ed. "La vie de l'impēratrice Sainte Irène." *Analecta Bollandiana* 106 (1988): 5–27.

Harl, Marguerite. *Origène et la fonctione révélatrice du Verbe Incarné.* Paris: Seuil, 1958.

von Harnack, Adolph. *Marcion: The Gospel of the Alien God.* Translated by John E. Steely and Lyle D. Bierma. Eugene, OR: Wipf and Stock, 2007.

Hick. John. *The Metaphor of God Incarnate: Christology in a Pluralistic Age.* Louisville, KY: Westminster Press, 2006.

Hussey, Joan M. *The Orthodox Church in the Byzantine Empire.* Oxford; Oxford University Press, 1988.

Junglas, Johannes P. *Leontius von Byzans: Studies zu seinen Schriften, Quellen und Anschauungen,* vol. 7, 3. Paderborn, Forschungen zur Christlichen Literatur- und Dogmengeschichte, 1908.

Karlin-Hayter, Patricia. "Iconoclasm." In *The Oxford History of Byzantium,* edited by Cyril Mango, 153–69. Oxford: Oxford University Press, 2002.

Kitzinger, Ernst. "The Cult of Images in the Age Before Iconoclasm." *DOP* 8 (1954): 83–150.

Koen, Lars. "Partitive Exegesis in Cyril of Alexandria's Gospel According to St. John." *Studia Patristica* 25 (1991): 115–22.

Konstantinovsky, Julia. *Evagrios: The Making of a Gnostic.* London: Ashgate, 2009.

Krivocheine, Basil. *In the Light of Christ: Saint Symeon, the New Theologian (949–1022), Life, Spirituality, Doctrine.* Crestwood, NY: St. Vladimir's Seminary Press, 1986.

Lambertz, Erich. *Concilium Universale Nicaenum Secundum: Concilium actiones I–III.* Berlin: Acta Conciliorum Oecumenicorum, 2008.

Larchet, Jean-Claude. *La Divinization de l'Homme selon Saint Maxime le Confesseur.* Paris: Cerf, 1996.

Leroy, J. "Un témoin ancient des petites catéchèses de Théodore Studite." *Scriptorium* 15 (1961): 36–60.

———. "S. Théodore Studite." In *Théologie de la vie monastique. études sur la tradition patristique*, edited by G. Lemaitre, 423–36. Théologie Historique 49. Paris: Aubier, 1961.

van Loon, Hans. *The Diophysite Christology of Cyril of Alexandria.* Leiden, Brill, 2009.

Louth, Andrew. *Maximus the Confessor.* The Early Church Fathers. Oxford: Routledge, 1996.

———. *St. John Damascene: Tradition and Originality in Byzantine Theology.* Oxford Early Christian Studies. Oxford: Oxford University Press, 2002.

Mango, Cyril, ed. *The Oxford History of Byzantium.* Oxford: Oxford University Press, 2002.

Mansi, Giandomenico. *Sacrorum Conciliorum Nova et Amplissima Collectio.* Vol. 11. Paris: H. Welter, 1902.

Maxwell, David R. "Christology and Grace in the Sixth-Century Latin West: the Theopaschite Controversy." PhD diss. Notre Dame, IN: University of Notre Dame, 2003.

McGuckin, John. "The Theology of Images and the Legitimation of Power in Eighth Century Byzantium." *SVThQ* 37 (1993): 39–58.

———. *St. Cyril of Alexandria and the Christological Controversy.* Crestwood, NY: St. Vladimir's Seminary Press, 2004.

Meyendorff, John. "L'Image du Christ d'après Théodore Studite." *Synthronon* 3 (1967).

———. *Byzantine Theology: Historical Trends and Doctrinal Themes.* 2nd ed. New York: Fordham University Press, 1979.

———. *Christ in Eastern Christian Thought.* Crestwood, NY: St. Vladimir's Seminary Press, 1987.

Mühlenberg, Ekkehard. *Apollinaris von Laodicea.* Göttingen: Vandenhoeck und Ruprecht, 1969.

de Navascués, Patricio. *Pablo de Samosata y sus adversarios: estudio histórico-teológico del cristianismo antioqueno en el siglo terzo.* Rome: Institutum Patristicum Agostinianum, 2004.

Norwich, John Julius. *Byzantium: The Early Centuries.* New York: Random House, 1988.

Ostrogorsky, George. *History of the Byzantine State.* New Brunswick, NJ: Rutgers University Press, 1969.

Ouspensky, Leonid. *Theology of the Icon.* Crestwood, NY: St. Vladimir's Seminary Press, 1992.

Parry, Kenneth. "Theodore Studites and the Patriarch Nikephoros on Image Making as a Christian Imperative." *Byzantion* 59 (1989): 164–83.

———. "The Medieval Mediterranean Peoples, Economies, and Cultures," 400–1453. In *Depicting the World: Byzantine Iconophile Thought of the Eighth and the Ninth Century.* Leiden: Brill, 1996.

Pelikan, Jaroslav. *A History of the Development of Doctrine 2: The Spirit of Eastern Christendom (600–1700).* Chicago: Chicago University Press, 1974.

———. *A History of the Development of Doctrine 3: The Growth of Medieval Theology (600–1300).* Chicago: Chicago University Press, 1980.

———. *Christianity and Classical Culture: The Metamorphosis of Natural Theology in the Christian Encounter with Hellenism.* New Haven, CT: Yale University Press, 1993.

Pratsch, Thomas. *Theodoros Studites (759–826): Zwischen Dogma und Pragma: Der Abt des Studiosklosters in Konstantinopel im Spannungsfeld von Patriarch, Kaiser, und eigenem Anspruch.* Berliner Byzantinistische Studien 4. Frankfurt am Mein, 1998.

Rankin, David I. *Tertullian and the Church.* Cambridge: Cambridge University Press, 1995.

Rappe, Sara L. "Explanation in 'Enneads' VI. 7.1–15." In *Neoplatonism and Nature: Studies in Plotinus' Enneads,'* edited by Michael Wagner, 71–99. Albany, NY: State University of New York Press, 2001.

Rees, Silas. "The Literary Activity of Leontius of Byzantium." *J. Theol. Stud.* 19 (1968): 229–42.

Roberts, Alexander, James Donaldson, Philip Schaff, and Henry Wace, eds. *Nicene and Post-Nicene Fathers.* 2nd series. Vol. 14: *The Seven Ecumenical Councils.* Peabody, MA: Hendrickson Publishers, 1994.

Romanides, John S. "St. Cyril's 'One *physis* (or *hypostasis*) of God, the Logos Incarnate' and Chalcedon." In *Does Chalcedon Divide or Unite?* edited by Paulos Gregorios, William H. Lazereth, and Nikos Nissiotis, 50–75. Geneva: World of Council of Churches, 1981.

Roth, Catherine. *St Theodore the Studite: On the Holy Icons.* Crestwood, NY: St. Vladimir's Seminary Press, 1981.

Russell, Norman. *Cyril of Alexandria.* London: Routledge, 2000.

Sachsen, Prinz Max von. *Der heilige Theodor, Archimandrit von Studion.* Munich: Georg Müller, 1929.

Sahas, Daniel J. *Icon and Logos: Sources in Eighth-Century Iconoclasm. An annotated translation of the sixth session of the Seventh Ecumenical Council (Nicea, 787), containing the definition of the Council of Constantinople (754) and its refutation, and the definition of the Seventh Ecumenical Council.* Toronto: University of Toronto Press, 1986.

Schaff, Philip. *Creeds of Christendom.* Vol. 1. Ada, MI: Baker, 1969.

Schneider, Georg. *Der Heilige Theodor von Studios. Sein Leben und Wirken: Ein Beitrag zur byzantinischen Mönchsgeschichte.* Münster: Heinrich Schöning, 1900.

Scott, Alan. *Origen and the Life of the Stars: A History of an Idea.* Oxford: Oxford University Press, 2004.

Sideris, Theodore. "The Theological Position of the Iconophiles During the Iconoclastic Controversy." *SVThQ* 17 (1973): 210–26.

Streza, N. "Aspect dogmatique du culte des icons chez Saint Théodore le Studite." *Studii Teologice* 29 (1977): 298–306.

Thomas Aquinas. *Summa Theologiae.* Translated by the Fathers of the English Dominican Province. Grand Rapids, MI: Christian Classics, 1981.

Thunberg, Lars. *Man and the Cosmos: The Vision of St. Maximus the Confessor.* Crestwood, NY: St. Vladimir's Seminary Press, 1985.

———. *Microcosm and Mediator: The Theological Anthropology of Maximus the Confessor.* 2nd ed. La Salle, IL: Open Court, 1995.

Treadgold, Warren. *The Byzantine Revival: 780–842.* Stanford, CA: Stanford University Press, 1988.

Völker, Walter. *Maximos the Confessor als Meister des geistlichen Lebens.* Wiesbaden: F. Steiner, 1965.

van de Vorst, Christian, ed. "La Translation de S. Théodore Studite et de S. Joseph de Thessalonique." *Analecta Bollandiana* 32 (1913): 439–47.

Walter, Christopher. *L'Iconographie des Conciles dans la Tradition Byzantine.* Paris: Institut Français d'Études Byzantines, 1970.

Ware, Metropolitan Kallistos (Timothy). *The Orthodox Church.* London: Penguin Books, 1964; 2nd, revised ed., 1993.

———, with Mother Maria, trans. *The Lenten Triodion.* Waymart, PA: St. Tikhon's Seminary Press, 2002.

Wheelwright, Philip E. *Heraclitus.* Princeton, NJ: Princeton University Press, 1959.

GENERAL INDEX

SCRIPTURE INDEX

OLD TESTAMENT

APOCRYPHA